Environment, Society an
International Relations

G000167964

'This is an important addition to the literature on the international relations of global environmental change. Dr Kütting's focus on eco-centrism challenges conventional analyses of regime implementation.'

Professor Marc Williams, School of Political Science, University of New South Wales

'In this useful book, Dr Kütting provides clear and direct discussion of an important problem. Her work has added value, both because it is rooted in a close study of two cases and because she makes a conscious effort to interrogate the adequacy of international relations theory from that basis. This book has much to recommend it.'

Dr Gwyn Prins, Senior Research Fellow, Royal Institute of International Affairs

What are the connections between environmental diplomacy and environmental protection?

What makes an international environmental agreement effective?

In the past thirty years the number of international environmental agreements has steadily risen to reach record numbers. However, the quantity of international environmental agreements recently concluded should not be taken as evidence of a necessary increase in quality. The number of agreements may be impressive but this does not mean that the terms of the negotiated agreement necessarily help to improve the state of the environment. These are the issues which Gabriela Kütting addresses in this cutting edge study of the effectiveness of international environmental agreements. Based on a critique of traditional regime theory, this book outlines the structures in which agreement-making operates and demonstrates that a fundamental reassessment of the relationship between environment and society is necessary.

Environment, Society and International Relations offers new insights into the study of social organisation and its effect on the environment. It also offers a compelling critique of neoliberal institutionalist thought, which has rarely been presented in such a thorough and convincing way. This ground-breaking volume is an essential resource for students and researchers of International Relations, Environmental Studies and International Political Economy, as well as for policy analysts.

Gabriela Kütting is a lecturer in International Relations at the University of Aberdeen. Her articles on International Relations/International Political Economy and the environment have been widely published in journals including *International Environmental Affairs* and *Environmental Politics*.

Environment, Society and International Relations

Towards more effective international environmental agreements

Gabriela Kütting

London and New York

First published 2000
by Routledge
11 New Fetter Lane, London EC4P 4EE

Simultaneously published in the USA and Canada
by Routledge
29 West 35th Street, New York, NY 10001

Routledge is an imprint of the Taylor & Francis Group

© 2000 Gabriela Kütting

Typeset in Baskerville by Taylor & Francis Books Ltd.
Printed and bound in Great Britain by St Edmundsbury Press, Bury St
Edmunds, Suffolk

British Library Cataloguing in Publication Data
A catalogue record for this book is available from the British Library

Library of Congress Cataloging in Publication Data
Kütting, Gabriela
    Environment, society, and international relations: towards more effective
    international environmental agreements/Gabriela Kütting.
    p. cm.
    Includes bibliographical references and index.
    1. Environmental policy–International cooperation. I. Title.
    JZ1324.K88 2000
    363.7'0526–dc21

                                                    99–053190

ISBN 0–415–21465–3 (hbk)
ISBN 0–415–21466–1 (pbk)

For Pavlos

Contents

Preface

This book arose out of the realisation that a gap needed to be bridged between the institutional international relations (IR) literature concerned with international environmental agreements and the environmental literature studying the social origins of environmental degradation. I hope that this book will prove beneficial for both camps: introduce a wider focus for IR by arguing the need for an inclusion of the study of the environment–society relationship and contribute to the environmental literature by showing how IR and the study of the environment can be linked.

Many people have helped in the completion of this project. I am particularly indebted to Julian Saurin, Marc Williams and Pamela Shaw for their intellectual stimulation, time, encouragement and interest in my work. Thanks are due to the MAP and CLRTAP secretariats who helped by providing access to officials as well as the British and German delegations to CLRTAP who gave me observer status during Working Group on Strategies meetings. Libby Assassi, Caroline Thomas, Barbara Adam, Detlef Sprinz, John Abraham, Branwen Gruffyth Jones, Sonja Boehmer-Christiansen, John Vogler, Evangelos Raftopoulos, the BISA Environment Group and the Sussex University IR and CDE research student discussion groups have helped me through comments and discussions. I have benefited from the friendship and emotional support given by my parents, Faiza Zaheer, Gaby Kittel, Zivka Mares Randic and Derek Shaw.

This book is dedicated to my friend Pavlos who sadly lost his mother last year. Pavlos and I share our interest in the state of the Mediterranean environment and I hope that he will be able to develop this and his other interests as he would have done without the tragic changes in his childhood.

Abbreviations

BAT	Best Available Technology
CAMP	Coastal Area Management Programme
CFCs	Chlorofluorocarbons
CLRTAP	Convention on Long-Range Transboundary Air Pollution
CO_2	Carbon dioxide
CSCE	Conference on Security and Cooperation in Europe
DDT	Dichlorodiphenyltrichlorethane
EC	European Community
EMEP	European Monitoring and Evaluation Programme
EU	European Union
GATT	General Agreement on Tariffs and Trade
IIASA	International Institute for Applied Systems Analysis
IR	International Relations
LBS	Land-based sources
LCP	Large combustion plant
MAP	Mediterranean Action Plan
Marpol	International Convention for the Prevention of Pollution from Ships
MEDPOL	Scientific component of the Mediterranean Action Plan
NGO	Non-governmental organisation
NOx	Nitrogen oxide
OECD	Organisation for Economic Cooperation and Development
PAP	Priority Action Programme
RAC	Regional Activity Centre
RAINS	Regional Acidification Information and Simulation model
SO_2	Sulphur dioxide
SPAMI	Specially protected area of Mediterranean interest
TOMAs	Tropospheric Ozone Management Areas
UN	United Nations
UNCED	United Nations Conference on Environment and Development
UNDP	United Nations Development Programme
UNECE	United Nations Economic Commission for Europe

UNEP	United Nations Environment Programme
VOCs	Volatile organic compounds
WTO	World Trade Organisation
WWF	World Wide Fund for Nature

Part I
Distinguishing between institutional and environmental effectiveness

1 Introduction

In the past 30 years, international environmental agreements have steadily risen to reach record numbers. There is a loose assumption that this is a good thing and that this rise has resulted in a commensurable improvement in environmental protection. But is this actually the case? In fact, is there a positive correlation at all or are there negative correlations? What are the connections between environmental diplomacy and environmental protection and how can environmental protection be achieved? That is the subject of this book.

It has been recognised that many, if not all, problems of environmental degradation are transboundary in nature and therefore need an international solution. National policy measures essentially cannot cope with international environmental problems because the source of pollution or the impact of pollution may not be within a particular state's jurisdiction. The growing and now substantial literature on international environmental agreements is testimony to the prominence of this characterisation, and to the assumption that there is a strong correspondence between the growing number of international environmental agreements and a purported increase in environmental propriety.

The quantity of international environmental agreements concluded recently should not be taken as evidence of a necessary increase in quality. The number of international environmental agreements may be impressive but this does not mean that the terms of the negotiated agreement necessarily help to improve the state of the environment. In fact, rather the opposite may be the case. In order to shed light on this key question, this book offers a two-pronged approach. It reviews the academic discourse relating to the evaluation of effectiveness of international environmental agreements and then examines the record of agreement effectiveness with reference to two cases, namely the Mediterranean Action Plan and the Convention on Long-Range Transboundary Air Pollution.

The conventional indicator for diplomatic success is the mere existence or completed negotiation of an international environmental agreement. However, if the paramount aim of an international environmental agreement is to deal effectively with a specific environmental problem (and in Chapters 3 and 4 the meaning of effectiveness will be explained in detail), then, as this book seeks to show, it is clear that neither the mere existence of an agreement nor possible high participation nor ultimate compliance should merit undue celebration without the crucial test of the adequacy of the international environmental agreement to deal with the specific problem nominally addressed. This argument has so far been neglected in International Relations (IR) thinking and even in the international policy-related literature, and it is to this crucial test that this book is focused.

In this introduction, through a brief overview of problems in the existing literature, I will outline the reasoning that gave rise to the ideas put forward here by surveying the problems identified in existing IR approaches to the study of the effectiveness of international environmental agreements. Further, the reasons for selecting the two agreements studied here will be explained. This will be followed by a description of the method of analysis used in this project and an outline of the chapters.

Outline of the problem of 'effectiveness'

Effectiveness means distinctly different things to different communities. To academics, effectiveness describes the ability of an approach to solve a particular issue. In this context, the scope of a solution needs to be discussed. Cox distinguishes between problem-solving theory and critical theory (Cox, 1981: 128). Problem-solving theory reproduces prevailing power and social relationships with the general aim of problem-solving being 'to make these relationships and institutions work smoothly by dealing effectively with particular sources of trouble' (p. 129). The term 'problem-solving theory' is confusing because it gives the impression that the main concern is the resolution of a problem. However, with regard to issues of effectiveness I argue that problem-solving relates to the resolution of political rather than substantial problems. Critical theory, on the other hand, stands apart from prevailing orders and structures by not taking institutions and social/power relationships for granted. Rather, 'it is directed towards an appraisal of the very framework for action, or problematic, which problem-solving theory accepts as its parameters' (p. 129).

It is from this critical perspective that I seek to develop the concept of effectiveness in this book. Institutions and existing social and power relations are not the defining boundaries within which effectiveness is analysed; they are given by the structures, origins and remedies of the problem of environmental degradation.

The state is still the foremost regulatory actor in international society. The doctrine of state sovereignty prescribes that the state holds a monopoly on legitimacy to enter international negotiations on environmental regulation. In turn, this doctrine is institutionalised in international law and the constitution of the United Nations system. In consequence, it is not surprising that international environmental agreements between states are seen as the principal form of international environmental cooperation. Thus, the development of international environmental cooperation on a large and organised scale is typically traced back to the 1972 UN Conference on the Human Environment in Stockholm although the first multilateral international convention relating to environmental matters can be traced as far back as the 1902 Convention for the Protection of

Birds Useful to Agriculture (Kiss and Sheldon, 1991: 33). The many single-issue or sectoral international environmental agreements which characterised the formative years of international environmental cooperation, and which continue to dominate international environmental agreements, were followed by the more comprehensive initiatives and agreements such as the Brandt Commission report (1980) and the Brundtland Commission report (1987), culminating in the 1992 Earth Summit, the UN Conference on Environment and Development held in Rio de Janeiro.

With the growing requirement in the IR and environmental literature that international environmental cooperation be seen to be convincing, the question of the effectiveness of such cooperation arises. The traditional realist and neorealist view of IR is that cooperation between states, as opposed to other forms of cooperation, is the only way to focus on international environmental problems. However, it is argued here that it is not necessarily an adequate or even appropriate way to do so.

The IR literature has nominally taken account of the problem of effectiveness in the growing body of literature on this subject. However, it has located the concept of effectiveness well within the traditional boundaries of the discipline. This means that it does so with the traditional analytical focus of the discipline, i.e. scrutinising and trying to explain the behaviour of actors in the international system rather than focusing on the problem giving rise to cooperation and its adequate solution. The same also applies to the study of the effectiveness of international environmental agreements. Literature on the subject is mostly limited to the study of how cooperation between states can best be *described* and to *the conditions in which institutions work*. Effectiveness, as defined by these criteria, means that an agreement can achieve a change of behaviour in an actor that would not have occurred in the absence of that particular agreement (Young, 1992: 161). This understanding of effectiveness does not require that environmental improvement occurs as a result of the agreement.

In this school of thought, the effectiveness of an agreement is assessed within conventional IR and regime theory terms, namely in relation to questions of international order and international organisation. Regimes are thus seen as a way to overcome the anarchy of the international system, which, in the realist view, characterises world politics, and to create a common code of conduct, or norms. This distorting focus places actor behaviour above environmental regulation. The relationship between the international cooperative effort and the environmental problem to be tackled is disregarded.

As Paterson (1995: 215) observes:

> Even though it is often accepted that IR as a 'bounded subject matter' may leak through into other areas, there are limits. Thus, for those who have written on global environmental problems, the question 'why have these questions arisen in the first place?' does not usually get asked – this is presumably left to political economists, geographers, or someone else. This question is left to others, as it is supposedly not an 'international' question

even though, if you reverse the lens, and start from an environmental perspective, it is of course of supreme importance. Thus the established academic disciplinary boundaries impede our overall understanding of environmental politics, and are one source of why the analyses of environmental regimes are so limited.

Although the main question to be asked in this book is not why environmental problems have arisen in the first place but rather, if international environmental agreements can rise to the challenge they pose, the point made by Paterson is of central importance. The question of how adequately an environmental agreement can and does tackle the environmental problem to be regulated can indeed be deemed to be outside the discipline's boundary, as Paterson posits, because it does not relate to the primary concern of IR, namely to define, or find a logic behind the interaction of the various international actors. However, I argue that this 'externalisation' (i.e. placing outside the discipline) is unjustified and needs to be remedied. Traditional IR approaches tend to be methodologically limited in their application to the study of effectiveness by concentrating on behavioural aspects of 'regime formation' and treating the agreement as a 'closed system'. These limitations and the remedial action proposed here will be discussed further below. However, first, the choice of agreements to be studied will be explained.

Choice of empirical studies

Two illustrative case studies have been chosen because they serve as good examples of the complexities involved in the study of institutional and environmental effectiveness. One of the agreements, the Convention on Long-Range Transboundary Air Pollution (CLRTAP), is generally considered an effective (in the traditional sense of institutional effectiveness) agreement while the other, the Mediterranean Action Plan (MAP), is not. However, neither can be described as effective in the important new, environmental sense that I propose. The aim of this book is to use these agreements as a means by which the concept of environmental effectiveness can be developed. These empirical studies serve as an illustration for an approach that can equally be applied to other global or regional agreements as well as other subject areas such as food or health.

CLRTAP has been chosen as an important and relevant empirical study because it is regarded as a success story in international environmental agreement-making. Although it was widely studied in the academic literature in the 1980s, hardly any literature exists on the developments that have taken place in the 1990s. In addition, because of its long-standing nature, CLRTAP provides a good study of change over time in an agreement and thus the literature produced in the 1980s is valuable as well.

The possibility to study change over time within an agreement offers an alternative to static approaches to the study of international environmental agreements. CLRTAP, established in 1979, is a particularly good example of the influence of Cold War animosities and ideology in 'high politics' on international environmental policy-making. The fact that CLRTAP is a regional rather than global agreement helps to keep the relationship between different factors of analysis in proportion without sacrificing complexity or over-simplifying the problems underlying international environmental policy-making. In fact, there are more regional than global agreements and therefore regional agreements are more representative of international policy-making.[1]

CLRTAP has a strong science and technology base. It therefore provides a good case study for analysing the role of science in the making of international environmental agreements. Likewise, the link between science and technology policy is relatively accessible to examination because of the open nature of the policy-making process in CLRTAP: it is a long-established institution that has well-defined regulatory structures and has developed strong institutional dynamics. All of this means that CLRTAP would be considered an effective agreement in traditional IR terms. Thus it is a good case to subject to wider analysis and to place in an environmental and holistic context. In this way, the strengths and weaknesses of traditional approaches can be evaluated and the results compared to the more comprehensive approach proposed in this book.

The Mediterranean Action Plan has been chosen because it is a controversial case. It is mainly known in the academic literature through Haas's study on epistemic communities which is based on MAP and sees it as an effective agreement thanks to the influence of epistemic communities (Haas, 1990). Otherwise MAP has largely been ignored by the IR academic community with the exception of a little-known study at the Fridtjof Nansen Institute in Norway which is more critical of its achievements (Skjaerseth, 1992b). However, I propose that the role of the epistemic community in MAP is negligible and has not contributed to either institutional effectiveness or environmental effectiveness. The state of the Mediterranean Sea was lamented at the 1972 Stockholm UN Conference on the Human Environment, with oil pollution being the main focus. A regional agreement was subsequently set up and the Barcelona Convention as the legal ingredient of this agreement signed in 1977.

MAP has to cope with the north–south divide in the region, thus reflecting the global development problem on a regional scale. In that sense it is a typical example of the tensions between environment and development, to be seen in both the UN Conference on the Human Environment in Stockholm and in the UN Conference on Environment and Development in Rio de Janeiro. The fundamental principle underlying these agreements is that environment and development are connected. Therefore, development needs to take place with reference to environment and vice versa the study of environmental degradation needs to consider development issues.

This agreement cannot be approached with an emphasis on the traditional foci of IR literature because it is not propelled by considerations of national or economic interest, or rather these considerations are factors to be explained themselves as opposed to explanatory factors in Mediterranean policy-making. This means that environmental policy is not based on considerations of national economic interest. On the contrary, they prevent the making of environmental policy. This raises the question: 'Why does this agreement exist at all since there is an apparent lack of motivation?' Traditional IR approaches find it difficult to answer that, which is perhaps the reason that this agreement has received so little attention.

The problem of structure and agency

In what follows, the orthodox regime theories, which dominate the International Relations of Global Environmental Change, are subjected to a wide-ranging and eclectic criticism. This means that not only economic and political relationships pertaining to either acid rain or to the pollution of the Mediterranean Sea will be studied but, in addition, a holistic approach will be used, taking account of social, political, economic, scientific, technological, bureaucratic and temporal structures and factors.

This alternative approach gives equal importance to structure and agency. Traditionally, IR has been concerned more with agency than with structure, especially in the field of the environment. Structures do not exist in isolation. An object or practice is always part of several or many structures. This makes it difficult to attribute causation to a particular set of structures. Structures are not static but historically specific, which means that they cannot be explained by studying their individual parts only. Systems, as opposed to structures, relate to the whole of this set of interconnecting parts. A system has structures and agents. There are open and closed systems. A closed system forms a unit. An open system interacts with other systems, structures and agents.

In IR terms, system refers mainly to the international system, which is described as anarchic by realists, i.e. without structure and dominated by power issues. However, if structure is seen as dialectical and taking account of the unintentional and intentional, even a supposedly anarchical international system is structured. In this book, the term system is not used in a closed sense but it is assumed that systems are open by their very nature. Therefore, structures in a system may not originate from this system but can come from elsewhere and vice versa. The same applies to agency. Therefore, sometimes the distinction between structure and system may not appear to be clearly defined, although with careful scrutiny one finds that distinctions can be identified.

This book, however, seeks to go beyond the analysis of the relationship between the actors in international environmental agreements and how the actions and behaviour of these actors can be contextualised in the structures within which they operate. This contextualisation will form only part of the analysis.

The second part of the analysis will be the re-embedding of international environmental policy-making in a context that includes nature or the environment. This means that environmental degradation is not seen just as a social problem but also as an environmental one, which then has an impact on its definition as a social problem. This means that an environmental problem cannot only be seen as an economic or health problem but needs to be seen in the context of ecosystem dysfunction. This dysfunction then has to be placed back in a social context in order to fully conceptualise the scale of the problem. I argue that conventional social science analysis in general disregards the link between nature and society and focuses on the social level only. This is inadequate since an environmental problem cannot be treated by analysing it on the social level only without reference to its environmental origin. It needs to be located in three dimensions – its structural, environmental and social origins – in order to be understood and redefined as a social problem.

The criticisms of orthodox approaches to international environmental agreements in general and to the concept of effectiveness in particular lead to the principal purpose of the book, which is the need to develop a new concept of effectiveness which overcomes the problems associated with methodological limitations of conventional approaches and which takes into account the linkage between society and nature. This is partly achieved by making a heuristic distinction between institutional and environmental effectiveness.

In order to move from identification of the limits of orthodox IR approaches to international environmental agreements to new, more useful notions of effectiveness, the book proposes particular innovations. Four key concepts have been singled out that are considered to be of prime importance for the understanding of the concept and actuality of effectiveness. These are, respectively, economic structures, time, science and regulatory structures.

Economic structures relate to power relationships, the role of production and cost considerations in international environmental policy-making. Previous analyses of environmental issues and economic structures or of political economies at play have tended to focus on single economic factors such as the role of the electricity industry or the automobile industry in the case of acid rain. This book takes a much wider view by including the effect of global and regional economic organisation.

The concept of time relates to the notion of change and introduces the concept of rhythmicity and irreversibility of environmental degradation. On the one hand, the time frames underlying regulatory proceedings indicate how seriously an international environmental agreement or its underlying environmental problem are taken. However, the concept of time does not only relate to clock and calendar time but is also concerned with the rhythms of ecosystems and how these rhythms interact with social rhythms, such as production patterns, energy consumption and regulatory procedures. It becomes obvious that environmental degradation very often leads to irreversible damage or change – a phenomenon that is not reflected in policy-making priorities.

Science has been chosen because scientific knowledge informs the policy-making process by providing not only information on its nature and origin but also the solutions to environmental degradation. Thus it plays an important role in the formation and revision of the international environmental agreements which are studied here. However, the traditional view of science as an objective tool that can establish definite cause–effect relationships is flawed and it will become clear here that scientific knowledge underlying international environmental policy-making is as much influenced by social, political and economic factors as it is by scientific findings. This means that a political economy of science is at work.

Regulatory structures provide the framework in which agreements are made and exist. They are the focus of regime theory and, as explained above, are traditionally taken as prime determinants of effectiveness. This view is examined and the current understanding of regulatory structures challenged. It becomes particularly clear that bureaucratic aspects of decision-making and administrative organisation mean that individuals in the policy-making process become increasingly specialised in one particular area and do not have an understanding of how their role is related to the policy-making process in general. This means that decision-making for environmental ends is overwhelmed by the bureaucratic battles of the policy-making process.

Chapter outlines

The following chapter, Chapter 2, discusses IR approaches to the environment and their adequacy for studying the effectiveness of international environmental agreements. This takes the form of a survey of how the subject of environmental degradation has been integrated into international relations. To this end, the main IR approaches, the international law perspective as well as game/rational choice theory are considered. The study of international environmental agreements is mostly a neorealist/neoliberal institutionalist pursuit and this theoretical approach therefore limits its explanatory adequacy.

Chapter 3 is dedicated to the effectiveness debate that takes place in the regime theory school of thought. Effectiveness is essentially defined in institutional terms, i.e. referring to factors that influence the role of regimes. These refer to ideology, the distribution of power, regime robustness, the capacity of governments to deal with the environmental problem in question or the coherence among member states to name but a few. In effect, this means that effectiveness is not a question of will-power or determination but one of pure luck or circumstance. Since most regime theorists believe that will-power and desire for order are the determinants of regime formation, it should follow that these factors are also responsible for the formation of effective regimes. However, this is not the case for environmental regimes. If the conditions are favourable for the formation of an institutionally effective regime, then it will happen. If they are not, then neither institutional nor environmental effectiveness will be achieved. In addition, effectiveness refers mainly to successful cooperation, but this does not automatically include a successful solution of the environmental problem in question.

Chapter 4 analyses the concept of effectiveness further and establishes a connection between the concept and actuality of effectiveness. This chapter introduces four key determinants that form the basis of effectiveness; namely, economic structures, time, science and regulatory structures. Chapters 5 and 6 study the consequences of ignoring environmental effectiveness with special reference to the role of science and time in relation to the empirical studies.

The Mediterranean Action Plan will be studied in detail in Chapter 5. It is an action programme that is composed of a legal, scientific, financial and policy-planning component. These institutional components are designed to interact with the scientific and policy-planning parts providing the basis for the legal component. The financial component regulates and distributes funding. As the research findings demonstrate, one key problem in MAP is its inability to make its four components interrelate. In particular, the science base has an extremely limited policy function. Therefore MAP has to be defined as an enabling and awareness-raising agreement rather than a form of focused policy-making.

In Chapter 6 the Convention on Long-Range Transboundary Air Pollution is studied in detail. It is an international legal agreement that deals with transboundary atmospheric emissions that are associated with the phenomenon of acid rain. It is composed of several protocols that focus on a particular substance each – a single-substance approach. It suggests to approach a reduction of emissions on a technological basis through the introduction of Best Available Technology (BAT) and technological standards. Thus it can be described as having a very 'symptoms-based' approach to acid rain-related degradation. Therefore it is not an enabling but very much a policy-related agreement that operates on tight time frameworks and clearly defined emission reduction values. However, the empirical findings suggest that it disregards environmental necessities in favour of institutional feasibilities.

Chapter 7 considers the social and structural origins of environmental degradation and puts forward a framework of analysis that overcomes the methodological limitations of existing approaches. In particular, the four key determinants of time, science, economic and regulatory structures are used to do so.

Chapter 8 affirms these points in an applied context. Acid rain regulation concentrates on the symptom of pollution rather than its origin and disregards other degrading characteristics of fossil fuel consumption. MAP does not propose specific policy solutions to environmental problems because it does not operate in a region with sufficient environmental awareness to put environmental regulation on a par with or above economic development. Thus in both cases the link between society and nature/environment is neglected. Therefore, these agreements cannot be effective by their very nature. Chapter 9 summarises the argument of this book.

2 International environmental cooperation and IR: what is missing?

In this chapter, existing approaches to the study of international environmental cooperation will be reviewed and their shortcomings highlighted. The chapter demonstrates that while existing analysis is able to examine the institutional workings of international environmental agreements, it is unable to assess either environmental effectiveness or the place of international environmental agreements in relation to environment and society.

The study of international environmental agreements is a predominantly realist/neorealist/neoliberal institutionalist field of study and here these concepts will be transcended. The existing mainstream literature has serious shortcomings limiting the extent to which international environmental agreements can be analysed.

This chapter is organised in the following way: first, realist, neorealist and neoliberal institutionalist approaches including international law approaches and game/rational choice theory are reviewed with reference to the concept of effectiveness; second, since regime theory has dominated the international environmental agreement debate, I will subject key aspects of regime analysis to criticism, once again paying primary attention to the question of effectiveness; and third, having identified a wide set of limitations in conventional analysis, I then begin to propose the need for alternative understandings and explanations of the effectiveness of international environmental agreements. Overall, this chapter is intended to explicate, with reference to the existing literature, those problems that are associated with the study of the effectiveness of international environmental agreements.

The regulation of environmental degradation and IR

In historical terms, the study of IR has been dominated by three interrelated strands of thought, namely realism, neorealism and neoliberal institutionalism. Because of their dominance of IR, their main tenets and contributions to the study of the effectiveness of international environmental agreements will be studied.

Realism

The historical foundations of IR are grounded in realist thought. Although it goes beyond the scope of this book to outline and explain the principles underlying realism, a brief summary will be given in order to assess its appropriateness for studying the effectiveness of international environmental agreements.

Briefly, the realist approach treats IR as a science that has the aim to 'deliver' international society (which, for realists, is a society of states) from the evil of war (Hollis and Smith, 1991: 21). It takes a pessimistic view of human nature grounded in Machiavellian and Hobbesian philosophy. However, it also purports to be rational and sees international politics as a science that is driven by objective laws. For example, one of the founding fathers of realism, Morgenthau, sets out six main principles governing the relations between states, the first one of which is that politics 'is governed by objective laws that have their roots in human nature'.

Because of its emphasis on the political sphere, the realist perspective reduces analysis of the relationship between states to issues of power and self-interest, i.e. national interest. It assumes that states are guided by a rationally defined national interest and that their primary interest must be to maximise power. The drive to maximise power leads to war as states compete for power. More powerful states will maximise their power by taking away power from other states. The way to prevent war is to create a balance of power in which all states are either equally powerful or form alliances with other states to create a balance of power of alliances.

The scientistic and power-focused analysis of realist approaches does not offer any help in analysing the effectiveness of international environmental agreements. Since environmental agreements are not about power but about common threats to livelihoods, there is a divergence of focus between the subject matter of environmental degradation and the realist concern with war and power. Therefore realism cannot grasp the concept of effectively regulating an environmental problem through international cooperation unless this happens through an incorporation of environmental concern in the concept of national interest. Therefore, in realist terms, an international environmental agreement can only be effective if effectiveness is in the national interest.

However, assuming that the effectiveness of an agreement is in the national interest of the member states to the agreement also assumes that the national interest and environmental effectiveness can both be objectively defined. This is clearly not the case. The view that national interest can be defined rationally assumes perfect, undisputed knowledge about the causes and consequences of environmental degradation, agreement on what types of time frames form the basis of policy-making (especially in the case of environmental problems that are going to affect future generations more than present generations), agreement on the value of a healthy environment as opposed to economic gain and, above all, it assumes that all states are equally affected by environmental degradation. If these conditions are not fulfilled, national interests do not converge and effectiveness cannot be achieved. Thus, realism does not provide a basis which allows for cooperation for any other reason than national interest and power politics. By sidelining moral, ethical and environmental concerns, it deprives itself of a basis that allows for the analysis of issues not primarily related to power and national interest.

Neorealism

Neorealism is also referred to as structural realism and this sums up the difference between realism and neorealism well. The neorealist approach to IR aims to explain the relations within the international system in terms of the structure of the system. Waltz distinguishes between three basic tenets of the international system (Waltz, 1986: 70–97). First, international systems are decentralised and anarchic. Therefore the different units of the system are equal. Second, the international system is composed of units and these units are states. They are fundamentally similar in their composition and can thus be designated as units although there are obvious differences in their wealth, power and ideology. Third, the structure of the international system is determined by the capabilities of the states/units in the system. Capabilities can change and therefore the composition or balance of the international system can change.

These basic principles of neorealist thought show that the difference between realism and neorealism is not very striking. States are still considered to be the most important actors and the system is still primarily anarchic. However, the focus has moved away from war as the major source of conflict. This development leaves room for cooperation between states to achieve a common aim, a phenomenon that was not considered possible under realist principles. However, even neorealism only accounts for short-lived and purely interest-oriented cooperation. Therefore it cannot explain the web of international environmental cooperation that has developed in this century. According to Paterson, neorealism explains such cooperation in two ways. First, cooperation necessitates the presence of a hegemonic state that will lead the cooperative effort. Second, game-theoretic approaches focus on cooperation under anarchy, i.e. the production of collective goods (Paterson, 1996: 94). Both these points will be examined here and their adequacy for studying the effectiveness of international environmental agreements assessed.

Hegemonic stability

Hegemonic stability theory assumes that a central, hegemonic actor in the system has been legitimated by the other actors to take a leading role. As Williams explains, 'hegemonic stability theory is based on the premise that the presence of a single dominant actor in the international system leads to collectively desirable outcomes for all states' (Williams, 1994: 30). There are two basic flaws in this argument, which diminish its explanatory power. First, the neorealist concept of hegemony is based on direct power, not structural power in Lukes' sense (Lukes, 1974).[1] Therefore it cannot explain patterns of behaviour that are not directly based on an actor's hegemony. However, especially in international environmental cooperation, the role of structural power, particularly in the form of agenda-setting, determines hegemonic relationships, not overt or covert power. Thus the concept of hegemonic stability is necessarily limited in its application. Second, none of the case studies in this book shows the existence of hegemonic actors and nor do many other agreements at the global and regional level. For example, neither the regional marine pollution agreements nor the agreements emanating from the Rio summit have a driving hegemonic actor responsible for their creation.

Thus the concept of hegemonic stability is limited in its explanatory power. In addition, it is only able to explain cooperation between states but not the quality or effectiveness of cooperation because it lacks the tools to do so. Therefore it is not equipped to study the effectiveness of international environmental agreements because such a concern is outside its remit.

Rational choice and game theory

Rational choice and game theoretic approaches assume that under certain conditions it makes sense for actors to cooperate and therefore widespread and long-term cooperation is possible under conditions of anarchy. Quite simply, rational choice and game theory predict actor behaviour on the basis of what would be the best choice rationally for an actor in a specific situation. As Stein and Pauly put it, 'advocates of liberal, realist and cognitive explanations all concur that assessment of gains and losses are central to decisions to cooperate' (Stein, 1993: 2). Thus the motivations underlying actor behaviour and the predictive capacities arising therefrom are the focus of game theoretic and rational choice approaches.

Rational choice approaches are widely used to explain cooperative patterns in international environmental agreements. The two major criticisms of this approach are the subjective nature of the data used for the classification of states and the simplicity of the criteria employed. A selection of the criteria determining rational choice cannot but remain a selection and rational choice presupposes perfect access to information, a non-arbitrary nature of information – and it also assumes that values, culture, ideology, ethics, public opinion and related concepts can be rationalised, i.e. have a rational, neutral, value-free basis that can be objectively determined. This is clearly not the case.

Another point is the parsimonious nature of game theoretical and rational choice approaches. The arbitrary selection of a few indicators denies the complexity of policy-making processes and takes them out of the context in which these processes take place. It also disregards the existence of social and institutional structures within which policy-making takes place, is shaped and is constrained. Although rational choice theorists are aware of this criticism and argue that their studies do not aim to be absolutely accurate in real situations, but rather profess to provide guidelines for the macro theorist, in practice they have failed to demonstrate the macro–micro link on the theoretical and empirical level (Mouzelis, 1995: 29–30).

As Leys (1996: 36) argues, rational choice reduces discourses to a very small number of general concepts such as institutions, organisations and their agents. Further, he maintains that the aspect of perceived reality modelled by the rational choice approach might not necessarily be a key aspect and that the chosen method cannot prove it is (p. 39). Thus there is a methodological problem with rational choice theory: it arbitrarily selects a number of 'variables' and assesses their influence on a certain event in a rational way, but this is a micro-theoretical approach and cannot sustain its argument on the macro-level. This is a common problem of institutional approaches and also of neorealism in general.

To summarise, neorealist approaches to IR cannot contribute to the study of effectiveness of international environmental agreements because of their limited nature. They primarily focus on explaining the behaviour of units, especially states, in the international system and do not include the object of cooperation, in this case environmental degradation, in the analysis. Therefore, neorealism is ill-equipped to assess the effectiveness of such cooperation. The two strands of neorealism that deal with environmental cooperation – hegemonic stability theory and rational choice approaches – cannot address the problem of effectiveness. Hegemonic stability can neither explain the existence of most environmental agreements nor analyse their effectiveness. Rational choice theory offers parsimonious explanations of actor behaviour but is too methodologically limited to provide an analysis of the effectiveness of cooperation. Thus, neorealism is of limited use for the analytical purpose of this book.

Neoliberal institutionalism

This approach evolved out of the Grotian and Kantian traditions and, in IR, centres on the work of regime theorists such as Keohane, Young or Levy. Its prominence in the 1990s is related to the growth of international interdependence and the advancement of regional or economic integration. Since it can be largely equated with regime theory, especially in relation to the effectiveness of international environmental agreements, it will be discussed in detail in that particular context. The legal approach has been included under the neoliberal institutionalist rubric because of its shared origins in the Grotian philosophy of international law.

The legal approach

The legal perspective is an institutional approach to the study of environmental degradation. International law is defined as a system of rules and principles that govern the international relations between states (Dixon, 1990: 2). These rules are created by states for states and cover almost any aspect of inter-state relationships. The sources of international law are statutes of the International Court of Justice, international treaties and custom.

International law is not concerned solely with the study of actor behaviour (not in explanatory terms but *vis-à-vis* its lawfulness) but also with the evolution and change of principles, rules and norms (Fawcett, 1970). In the general environmental field, this would mean the study of the nature and content of the principles in global conventions from the 1972 Stockholm UN Conference on the Human Environment as the advent of large-scale international environmental regulation to the present and the search for trends. Trends in this context means legal developments such as a convention-plus-protocol approach, convention-plus-annex approach, special area status, or protocol-plus-declaration (Sand, 1990). In a more specialised field, such as air or marine pollution, an international law analysis would include the first inter- or binational attempts to tackle a specific problem, a history of international legislation and a discussion of various conventional approaches in use (for example, Rosencranz, 1981). However, such discussions are limited to the legal consequences of a specific approach and do not include an analysis of, for example, the scientific method underlying a legal approach, social consequences or economic cost.

Another area of international law focuses on the study of compliance with international environmental agreements (Cameron *et al.*, 1996). Again, this approach is restricted to studying legal technicalities related to the improvement of compliance.

As compared to various IR approaches, the international law perspective analyses processes as well as actor behaviour. In this sense, it is broader than, for example, regime theory. However, the study of processes in international law presupposes that the legal approach is the best problem-solving approach in the international system, i.e. is centred on explicit norms and rules. The view that the legal approach is the best problem-solving approach in international environmental policy-making neglects the insight that the international law perspective is fed by many other disciplines such as the natural sciences, sociology, politics, economics or geography. The assumptions delivered by the mainstream of these disciplines inform the legal process but their validity is not usually questioned. There is little questioning of underlying or open assumptions in the legal analysis of international environmental agreements. Further, the international law perspective does not relate back to the subject matter it is supposed to regulate but concentrates on legal feasibilities.

To summarise, international law is a discipline that is informed by other disciplines but is not always aware of its dependence on them. It does not question the social origins of problems and thus cannot deal with them on a deeper level. It does not try to analyse or change society but just applies regulations, i.e. it is a purely reactive problem-solving approach.

From the point of view of short-term regulation of an environmental problem, the legal approach with an emphasis on institutional arrangements can contribute to the study of international environmental agreements but cannot provide a satisfying analysis of their motivations, usefulness, problem-solving capacity, social origin or environmental benefit. Therefore, the study of international law cannot lead to any new insights that are relevant in the field of international relations, except for some limited usefulness in the field of regime theory.

Regime theory

The regime theory tradition evolved out of more general developments in IR theory, in particular the further development of neorealism. Regime theory studies order in the international system and assumes that order is a function of will. This was guided by the need and desire for norms and rules which govern interaction between states. The concept of regime was first used in the international politics literature in the 1970s by Ruggie and described by Keohane (1984: 57) as

> a set of mutual expectations, rules and regulations, plans, organisational energies and financial commitments, which has been accepted by a group of states.

This description was narrowed down to the definition in Krasner (1983: 2), which was widely accepted during the 1980s:

> Regimes can be defined as sets of implicit and explicit principles, norms, rules and decision-making procedures around which actors' expectations converge in a given area of international relations. Principles are beliefs of fact, causation and rectitude. Norms are standards of behaviour defined in terms of rights and obligations. Rules are specific prescriptions or proscriptions for action. Decision-making procedures are prevailing practices for making and implementing collective choice.

This definition was still confusing and the distinction between international system and international regimes was blurred. Puchala and Hopkins, for example, even went as far as to describe colonialism as a regime (1983: 61–92). By that account, Lloyds of London insurance market would be a regime just as well as the bipolar balance of power system of the Cold War. It was realised that the wide pitch of the definition inhibited its explanatory power. In the 1990s, therefore, Keohane has narrowed the definition down to

> institutions with explicit rules, agreed upon by governments, which pertain to particular sets of issues in international relations,

which is a clearer and more focused definition (Hurrell, 1993: 54). So, mainstream regime theory in the 1990s can largely be equated with the study of formal international agreements since emphasis has been placed on explicit rules.

According to Krasner, there are three varieties of regime theory: realist/structuralist, modified realist/structuralist and Grotian (Krasner, 1983: 6–8). The realist variety conceives of the world as consisting of state actors engaged in a struggle for power maximisation. Regimes are a method by which powerful states set up rules that best represent their interests. Therefore, the realist view of regimes has nothing to offer in the analysis to IR that has not already been discussed elsewhere in the realist literature with a different terminology.

The modified/structuralist view of regime theory is based on the idea of rational choice and moves away from the idea of pure power politics to more functional areas of international cooperation, such as social or technological issues. Regimes are seen as the result of bargaining and negotiations and these results are often, but not necessarily, analysed in a game theoretical framework. The basic approach of the modified realist view is state-centric although it takes into account the existence of non-state actors (for example, Choucri, 1993).

Last, the Grotian model emphasises social factors in the study of international relations. In addition, the importance of domestic and transnational actors is stressed although the state is seen as the central actor in the international arena. The Grotian argument is that the actors are necessarily bound by certain norms and rules to be observed when social interaction occurs. These may be overt or covert rules and norms, that means open and tangible or implied, structural, or even moral. These points are not covered by more formalistic approaches to regime theory (Evans and Wilson, 1992: 331).

Problems with regime theory

Writing in the 1980s but still having validity, Strange (1983: 337–354) criticised the study of regime theory, arguing that it is a passing fad arising out of a temporary reaction to developments in world history; that it is too vague; too value-laden; too static in analysis and rooted in a state-centric outlook. The first of her criticisms has to be rejected since, in the 1990s, regime theory is well and truly alive, if in a different form, and therefore the contention that it is but a passing fad is wrong. The other criticisms will be addressed below.

One of the problems with these earlier and more general studies in regime theory is that they are used to explain the nature of the whole subject of International Relations for which it is clearly not suited. The early definition of regime is so vague that it basically covers any form of interaction between two actors. The procedure surrounding a letter of credit is as much a regime as the Nazi–Soviet Pact of 1939. The analytical tool of regimes is therefore not sufficiently sharp and focused, being of limited value as an explanation of inter-, cross- and transnational action. The Grotian view that takes into account the necessity of rules and norms for the guidance of social interaction has a more thorough basis for analysis than the other two strands but cannot overcome the methodological problems associated with regime theory, i.e. actor-centric institutional focus.

However, the Grotian view has continued to influence the proliferation of regime theoretical analysis in the 1990s. For example, Hurrell (1993: 50–51) argues that the central question of regimes has retained its validity:

How is cooperation possible between states claiming sovereignty but competing for power and influence in a situation of anarchy? What is the relationship between law and norms on the one hand and power and interests on the other?

This view stresses the importance of studying the factors determining cooperation. However, despite the consideration of power structures, Hurrell only takes into account actor-centric, closed-system institutional considerations. This is a problem associated with methodology. Regime theory tends to pursue and analyse a selection of variables and attempts to assess their significance with counterfactual means by assuming that these variables operate outside a temporal context and in a social vacuum, i.e. they are not interacting and interconnecting with other 'variables' or social processes.

As an illustration, a typical 1990s regime theoretical approach is that of Young and Osherenko (1993: 223–251) in which they propose that power-based, interest-based, knowledge-based and contextual hypotheses be tested in order to find the determinants of success or failure in efforts to form international regimes. They assume that the formation of international regimes reflects the distribution and configuration of power in the region, or indeed at the global level and is the result of the cooperation between self-interested parties with the aim to benefit jointly, for which the likelihood of a joint gain is a precondition. Common knowledge and interpretation of causal mechanisms as well as known knowledge brokers have an important influence on regime formation, as may factors that are not directly related to the regime formation process.

This approach has several shortcomings. First and foremost, it places emphasis on regime formation but not on regime quality or the likely effectiveness of a regime or agreement. This is a problem of focus. The contents and adequacy of the regime and the ways in which they are determined are neglected in favour of diplomatic history-type analysis of regime formation. Second, the approach concentrates on the negotiation stage of regime formation and neglects processes before and parallel to the negotiation stage. This ties in with the aforementioned point that diplomatic history-type accounts concentrate on actor behaviour rather than social and knowledge-related processes. Although Young and Osherenko argue that knowledge-based and contextual factors should be included in regime analysis, they only refer to factors directly related to the regime in question, thus treating the regime as a closed system that is not influenced by other events, developments or processes. Third, it provides no mechanism for explaining regime change/evolution. These are only explained in terms of changes in actor behaviour. Again, this presupposes that the regime exists in a social vacuum, i.e. is a closed system. Fourth, the approach is state-centric and static, and fails to consider many non-state actors and processes. Although non-state actors have found their way into regime analysis, they are considered to be secondary actors compared to states. The relationship between different types of actor is not analysed with reference to structural and systemic considerations. In short, the Young/Osherenko approach raises a list of very interesting and relevant questions but largely fails to apply them in context. This is characteristic of regime formation analysis.

Saurin (1995) brings regime theoretical shortcomings to the point:

> The inadequacy of regime theory, particularly in its rational choice approach, is that it avoids dialectical, relational and social thinking … The notion that thought and action are mutually constitutive is alien to regime theory.

To this should be added that it is not just thought and action but also structure that are mutually constitutive. Regime theory concentrates on action, or behaviour, but without seeing this action as part of a wider social, even historical, process and context. Crespi (1992: 5) makes a distinction between action and behaviour along the following lines. Behaviour is not related to intentionality but rather to instinct. Animals, for example, behave but they do not act. Action, on the other hand, assumes a degree of intentionality and is unique to humans. According to this definition, regime theory deals with both action and the behaviour of states, without placing either in a wider framework. Thus the object of study is isolated and stripped of its spatial, social and temporal meaning. The object of study becomes a deliberate, rational concept because it is seen as a rational design, wilfully and intentionally created. However, the lack of explanatory power of these approaches clearly demonstrates that this reductionist method of analysis cannot advance our understanding of the way society interacts.

Gale (1998) argues that regime theory can be deployed outside neorealist and neoliberal institutionalist frameworks. Therefore, he maintains, the criticisms of regime theory are really levelled against the neorealist and neoliberal institutionalist framework in which it is used rather than regime theory itself. However, he fails to provide convincing evidence for this argument and does not demonstrate how an alternative type of regime theory would operate.

Epistemic communities

A different approach within regime formation theory has emerged and become very popular in the past decade, namely Haas's epistemic communities approach. Although state-centric, this approach focuses on the effect experts and knowledge-based communities have on governmental learning and the development of new state objectives. As Haas (1990: 52) puts it:

> Such an approach looks at the conditions under which behaviour may change based upon a new understanding of the causal relationship in the world. Writers from this tradition look at policy-making in terms of such nonsystemic variables and actors as ideas, knowledge, beliefs, experts and scientists. Arguing that structural analysis alone overpredicts inter-state conflict and underpredicts co-operation, such writers rely on insights from

organisation theory, policy sciences, social psychology, the philosophy and history of science, the sociology of knowledge, and international relations to explain the choice of state ends to which resources will be deployed and the precondition for and forms of international co-operation.

In the environmental field, advances in science and technology play an important role as they form the basis on which possible solutions to environmental threats are considered. They also form the basis of the identification of problems. For this reason, governments or policy-makers attach great importance to the opinion of scientists who are considered experts in the relevant field. These experts are called an 'epistemic community', i.e. a group of professionals that share a common interpretation of cause and effect relationships, means of testing them and have a common value basis. This 'monopoly on truth and expertise' gives the epistemic community a power base from which it can operate.

The epistemic community approach takes the emphasis away from the level of governmental negotiations and attaches importance to the role of the expert adviser and the potential transnational dimension of the epistemic community concept. However, there are several problems with this approach. First, important as an epistemic community may be, it is never the only actor in the process of developing an international environmental agreement and the epistemic community approach fails to place itself in context. Second, although this approach criticises state-centrism, it is state-centric itself in the way it is applied, which means that it neglects the role of wider processes and knowledge as such (independent from the knowledge holder). In Haas's Mediterranean case study, the influence of epistemic communities is measured by membership of scientists in policy-making national bodies, thus reducing a potentially transnational concept to state-centric analysis. Litfin (1994: 47) makes the additional criticism that the epistemic community approach does not explain the source of the epistemic community's power and that it provides no coherent conception of knowledge. These points will not be elaborated as the concern of this book is with effective environmental cooperation rather than concepts of power and knowledge *per se*.

Conclusion

To summarise, although there are several strands of regime theory, which are quite different from each other, they all limit their study to the behaviour and motivations of actors and thus limit their scope. Regime theorists are trying to develop sets of 'laws' under which cooperation occurs, but this attempt is bound to fail as each case study has its specific characteristics and cannot be generalised. As long as actor behaviour remains the centre of regime analysis, it cannot be expected that regime theory can lead to substantial new insights.

Regime theory has an inherent internal logic which is limited to studying a cooperative effort at the institutional level only, treating an agreement as a closed system. Therefore its shortcomings are founded in its methodology.

Actor-centric, closed-system analysis cannot capture the complexity of social and environmental problems and confines itself to modelling institutional set-ups. The variations in regime theoretical approaches are found at the modelling level, not in methodology. However, the study of effectiveness of international environmental agreements necessitates a meta-theoretical approach for which the regime theory method is ill-equipped. Before developing this point in more detail, the effectiveness strand of regime theory will be analysed in the next chapter.

3 IR theory and effectiveness

There is an active debate on effectiveness within the regime theory school of thought which is conducted by various authors. The debate is concentrated in two camps: in Norway and in the United States. One of the initiators of the debate is Arild Underdal with his article on 'the concept of regime effectiveness' (1992: 227–240). Another main contributor and initiator on the other side of the Atlantic is Oran Young and his research on resource regimes (1982).

In this chapter, the definition of the term 'effectiveness' and its adequacy in the existing literature are examined. This includes an analysis of the research questions the above writers ask. The rationale for this is that the definition of effectiveness each author gives is closely linked up with the research questions asked. For example, if the research question centres on how institutions have to be organised in order to be effective, then the definition of effectiveness will focus on institutional details. This relationship needs to be studied before concepts of effectiveness can be looked at in detail.

The Norwegian school

Underdal tries to find indicators which examine the conditions under which a cooperative arrangement will be effective (1992: 227). He does not give an explicit definition of effectiveness but rather offers three questions that need to be asked in order to study regime effectiveness systematically. These refer to the establishment of the object to be evaluated and the standard against which effectiveness is measured. In addition, Underdal surmises that effectiveness is a relative concept that needs to be defined individually in the case of each regime. This approach aims to serve as a basis in an applied context but is vague on where effectiveness is situated, e.g. problem-solving adequacy, institutional set-up, implementation or compliance.

Underdal's argument relating to the introduction of standards raises an important point which leads to two consequences. First, it shapes the concept of effectiveness and helps get over the general vagueness which is present in other approaches. Second, it introduces arbitrariness to the definition of effectiveness since standard-setting is a subjective process. The standard is dependent on what the aim is. A regime theorist's standards differ from those of an environmental activist. This point has been neglected in the effectiveness debate despite Underdal's role as an initiator. Thus, Underdal's approach needs to be incorporated into a definition of effectiveness although on its own it is too narrow.

Wettestad and Andresen elaborate on Underdal and have developed a series of indicators which show that their main research question is whether the institution in question is actually dealing with the environmental problem it is supposed to solve or improve. These indicators are:

- the achievement of the institutional goals set by its member states,
- the degree of correspondence between expert advice and actual decision taken,
- the degree of improvement compared to the pre-institutional state of the environment, i.e. what the state of the environment would be without the institution.

(Wettestad and Andresen, 1991: 2)

This definition is the most detailed given by all writers and it includes institutional and environmental criteria by which effectiveness is measured, which is unique to the Norwegian school. Wettestad and Andresen's approach builds on Underdal and on Kay and Jacobson (1983).

Wettestad and Andresen, following Underdal, differentiate between the effectiveness of a solution and that of a problem-solving effort. This is a distinction between what the agreement sets out to do and what it actually does. Wettestad and Andresen focus on solution effectiveness since they believe that an evaluation of the problem-solving effort should include e.g. transaction costs and do not consider this practicable. This separation is a temporal distinction with the concept of a problem-solving effort referring to the agreement-making stage and the concept of a solution to the implementation of the agreement. It is arguable that a solution is easier to evaluate than an effort, even more so since one of Wettestad and Andresen's indicators is the evaluation of the change a regime has brought about as compared to the state of the environment without that particular regime. This is not an indicator that can realistically be used (see below). In addition, their second indicator of effectiveness relates to the degree of correspondence between independent expert advice and the actual decision taken, which evaluates the effectiveness of a problem-solving *effort*. Hence, there are several weaknesses in the internal logic of Wettestad and Andresen's approach.

However, some points raised by Wettestad and Andresen need to be taken into consideration for contextualising the concept of effectiveness, namely the distinction between problem-solving effort and solution as well as one of the indicators of effectiveness using independent expert advice as a standard against which goal achievement can be measured. This is an environmental indicator and a standard as proposed by Underdal. However, this indicator can only be used in the full awareness that independent scientific advice does not mean value-free or objective scientific advice. The implications of this point are discussed in the following chapters. So, there are some lessons to be drawn from the Norwegian school although it has not gone beyond the methodological limitations of regime theoretical approaches.

The American school

Young (1992: 161), as the major representative of the American school, asks the following question:

> How can we assess the significance of institutions as independent or intervening variables with regard to individual and collective behaviour at the international level and, in so doing, resolve the conflict between these divergent points of view?

This question shows clearly that for Young effectiveness is defined by looking at the role of the international environmental institutions in question. For him, an institution (p. 161)

> is effective to the extent that its operation impels actors to behave differently than they would if the institution did not exist or if some other institutional arrangement were put in its place.

Thus, Young defines effectiveness as lying in the performance of the institution. Other determinants such as environmental criteria are reflected in the performance and therefore influence effectiveness indirectly. Measurement of effectiveness of an agreement is purely performance-related. No connection between problem-solving adequacy of the regime and its performance is made. This is a classical case of what Cox calls problem-solving theory (1981).

Young has established a list of factors that influence the role of regimes (1992: 176–194). These are divided into exogenous factors relating to the social environment in which the regime operates, and endogenous factors relating to the character of the regime: transparency, i.e. the ease of monitoring or verifying compliance; robustness of social-choice mechanisms; transformation rules, i.e. ability to adapt to change; capacity of governments to implement provisions; distribution of power such as material inequality between member states; the level of interdependence among member states; and the intellectual order expressed as ideology and the power of ideas. All these factors can help or impede the effectiveness of a regime. An effective regime would need high transparency, high robustness, good transformation rules, high capacity of governments, equal distribution of power, high interdependence and a constant intellectual order. All these factors relate to regime performance.

Levy, Young and Zürn name three dimensions of regime consequences: direct versus indirect effects, internal versus external effects and positive versus negative effects (1994: 21). The direct/indirect dimension depends on the length of the causal chain connecting regime and behaviour. Direct effects have short causal chains and indirect ones larger ones. Internal/external effects refer to regime consequences within and outside the issue area treated. The distinction between positive and negative effects is obvious and does not require further explanation. These levels of analysis, the authors argue, have to be incorporated into the regime theory measurement of effectiveness, namely the causal connection between regime and behavioural change. This causal connection consists mostly of external and internal factors. External factors are patterns of interests, distribution of influence, nature of the issue area, while internal factors are design features and programmatic activities (Levy, 1993a: 21–27). Again, the above criticism of regime theoretical approaches and the specific criticisms made with reference to Young apply.

This separation of variables of effectiveness into endogenous and exogenous factors or internal and external effects poses a serious problem. Since for regime theorists order is a function of will, the achievement of effective order should be a function of will as well. However, if effectiveness is largely dependent on exogenous factors as Young (and Levy below) argue, then it is not a function of will but dependent on the nature of the problem, the particular membership of the regime and other circumstantial factors, thus becoming fortuitous. From this it follows that it may not be possible to have an effective (in whatever way) regime even if all the members are ambitious to form one. Therefore effectiveness is not a function of will.

This point questions the foundations of regime theoretical assumptions. The general criticisms of regime theory mainly refer to questions of method. However, this point affects the intrinsic logic. Regime theoretical focus on actor behaviour can be defended by arguing that the definition of behaviour encompasses not only actor behaviour but also the outcome of interactive processes involving members of international society (Young, 1992: 162). This refers to the regime theoretical argument that actors make processes and that the distinction between actors and processes is therefore minimal as processes are merely the outcome of action. However, even a regime theorist will have to admit that exogenous factors are a characteristic of exogenous processes, thus confirming the existence of processes, structures and systems that are not directly related to actor behaviour. This clearly means that closed-system actor-centric analysis as defined by the institutional framework used in regime theory is insufficient for an understanding of effectiveness and that regime theory cannot account for this fault in its internal logic.

Spin-offs from Young's work include Levy's. Levy also follows the tradition of defining effectiveness in institutional-behavioural terms. However, he expands:

> Effective international institutions, in the comprehensive sense, not only redirect behaviour; they also solve environmental problems; and they do so in a more efficient and equitable manner than available alternatives.
>
> (Levy, 1993a: 17)

This is very similar to the definition given by Haas *et al.* (1993: 7). They, too, focus on institutional effectiveness: 'Is the quality of the environment better because of the institution?' This implies that an effective institution should initiate change that would not occur otherwise. However, this point does not relate to the environmental problem and its needs. It is limited to any type of change without indicating how such change can be measured or how change can be causally attributed to the institution in question rather than some regime-external developments.

Haas, Keohane and Levy refer to the 'three Cs' that are preconditions for effective institutions: concern, the contractual environment and capacity. They do not subdivide them into categories as Young or Levy do but implicitly the distinction between exogenous and endogenous factors is there. Again, upon close study of the argument, it transpires that the achievement of effectiveness as defined by the authors is not necessarily in the hands of the institution's members. However, given regime theoretical definitions of effectiveness, it should be. According to Levy, it is up to the institution to raise its ability to achieve effectiveness and this is what effective institutions do (1993a: 20). This argument is simplistic and cannot be sustained. It implies that an effective institution's members all score highly on the 'three Cs' and now try 'to spread the gospel'. However, the 'contractual environment' and 'concern' are circumstantial factors, making effectiveness a fortuitous concept rather than a function of will.

The arguments concerning the regime theoretical approaches show clearly that this definition of effectiveness only leads to ambiguities and contradictions. It is vague in that it focuses on 'regime consequences' (i.e. implementation) as measures of effectiveness but does not measure the consequences against a set standard. In addition, as shown before, there is no explanation of how change incited by the regime can be measured as development since the pre-regime state need not necessarily be due to the regime but to external developments or pure fortuity. The suggestion to model the state of affairs as would have been without the regime is practically impossible for exactly this reason. It demonstrates again that the regime theory approach is limited by its own method and cannot reach beyond its self-imposed limitations.

Rational choice, regime theory and effectiveness

A related approach is that by Bernauer who combines his rational choice framework with Underdal's concerns by asking under what conditions states cooperate and if international institutions can contribute to successful international environmental collaboration, and if so, under what conditions (Bernauer, 1995: 351). Again, the research focus disregards how institutional efforts relate to the environmental problem in question. He believes that effectiveness can be measured in terms of goal attainment, namely by assessing the change in actor behaviour or the state of the natural environment over time along 'dimensions identified by institutional goals and end points defined by institutional goals'.

Bernauer concedes that there are major evaluative and analytical challenges to be met if institutions are to be measured as 'explanatory variables' or if their effect is to be assessed and these evaluations then compiled into a theoretical approach explaining success or failure. He recommends (p. 353) that

> to arrive at practical recommendations for the design and operation of insti-
> tutions, we have to assess and compare institutional performance
> systematically and explain when and why specific types of institutions influ-
> ence the behaviour of governments, businesses and other actors in a direction
> that solves the environmental problems that motivated their establishment.

There is a basic assumption that a set of rules and norms leading to effectiveness in agreement-making *can* be established and that these rules and norms can
be identified through systematic study and comparative analysis of existing international environmental agreements.

As already discussed in the context of rational choice approaches, comparative analysis presupposes the existence of rules and norms where there might not
be any. Bernauer's method leads to questions about the feasibility of compara-
bility. Comparative study is based on the comparison of like with like. However,
each agreement arises out of its own unique circumstances and therefore
comparative studies are of limited use since the only generalisations that can be
drawn are the obvious.

In order to see how Bernauer tackles this problem, let us see how he would
evaluate the effect of institutions:

- The effect of the agreement is measured according to its goal attainment,
  i.e. 'the difference over time or across cases, between actor behaviour or the
  state of the natural environment along dimensions identified by institutional
  goals on the one hand, and certain endpoints defined by institutional goals,
  on the other'.
- It needs to be measured how far the institution, as compared to other
  factors, has contributed to goal attainment. Together with the first point,
  this comprises a measurement of institutional effectiveness.
- The effect of the specific institutional framework of an agreement is analysed and compared (p. 364).

In fact, this does not offer anything other regime theorists or Susskind (see
below) have not already offered. Although Bernauer bemoans the fact that no
rational choice analyses have yet been made of international environmental
agreements assessing their success or failure and that existing approaches are ill-
defined and too vague, he does not offer a viable alternative. However, it can be
assumed that even with empirical studies, the findings would not lead to substantial new insights as the basis (that such rules and norms exist) is not convincing.
In addition, Bernauer repeats the mistake of other regime theorists to assume
that it is possible to attribute goal attainment to the institution in question or to
other factors. Therefore, Bernauer's approach suffers from the same shortcomings as the other works discussed here.

International law and effectiveness

Susskind, following the legal tradition, asks how we can negotiate more effective global agreements but does not offer an explanation of what is to be understood by 'effective'. However, from his outlined argument it can be deduced that he is concerned with the improvement of institutional structures on the one hand and the political weight and integration of environmental issues on the other, i.e. a move away from an 'isolationist' environmental policy (Susskind, 1994: 7). Thus he also places himself among the institutionalists albeit with a different focus.

Susskind's book suffers from the absence of a definition of effectiveness although he identifies four areas in which most of the failures of global environmental negotiations have occurred. This is a pragmatic-subjective approach that is not based on the effectiveness debate. This may be because Susskind is first and foremost concerned with negotiations and not with institutions.

The four shortcomings he identifies are:

- lack of fair representation and voting procedures in negotiations,
- uneven balance between scientific and political considerations,
- failure to adequately link environmental policy to other policy issues,
- failure to implement effective monitoring and enforcement mechanisms.

These four points all relate to the negotiation process and not to the agreement itself. However, since the negotiation process is quite a substantial part of the agreement-making process, these four points do have relevance for the definition of effectiveness. The fourth point seems to be occupied with implementing parts of the agreement and it is difficult to see how this relates directly to the negotiation process. The first and fourth points focus on institutional framework issues while the second and third points deal with the issue area in question.

Susskind comes from a legal background and therefore the criticisms made in relation to International Law approaches apply. His ideas of effectiveness are conceived in a legal framework which will necessarily lead to a certain narrowness although they go beyond traditional legal concerns of compliance. However, some parts of the debate can be recognised from regime theory arguments. For example, Susskind distinguishes between idealists and pragmatists with the pragmatists taking the role of regime theorists. They argue that the existence of many agreements presents huge progress since it is an exercise in awareness-raising and puts environmental issues firmly on the agenda. However, for the idealists nothing short of positive action will suffice. Susskind takes over the role of the idealist and analyses the flaws in the legal system.

From this point of view his work is helpful and has valuable contributions. He critically analyses issues such as sovereignty, traditional structures of international environmental agreements and incentives that initiate bargaining processes in separate chapters. These are all issues that need to be considered for assessing the performance, or performance potential, of international environmental agreements without some of the methodological constraints of regime theory.

However, for a wider definition of effectiveness, Susskind's approach is too limited as it is not concerned with, for example, standards set by an agreement and how they relate to the environmental problem in question, how wider social processes feed into the process, what role time dimensions play to name but a few of the points raised later. Since Susskind is not concerned with defining effectiveness but with tightening negotiating processes, this is not a limitation of the approach but of the method.

A body of literature in international environmental law is concerned with the study of compliance (Cameron *et al.*, 1996). Although it is conceded here that compliance as a form of implementation does indeed relate to the concept of effectiveness,[1] compliance theory itself recognises that 'greater compliance is neither a necessary nor sufficient condition for effectiveness' (Mitchell, 1994: 25). However, it is one aspect of effectiveness and as such needs to be mentioned despite its methodological limitation.

These are summaries of the effectiveness authors' definitions of the concept and their starting points or motivations respectively for analysing effectiveness. It becomes clear that the motivation for studying effectiveness is reflected in its definition. It also becomes obvious that there is no clear definition or consensus on what effectiveness actually means. This needs to be taken further. Since these issues are so intertwined and at the same time crucial for the understanding of the effectiveness literature, this task needs to be carried out in this introductory part of the book. First, we will distil what is meant by effectiveness and then relate it back to the underlying research motivations.

What is effectiveness?

One insight that has emerged from a review of the various definitions of effectiveness is that there is no real understanding of what it actually means and how it can be measured. As Paterson (1995: 214) argues:

> Conventional approaches to regimes 'depoliticise' international environmental problems by providing criteria by which responses can be judged in a supposedly neutral manner … Yet these cannot be isolated from other criteria. Environmental questions cannot be neatly boxed off from other political questions. The regimes established to resolve transnational environmental problems always benefit some social groups more than others, whether or not they are successful from a purely environmental point of view and they also preclude the broader questions of whether the existing political, social and economic orders may themselves generate environmental crises.

Within the effectiveness debate in regime theory, two approaches have crystallised. On one level, effectiveness is seen in terms of institutional workings through good institutional structures. On another level, effectiveness is measured on the basis of environmental impact. It seems that a distinction can be made between institutional and environmental effectiveness. The approaches analysed here are mainly concerned with institutional effectiveness. Although Haas, Keohane and Levy's interest in environmental impact could be construed as being concerned with environmental effectiveness, I argue that their concern is predominantly with the change that an institution can bring about rather than environmental quality *per se*. Therefore, their approaches should still be classified as institutional. The Norwegian school constitutes a partial exception to this point although later works (Andresen and Wettestad, 1995) also focus almost exclusively on institutional aspects.

Institutional effectiveness is related to the behaviour of the member states in an agreement and the institutional, or agreement, structure. The main indicator of institutional effectiveness identified so far seems to be the incitement of change in actor behaviour, thus resulting in a change in the state of the environment that would not have occurred without the institution.

This poses two problems. First, a change in actor behaviour may result in some action taken but this may not actually improve the state of the environment. For example, the 1985 CLRTAP Sulphur Protocol led to a 30 per cent reduction in national sulphur dioxide emissions by 1993 but that did not stop the forests from dying or lower the rate of respiratory diseases. Young (1994: 143–144) does take account of this problem in his later works in which he distinguishes between six dimensions of effectiveness (effectiveness as problem-solving, as goal attainment, behavioural effectiveness, process effectiveness, constitutive effectiveness and evaluative effectiveness). His point of effectiveness as problem-solving as distinct from effectiveness as goal attainment does indeed come to the same conclusion, namely that goal attainment does not necessarily lead to the solution of the environmental problem in question. However, this point is not taken further and is used only in a descriptive context. Young's analytical distinctions do not serve the purpose of improving effectiveness but are limited to creating a taxonomy.

Alternatively, the change may result in an improvement in the state of the environment as compared to the pre-agreement stage but this may not actually be sufficient to solve the environmental problem. For example, the Mediterranean Action Plan is generally assumed by its policy-makers to have led to an improvement in the state of the marine environment between the 1970s and 1980s but this was offset by a higher level of industrialisation in the region.

Second, a problem of measurement exists. It is impossible to isolate the processes that led to the conclusion of an agreement from larger social, historical, political, economic, technological, scientific and environmental processes and therefore the impact of an institution/agreement cannot be measured. After all, the larger social processes that led to the creation of the agreement quite possibly also led to changes on other levels and therefore change cannot be attributed to the institution/agreement alone. It is impossible to analytically isolate the effects of the agreement from, for example, the larger consciousness developed in general. Therefore, it needs to be argued that a definition based on institutional effectiveness alone is lacking in many respects.[2]

Although Wettestad's working paper argues that the primary aim of an effective analysis of environmental regimes has to be their capacity to solve the environmental question behind it, he realises that environmental problems have 'objective and subjective dimensions' (1995: 15). These dimensions are not static, i.e. they change over time. Therefore, Wettestad argues, that 'this comprehensiveness strengthens the case for focusing most attention on the outcome/behavioural change part of the concept [of effectiveness]' because other issues are too difficult to measure. Likewise, Young (1997: 13) argues:

> Intuitively it makes sense to regard international regimes as successful or effective when they serve to solve or alleviate the problems that motivate their founders to create them. As it turns out, however, empirically demonstrating effectiveness in this sense is extremely difficult, which has led to a variety of other perspectives that emphasise variables such as goal attainment, implementation and compliance, behavioural change, social learning and the initiation of social practices.

Again, this is a methodological constraint of regime theory and an avoidance of the environmental quality issue. Environmental effectiveness measures the improvement of the environment against a particular standard. Wettestad and Andresen mention two environmental indicators, namely goal achievement of the agreement (which doubles as a criterion for institutional effectiveness and becomes an environmental indicator only in an appropriate framework) and how far agreement content is equal to expert advice on what measures should be taken (1991: 2). The first indicator faces the criticism of vagueness as goal achievement can be measured over time and at different institutional or environmental stages. Does the signing of an agreement constitute goal achievement or its ratification, implementation on the national or local level, and what significance is given to the time dimension? This indicator is too vague to be significant and needs to be qualified by introducing standards. The second indicator gives a standard against which the contents of an agreement can be measured but independent expert advice is only of limited use as a standard because of the controversial status of scientific advice. However, independent expert advice from various sources is quite a good indicator for partial environmental effectiveness. This leads to the conclusion that the definition of environmental effectiveness needs to be developed. In order to elaborate this issue, the motivations for studying effectiveness need to be considered in order to put the definitional problems into perspective.

Why study effectiveness?

As the above review shows, the motivations for studying effectiveness are not as straightforward as they seem. The institutional school of thought studies effectiveness mainly because it relates to the issue of institutional performance. These writers are mainly regime theorists and as such believe in the vital importance of international institutions/agreements, or regimes, as a form of international order. Effectiveness is used as a measure for regime strength or weakness and thus an effective regime must necessarily be one with a high level of cooperation. The issue of how well this cooperation deals with the problem giving rise to it takes a secondary position. In the traditional environmental effectiveness strand, the concern is with the environmental problem necessitating the agreement. However, so far these concerns form only part of a wider institutional analysis rather than the principal concern.

The subordinate role of environmental effectiveness is related to research focus. Regime theorists assume that a significant and cooperative institution will incite change and change will improve the pre-institutional state of being. However, change might, for example, only be an exercise in awareness-raising but for the regime theorist this is a success since it has resulted in an improvement on the pre-regime situation. The standard by which effectiveness is measured is not set in relation to the problem to be dealt with by the regime but by the ability to bring about change. However, this standard is lacking because change by itself is no measurement and does not hold any evidence for a well-functioning institution, nor for environmental improvement. Again, this issue highlights the methodological constraints of regime theoretical assumptions.

This discussion on the underlying foci in the study of effectiveness has demonstrated quite clearly that at the very least there has to be some reference to the environmental problem giving rise to the agreement and one or several standards against which effectiveness can be measured.

Therefore it seems that regime theory cannot offer a useful or workable definition of effectiveness. However, what we can learn from regime theory is that in order to have effective environmental agreements we need to have functioning institutions. Since institutions are what regime theory focuses on, the experience of this research has to be valued but treated with caution due to its limitations and its treatment of agreements as closed systems. It has to be placed in a different analytical framework.

This analysis of existing concepts on the effectiveness of international environmental agreements has demonstrated that there are vast differences in opinion on what effectiveness is and how it should be measured. The definition of it largely depends on the research focus that is given by the writer. However, none of the schools of thought discussed here relate effectiveness back to environmental degradation as the main focus of research.

Several points need reiterating here. First, it seems possible to make a distinction between institutional and environmental effectiveness and a good definition needs to incorporate both concepts. However, this distinction is heuristic and for analytical purposes only. Environmental and institutional effectiveness are not two separate concepts but are interconnected and two sides of the same coin.

Second, there are certain weaknesses in the definition of institutional effectiveness that need to be improved. The premise favoured by many authors that the effectiveness of an agreement can be measured by comparing the achievement of the agreement with a hypothetical state of affairs in the absence of the agreement is not feasible. Moreover, one should not necessarily conclude that an agreement is effective simply because environmental improvement has occurred subsequent to the agreement. This is not feasible as agreements do not exist in a social vacuum. It neglects the consideration of parallel social, environmental, economic, technological and knowledge processes that exist or might exist at the national, regional and indeed global level and influence policymaking. Thus, environmental change cannot automatically be attributed to the existence of an international environmental agreement.

Third and importantly, the regime theory school attributes major importance to exogenous factors, thus implying that regime effectiveness is not a function of the members' will. Since regime theory's main tenet is that order is a function of will, it is a contradiction to suppose that effective order is not.

Fourth, it remains unclear why the effectiveness of an agreement is only related to environmental indicators in a very few cases. The difficulty associated with the task of relating environmental indicators to effectiveness cannot be the cause of this as some institutional indicators used (for example, the attribution of environmental change to the regulatory efforts of an agreement) are far more difficult to measure.

Finally, there is a vagueness surrounding these existing definitions as they all operate outside a time frame, yet effectiveness should be an issue very much associated with time constraints. Environmental change is usually irreversible and thus it seems imperative that a process of degradation has to be halted as early as possible to minimise irreversibility.

From institutional to environmental effectiveness

So far, effectiveness has basically been defined as a well-working institution whose performance can achieve change in its members' behaviour. This emphasis has led to a prioritising of the analysis of agreement implementation rather than agreement formation. In turn this has meant that effectiveness has come to refer to changes actually achieved by the agreement in question – whether good or bad. In contrast, the prescription of remedies in the first place has been neglected in analytical terms which means that environmental amelioration as a concept does not form a major part of analysis. This latter notion is what I seek to develop here. The distinction between institutional and environmental effectiveness is made most obvious in this context: institutional effectiveness is mostly concerned with the performance of the institution in question while environmental effectiveness as I propose it as a concept makes the eradication or prevention of environmental degradation its priority. Neither of the two types of effectiveness are exclusive in their approach and therefore the distinction between the two can only be made heuristically.

In addition, traditional institutional effectiveness is actor-centric and pragmatic, i.e. concerned with feasibility. Environmental effectiveness, on the other hand, takes a holistic approach and is idealistic in the sense that it concentrates on necessity rather than feasibility. In this sense, the concept of institutional effectiveness is used to describe existing approaches with slight improvements made. However, environmental effectiveness as a concept overcomes the methodological limitation of institutional effectiveness by incorporating its concerns in a wider framework that makes the institution in question part of a web of social, political, economic and environmental relations. It studies the effectiveness of international environmental agreements not from a problem-solving theory aspect but takes recourse to critical environmental theory using critical theory in Cox's sense (Cox, 1981).

Institutional effectiveness

The concept of institutional effectiveness can be largely equated with the definition of effectiveness as put forward by the regime analysts but taking account of and improving on its shortcomings. However, the proviso should be added that an agreement can be called institutionally effective when its administrative framework and working process are actually geared towards solving the problem in response to which it was formulated. There are five essential prerequisites to an institutionally effective agreement:

- participation includes all those affected by the problem, both polluter and polluted,
- the framework includes provisions for increasing knowledge on the environmental problem and is able to incorporate the knowledge created,
- linkage of environmental policy to other policy issues (Susskind, 1994),
- high degree of good will,[3]
- achievement of the institutional goals (Wettestad and Andresen, 1991).

The exogenous–endogenous factor distinction made by Young and other points relating to order have been deliberately ignored because they are directed towards determining the *sources* of effectiveness (i.e. they are based on the assumption that there are sources of effectiveness which can be tapped) whereas the above list refers to the *conditions* of effectiveness. The focus on conditions of effectiveness implies that the achievement of institutional effectiveness depends on certain conditions and they may not be met in the case of each and every agreement. In fact, empirical evidence suggests that they are unlikely to be met in most cases. Therefore the effectiveness of an agreement is not dependent on sources of effectiveness but rather on conditions that have to be met, i.e. is not a foregone conclusion. Since the focus of this book is to determine how agreements can be made more effective rather than to explain the behaviour of states and the creation of order, the discussion on the conditions of institutional effectiveness will take place in the context of the section of regulatory structures in the next chapter, i.e. as part of a larger whole.

As already argued in the preceding chapter, institutional effectiveness is an actor-centric and closed-system concept and is methodologically limited unless placed in a wider systemic and structural context. The concept of environmental effectiveness can provide such a wider framework because it treats agreements not as closed systems but as interconnected parts in a much wider social, political, economic and environmental web, which needs to be studied in order to understand the complexities underlying environmental degradation.

Environmental effectiveness

The environmental effectiveness of an international environmental agreement refers to the degree to which the degrading or polluting processes and consequences are arrested or reversed. On the surface, this definition does not seem to be any different from Haas, Keohane and Levy's definition stipulating that an effective agreement/institution is one resulting in change as compared to the pre-agreement state (1993). However, there are vital differences.

First, it is not necessary that the reversal of environmental degradation is directly attributable to the agreement in question. If the agreement set in motion other social processes that lead to an arrest or reversal of degradation, then the agreement has been indirectly effective. Second, this definition does not only take change in actor behaviour as its basis but a clearing up, or solution, of the problem in question. This point is not included by Haas, Keohane and Levy or other authors. Third, the new definition places the agreement in a wider context, both in the societal and environmental sense, by studying it with particular emphasis on the four determinants of effectiveness, i.e. science, time, regulatory and economic structures. Existing approaches do not go beyond institutional concerns. Without prejudging the later, more detailed analysis of these four determinants, it is worth signalling the general significance of these determinants here.

Economic structures encompass the structures of economic organisation of society and not just those with an immediate rapport to the agreement. Time as a concept is applied on a multitude of levels. Suffice here to say that in critical terms, time frames associated with bureaucratic feasibilities are not considered effective since they do not take account of environmental necessities. Again, what is meant by environmental necessities shall be discussed in the next chapter. Science is the tool used by policy-makers to determine the causes of and remedies for environmental degradation. Due to the complexity of issues involved in determining scientific cause–effect relationships, scientific advice is not usually considered universal, absolute and value-neutral. Therefore, Wettestad and Andresen's indicator of effectiveness being achieved when the degree of correspondence between independent expert advice and the terms of the agreement is high can be misleading and difficult to measure due to the nature of scientific advice. Regulatory structures refer to the institutional and bureaucratic structures in which agreements operate (not just the structures of the agreement).

It is considered necessary to place an agreement in the context of these four determinants in order to define its relationship with society and the environment. A definition of this relationship is vital for determining an agreement's effectiveness. This means that there cannot be one definition of environmental effectiveness that is valid for every international environmental agreement studied. Rather, the effectiveness of an agreement has to be determined by studying its social and structural origins in the context of the four determinants of effectiveness. This point will be developed in the next chapter.

4   The four determinants of environmental effectiveness

The new concept of environmental effectiveness as opposed to the traditional view of institutional effectiveness is not based on a set of indicators of effectiveness but rather explores four areas which are vitally important for understanding the relationship between environmental degradation and its regulation. These determinants define the relationship between an agreement, the environmental problem it is supposed to regulate and the social and societal structures in which it is placed. They are not sources of effectiveness, instead they highlight the issue areas that have to be considered for an environmentally effective agreement.

These four determinants do not all operate on the same level. While regulatory structures are an issue at the level of the agreement which are only highlighted from a different angle than their usual actor and interest-based focus, economic structures are a determinant that goes right to the roots of the way society is organised. The same applies to the time determinant. Science, on the other hand, is a more specific determinant, analysing the relationship between scientific knowledge informing international environmental agreements and its status as policy basis.

Economic structures and the environment

Economic structures form a very clear determinant of effectiveness because of the nature of social organisation. Economic organisation determines the form and shape of social organisation in general. It also determines the way the environment is perceived by society. For example, the view that green technology can overcome environmental degradation and the connected idea of sustainable development are based on notions of liberal and neoclassical ideology presuming that economic growth can continue indefinitely. The link between society and its environment is not fully understood.

At the institutional level, this means that regulatory structures reflect this economic determinism and negotiations are guided very much by economic considerations and feasibilities. The sheer fortuity of an economically viable environmentally friendly alternative to existing processes determines institutional success or failure. Again, this point demonstrates the poverty of regime theoretical analysis as the will to achieve order clearly plays a secondary role. In terms of environmental effectiveness, economic structures provide the framework through which environmental degradation occurs and through which it can be avoided.

At this point it is timely to discuss Cox's writings on social forces and world order because of their relevance to the arguments and structure of this book. Although Cox's main concerns are production and power and not environmental degradation, his critical approach nevertheless has some applicability for the structure of this book.

Cox's distinction between problem-solving and critical theory has already been discussed and applied in the context of this book to go beyond the closed-system approach of regime theory to the effectiveness of international environmental agreements. Cox (1981) cites five basic premises that a critical theory approach has to fulfil. It needs to realise the existence and constraints of the framework within which it operates, but go beyond it. Likewise, it needs to be conscious that theory and action are mutually constitutive and operate in the same paradigm, which needs to be overcome by critical theory. Critical theory needs to understand change and be able to react to it. In this context, the study of historical structures is vital. Last, an arena of action needs to be studied 'from the bottom or from outside in terms of the conflicts which arise within it and open the possibility of its transformation.'[1]

Cox uses his critical theory to study the changing role of the forces of production in world order over time and identifies changes in political world order that go hand in hand with changes in the configuration of social forces, particularly forces of production. Therefore its outlook and concerns are related to world history and the history of social change. The concern of this book is with social change relating to environmental degradation, which is outside the remit of Cox's approach. However, a link can be made between Cox and this book in terms of the four determinants of effectiveness, particularly economic structures. This link is based on the premise that

> production creates the material basis for all forms of social existence, and the ways in which human efforts are combined in productive processes affect all other aspects of social life, including the polity.
>
> (Cox, 1987: 1)

Power and production influence each other. This holds for the four determinants of effectiveness: regulatory structures, economic structures and the political economy of science are determined by productive processes and their dominant role as social forces. Even the temporal organisation of society is dominated by the consideration of production. However, this is exactly where the issue of effectiveness becomes important. Because social organisation is so intertwined with production, the degrading consequences of the productive process cannot be incorporated in a social framework that is geared towards facilitating production. Cox (1996: 516) recognises this:

The global economy, activated by profit maximisation, has not been constrained to moderate its destructive ecological effects. There is no authoritative regulator, so far only several interventions through the inter-state system to achieve agreement on avoidance of specific noxious practices.

However, Cox sees the main analytical challenge in this to be the effect on the state system and sovereignty rather than the challenge to overcome environmental degradation. This is the limitation of his approach in relation to the study of environmental effectiveness because it demonstrates that Cox's critical approach still operates within the orthodox concerns of the IR discipline, i.e. is concerned with actors in the international, or global, arena. It does not offer an opportunity for incorporating the concern of effectiveness in relation to international environmental agreements and resulting environmental improvement, as is made abundantly clear (p. 517):

The biosphere has its own automatic enforcers for instance, in the consequences of global warming; but who will negotiate on behalf of the biosphere? That must be one of the questions overshadowing future multilateralism.

In fact, the critical approach taken in this book implies that the question overshadowing environmental degradation is not who will negotiate and how, but how environmental degradation can be remedied given the mutual constitution of power and production. Here, Cox cannot give any answers because he is not concerned with this question.

Therefore, existing IR approaches are not really well suited to study the environment since they operate on the premise that social systems are the only, or at least major, systems in existence. However, it is not sufficient to incorporate the environment as a new subject or actor in existing modes of analysis because clearly this is not what it is. Rather, it is a system of which all other (human/social) systems form part. Thus actor-centric analysis will not be very fruitful and a systemic/structural approach must be chosen that goes beyond the sole consideration of social structures and forces. However, such an approach needs to include the environment not as another system but as a system of which all other systems are part.

This is clearly a difficult task since it goes against prevailing concepts. A study that attributes causal liability to the functioning of environmental systems must therefore displace the exclusive preoccupation with institutional factors, and instead concentrate on environmental effectiveness, or compatibility.

Time and the environment

This section is concerned with the relationship between time and the environment and the bearing of time on the effectiveness debate. This is a relatively unresearched and therefore new area to study in the context of environmental regulation.[2] The concept of time has implications for all other determinants of effectiveness as it affects their organisation.

Time is not just a measurement according to which we plan our schedules, be it short-term, long-term, day-to-day, life, social, historical, etc., but can be institutional or social, cyclical or linear, perceived or measured, according to the focus of analysis. Time in its various forms is such an important issue because of the irreversibility of environmental degradation and also because it dominates every society and individual's life as all organisation is ultimately based on temporal issues. Therefore, analysing the significance of perceptions of time in relation to environmental degradation has a central place in policy terms as the irreversible loss of something is to be prevented.

Environment and society are treated as separate phenomena by social scientists. The environment is subjected to human perceptions of time in the way it is treated and analysed. However, it operates under non-human time frames. Therefore, it is in a special position compared to social problems that are studied. This special status and its consequences will be investigated here. Adam (1994: 93) describes this phenomenon:

> How can [we] make sense of the different definitions, approaches and proposals for solutions [to environmental degradation] when [they] have been established on the irreducible distinction between nature and culture, the natural and the symbolic environment, evolution and history, when the environment as a subject matter so clearly falls outside [this] traditional bounded domain? One strategy has been to stay clear of the substantive issues and to focus instead on environmentalism, the rise of green issues on the political agenda, on assumptions underpinning deep and shallow ecology, as well as the social construction of those scientific 'facts'.

This statement emphasises that social science is concerned with the study of society and the realisation that the environment is not a 'given' within which society operates is relatively new and thus has not really filtered through. This lack of acknowledgement explains the literary vacuum on the study of time and the environment and it also demonstrates the need for an interdisciplinary approach to it. However, Adam is mainly concerned with the role of time in environment–industrial age interaction, which is the period that sees the rise of humans as 'dominators' of nature. The focus of her work is the incompatibility of perceptions of time in nature and society, which becomes even more obvious in the age of what is generally referred to as globalisation. This (missing) link between nature and society will be discussed further in Chapters 7 and 8.

Relating to the effectiveness of international environmental agreements, there are two primary time issues that are important. First, at an institutional as well as an environmental level, time frames of international environmental agreements need to reflect environmental necessities. Institutionally this means that the administrative process from the formation of an agreement to its implementation and the time frames imposed by the agreement need to reflect the urgency and irreversibility of the environmental problem to be regulated.

Time and regulatory structures in agreement formation

An agreement has to go through a process of negotiation, signature, ratification, entry into force and then implementation. The text of the agreement may or may not prescribe targets and the time period in which the provisions of the agreement have to be achieved. For example, no protocols of the Barcelona Convention (MAP) include any time limits for the introduction of its regulations. CLRTAP, on the other hand, includes various time limits. Ratification times can vary from two to up to more than a dozen years. For example, the UN Law of the Sea Convention was signed in 1982 but only collected sufficient ratifications for entry into force in 1996.

Administrative time frames relate to the institutional level and should thus be an issue or condition of institutional effectiveness. However, the concept of time has been neglected by the institutional effectiveness school of thought as an indicator of effectiveness. This neglect applies to time frames as a measure of institutional effectiveness and to the connection between time frames and environmental amelioration.

Natural and mechanical rhythms

The other primary time issue relates to rhythmicity and how social activity can disrupt environmental rhythms. Social activity impacting on environmental processes can primarily be found in the industrial sector, particularly mechanical and technological processes.

Environmental and technological processes do not share the same underlying principles according to which they evolve or function. Environmental processes are highly interactive, rhythmic, cyclical and 'renewable' (Daly, 1992; Lovelock, 1988). Technological processes, on the other hand, are linear (i.e. non-renewable after their life span expires, and also producing waste). Although some social technological processes can be interactive and rhythmic, technological products used in the production process certainly are not. A machine's life is mechanical and non-renewable, i.e. functions according to Newtonian principles (Adam and Kütting, 1995: 243), which means that a technology-centred economy is based

> on the principles of decontextualisation, isolation, fragmentation, reversible motion, abstract time and space, predictability, and objectivity, maxims that stand opposed to organic principles such as embedded contextuality, networked interconnectedness, irreversible change and contingency.

Therefore, two systems – namely, the environment and industrial society – that are based on opposing principles have to cohabit. Industrial society interferes with the rhythm of nature and thus disturbs its careful balance. This phenomenon can be summarised by distinguishing between mechanism and organism. Mechanical systems such as machine-based production societies draw on Newtonian concepts and assumptions. This view of science is still dominant today. A mechanical view of nature implies that nature/environment can be neatly compartmentalised into constituent parts and that these parts are not interdependent. They can be replaced easily by new parts, i.e. the focus is on the part, not on the functioning of the whole. An organic view of the world, on the other hand, can be described as focusing on the connection and dependent relations of nature, thus stressing the holistic aspect. This view also highlights the cyclical, evolutionary and irreversible nature of environmental rhythms.

This summary demonstrates that mechanical systems work differently from organic systems, with the main difference being that organic systems produce and feed back into the system what they have produced, thus creating a constant cycle. The phenomenon of the rain cloud 'dropping' its water into the ocean only to have the water evaporate and then form new rain clouds is a good example. Another main characteristic of organic systems is their interconnectivity. For example, heavy metal deposits in coastal zone fish will pass through the food chain and affect animals and humans in places removed from the source of pollution. Mechanical systems, on the other hand, produce, but the final product does not feed back into the system, i.e. energy is drawn but not replaced. Instead, wastes occur during the production process that are released in the form of pollution. Since the drawing of energy and its replacement with pollution affect organic systems, the mechanical systems exist at the cost of organic systems. In time terms this means that the cyclical, regenerative nature of the environment is disturbed. By removing resources from the environment and returning them in the form of waste only, mechanical systems, or industrial society, endanger the functioning of these cyclical, regenerative phenomena, which results in environmental degradation, which then in turn affects society.

The role of science in agreement-making

The IR literature on international environmental agreements largely limits the role of science to the input of science into agreement-making (Haas, 1990; Susskind, 1994; Sjöstedt, 1993). However, this limitation does not do justice to the influence of science in all social spheres. Science determines the everyday life of society and has an all-pervasive influence since late twentieth-century Western lifestyle is largely based on rational, scientific logic. In Western culture, science has become an ideology or even more than that, replacing the role of religion and providing the core values of society (Midgley, 1992). However, this aspect of science need not be discussed in detail for studying the role of science in agreement-making. Only a relatively small aspect of science will be considered in relation to environmental policy-making, i.e. those aspects relating to international environmental agreements in a wider sense. In this context, science is taken to mean the activity, and its results, carried out by a professional group of people in universities and other research institutions (the scientists) trying to find laws and correlations in their study of phenomena occurring in the physical environment by simulating these in a laboratory environment (adaptation of Kuhn, 1982: 75). This method of analysis isolates the environmental problem from its ecosystemic context, and this practice may lead to complications when applied. As Jasanoff (1995) argues, 'scientific inquiry, contrary to expectation, does not always lead to the same explanation for the same observed phenomenon'. This point will be taken further in some empirical studies below. However, the main issue at stake is that scientific activity is not an isolated social activity but one that is interconnected with other social processes, and the other arguments then arise thereof.

Usually, before formal negotiations start on an international environmental agreement, there is a call for research in the area of environmental degradation to be regulated. In the case of CLRTAP, the underlying science has become more focused in the course of the agreement's history. Before CLRTAP's existence and until the first sulphur protocol, published scientific research concentrated mainly on the pathways of pollutants but not on preventative action and its requirements. As a consequence, the first sulphur protocol and its 30 per cent reduction requirement did not have a scientific basis (Anon., 1995b: 18). However, scientific research can be seen as the trigger for the NOx and VOC protocols – although not for their provisions.[3] The realisation that it was not SO_2 alone but a cocktail of substances that caused acid rain is also the result of scientific research. As will be discussed in detail below, the second sulphur protocol is based on environmental modelling and, to a large extent, so too are the protocols currently under negotiation. In CLRTAP, the scientific community has a permanent and continuous set of tasks and interacts with the policy-makers in this process, i.e. is part of the institutional make-up of CLRTAP.

In MAP, the scientific community works on a commission basis, receiving its projects from the UNEP Coordinating Unit. This pattern of scientific work is related to MAP's financial organisation since MAP has only limited funds and can only budget for the current financial year. However, since UNEP/MAP does not have an 'in-house' science base as such, there is less communication between scientists and policy-makers than in CLRTAP's case. The MAP Coordinating Unit decides the projects that will be undertaken and the institution that will carry them out.[4] Although the same institutions tend to get contracts,[5] the link between the scientific community and the policy-makers is neither direct nor permanent. However, there is a permanent link between scientific coordinators in the Coordinating Unit and policy-makers. Thus the scientific community in MAP is also institutionalised but in a different and perhaps more *ad hoc* or fragmented form of bureaucratic organisation.

These varying practices of scientific organisation have implications for the debate on epistemic communities. However, in this context it is not the regime theoretical method related to epistemic communities that needs to be discussed but the concept of epistemic communities as such. The Mediterranean Action Plan is often used as an example of how scientists affect policy-making in what Haas (1990) calls the epistemic community. Haas's study of the early stages of

MAP found that the epistemic community significantly influenced policy-makers in MAP, thus leading to an epistemic community power base. This research was identified as a substantial new contribution to IR theory and has been accepted as such. However, the idea is not new and nor is the idea that politics and science are linked. It goes back to the works of E.B. Haas and G. Ruggie and also the sociology of science literature. Therefore the success of this approach is surprising and has to be seen as a reaction to the growing interest in international environmental organisation, for which it provides a useful analytical tool.

There are methodological criticisms of Haas's approach other than the general regime theoretical methodological constraints. For example, Haas uses the number of scientists in national delegations at MAP intergovernmental meetings as an indicator of the influence of epistemic communities. Members with a 'scientific' representation are found to be those that are very active in developing or expanding an environmental policy and are considered active MAP members (Haas, 1990). Again, this point focuses on institutional aspects of science in agreement-making. However, irrespective of this apparent correlation, Haas neglects other vital social factors such as the role of EC environmental legislation and the need to comply with it, the institutional *status quo ante* in a member state, political culture and traditional forms of representation at governmental meetings, the role and organisation of environmental administration in the respective country or the infrastructural make-up of a member state.[6] Out of the five MAP members with influential epistemic communities, two are EU states (France and Greece) and another is Israel with a high degree of bureaucratisation. Only Algeria and Egypt support Haas's case. However, Algeria only acceded to the legal part of MAP later on (in 1981) and did not sign the convention and protocols in the beginning. It is not conclusive by any means therefore that the influence of epistemic communities in these countries led to the successful espousal of MAP's ideas as portrayed by Haas and his assertion remains unproved. In any case, only 5 out of the 18 member states had an influential epistemic community according to Haas's argument, which itself cannot be considered overwhelming evidence in support of his epistemic community approach.

It is deceptive to see the epistemic community as an army of 'lab coats'. For Haas, the epistemic community is not so much the research scientist at the bench but rather a figure like the MAP scientific coordinator and his national counterparts, i.e. a community dealing with and including policy-makers. However, it could be argued that, contrary to Haas, scientific representation in a national delegation demonstrates a prioritising of MEDPOL and is an expression of financial and strategic interest to win more research contracts. This could also serve as an explanation for the phenomenon that the epistemic community of MAP was strong in the early phase but has since lost its importance.[7] After all, in the early stages of MAP many members hoped that MAP would achieve environmental regulation by developing scientific capabilities in the southern Mediterranean region but then it became apparent that the budget of MAP was too limited and that the research contracts were not very lucrative. Thus the member states lost interest.[8] This is an indication of the fact that science is an economic activity and thus subject to the workings of political economy.

Jasanoff takes up this point in a different manner. She quotes Brooks to make a distinction between *science in policy* and *policy for science*:

> The first is concerned with matters that are basically political or administrative but are significantly dependent on technical factors – such as the nuclear test ban, disarmament policy, or the use of science in international relations. The second is concerned with the development of policies for the management and support of the national scientific enterprise and with the selection and evaluation of substantive scientific programs.
>
> (Jasanoff, 1990: 5)

This distinction is not mutually exclusive. Policies for science necessarily need to be made with the advice of scientists and science in policy obviously needs to be conducted in such a way as to fit in with administrative and regulatory structures. This makes the distinction more confusing than helpful in places but also shows that science is not a separate domain but just another sector of social organisation. Likewise, the distinction of scientific expertise as determined by the background of the scientist (environmentalist or industry representative) shows that science and economics are intrinsically linked (Rodricks, 1992). Jasanoff's work also shows that science is preoccupied with institutional effectiveness rather than environmental degradation. As she argues in relation to risk in policy-making:

> Judgements about risk inevitably incorporate tacit understandings concerning agency and responsibility, and these are by no means universally shared even in similarly situated Western societies. Against this background it makes little sense to regulate public demands, and claims to superior expertise. Environmental regulation calls for a more open-ended process, with multiple access points for dissenting views.
>
> (Jasanoff, 1997: 13)

In agreement-making terms this means that scientific advice is definitely not an objective source of knowledge that needs to be tapped in order to make good policies and agreements, as implied in the IR literature. Therefore the notion of independent expert advice providing guidelines for effective policy-making is misleading.[9]

The critical loads approach under CLRTAP illustrates this point well. This new technique in environmental policy-making is a move away from uniform emission standards (such as flat-rate reductions for everybody) or environmental quality standards (such as the EC bathing water criteria) and towards a modelling-based approach using scientific knowledge determining a region's threshold above which environmental degradation will occur.

The critical loads approach

The critical loads approach has long been incorporated in CLRTAP, but only the 1994 protocol on further sulphur reductions uses the critical loads approach as the basis for emission reductions. For each state, maps have been developed which indicate levels of acid deposition and acid-sensitive areas. These are the basis of calculations which show the sulphur dioxide emission reductions necessary in order to reach an overall 60 per cent reduction target (Weir, 1993: 20–21). This means that the role of scientific experts advising on threshold values, emission trajectories, ecosystem tolerance, etc., is becoming increasingly important in the CLRTAP policy-making process.

While the first sulphur protocol (1985) was based on a uniform 30 per cent reduction target, the protocol on nitrogen oxides had a special declaration of one group of states setting higher aims than the lowest common denominator and the VOC protocol was flexible in base year and also introduced the concept of Tropospheric Ozone Management Areas (TOMAs). The case of the new sulphur protocol is very similar in some ways.

This protocol was signed in June 1994. Its main provision, stated in article 2, paragraph 1, is that the member states

> control and reduce their sulphur emissions in order to protect human health and the environment from adverse effects, in particular acidifying effects, and to ensure, as far as possible, without entailing excessive costs, that depositions of oxidised sulphur compounds in the long term do not exceed critical loads for sulphur given, in annex I, as critical sulphur depositions in accordance with present scientific knowledge.

Critical loads is an attempt to calculate the threshold below which levels of air pollutants do not represent a danger to the environment or human health according to present knowledge. During a major international conference in spring 1988 in London, the critical load level for sulphur was set at a maximum of 3 kg per hectare per year (Swedish Environmental Protection Agency, 1993). If this amount is exceeded, acidification damage may occur. Of course, this acidification process depends on geographical conditions such as type of soil, which has been taken into consideration in the models. Some areas can cope with acidification better than others. Southern Scandinavia, for example, is an extremely sensitive area. The new sulphur protocol is based on the predictions of the RAINS model which foresees an overall 60 per cent gap closure scenario, i.e. an average 60 per cent reduction of SO_2 emissions as compared to 1980 levels (see below).

Maps of critical loads for the European region have been designed using a standardised method which was developed by a Task Force on Mapping and agreed by the relevant UNECE working group (Hetteling *et al.*, 1991). The critical loads are aggregated to 150 × 150 square km grid squares by constructing cumulative distribution of critical loads for ecosystems in each square. All maps are produced on a five percentile basis, which means that if the input of acid does not exceed the rate indicated (in equivalents/hectare/year), 95 per cent of the ecosystems in the grid will be protected. Predictions of depositions, derived from long-range transport models developed by EMEP are available on a comparable scale. These data have to be used to work out critical loads exceedance maps. There are several computer models available which have done this. The model chosen by the UNECE is the RAINS model by the International Institute of Applied Systems Analysis in Laxenburg, Austria. It is composed of a range of smaller models that deal with pollution generation, pollution trajectories, deposition and environmental effects. The emission forecasts are based on energy consumption data as well as characteristics of fuels under different combustion conditions.

The targets put forward by the RAINS model were not deemed achievable in practical terms and therefore a compromise solution was negotiated which foresees that the discrepancy between the five percentile critical loads model and actual sulphur depositions in 1990 had to be reduced by 60 per cent, hence the '60 per cent gap closure scenario'. Only in the grids where the model's aim had already been achieved (parts of Portugal, Spain and Russia) were its figures used for the protocol (Klaassen, 1996: 194). In practice, this process can be described as the economic and political integration of the model.

There has to be a general acceptance by the governments involved that the proposed data are reliable and can be used as a fair representation of damage control. There is no guarantee that a negotiating party will accept the data proposed for its country and it may argue for more lenient targets or time scales on economic grounds, 'not entailing excessive costs'. In the case of the new sulphur protocol, such 'spanners in the wheel' have been avoided by incorporating desires for more lenient targets in the model in order to ensure that as many states as possible sign the agreement. This shows that the model is not solely based on scientific criteria but that political and economic considerations have been incorporated in the model.

This empirical study has repercussions on how IR views science in international environmental agreements. Conventional IR approaches disregard the consequences of the fact that the environment is a field where diplomatic negotiators are dependent on expert advice in order to understand the causes of and solutions to environmental degradation. Regardless of the inevitable absence of 'objective truth' and unambiguously established causal connections, an outside body of knowledge exists whose input is necessary for policy-making and can only be obtained by policy-makers through relying on expert advice. This phenomenon has to be abstracted from discussions on the objectivity of scientific advice and epistemic communities and seen as a process in international environmental policy-making. When the first sulphur protocol to CLRTAP was signed, the 30 per cent reduction in sulphur emissions required by the signatories was an arbitrary figure and not suggested by a scientific community. It was negotiated. However, since then the role of science has changed in CLRTAP and also in other agreements such as the Montreal Protocol.[10] Therefore, the role and nature of expert advice/science needs to be taken into account more clearly in the analysis of international environmental agreement-making than has happened so far.

This does not mean that the science underlying agreements is unambiguous. Skeffington from National Power Research and Engineering, for example, argues that

> there is no consensus on many aspects of the models, criteria are not objective, and the results of the exercise are as much a product of political negotiations as of science. There are many reasons for this. One is the large uncertainties which exist over both the effect of emission reductions on deposition and on how critical loads ought to be calculated. Another derives from how such bodies as UNECE operate, which does not ensure that the best available scientific information is used in decision making.
>
> (Skeffington, 1994: 93)

In a personal communication on 12 September 1996 in Birmingham, Skeffington gave an example of the arbitrariness of scientific data used. For a study on forest acidification, IIASA scientists used data collected on 12 trees in the suburban forests of Berlin, which were then extrapolated and used for a European forest acidification map. Although Skeffington's comments have to be seen in the context of his position with an agency that would rather deny the relationship between power plant emissions and acid rain, it is clear that the main criticism is that science cannot deliver objective results but is related to the moral, political, philosophical and other values held by the scientists or funding agencies in question. These results are dependent on the scientists' relationship with the environment, if it is seen as independent of human systems, subjected to human exploitation, something that needs to be preserved in order to keep its economic value or something that needs to be kept as pristine as possible for its own worth, etc. These underlying attitudes make it impossible to give scientific expertise a superior, objective status.

The critical loads concept has to change the analysis of the CLRTAP negotiation process despite its arbitrary nature. With the focus on environmental data such as pollution trajectories, tolerable emission limits and so on, it will be more difficult for academics to use conventional neorealist/neoliberal institutionalist analysis since the context of the negotiations can be measured against the environmental data available and introduces environmental quality into the debate. This means that negotiation processes could become more transparent and actors thus more accountable in environmental terms. However, since science is of such an institutional nature, this might not actually be of any importance. After all, science might only reproduce a certain institutional set-up and not reflect environmental concerns.

The science base and its underlying values gain significance as compared to traditional agreement-making. This means that the scientific approach chosen as the basis for critical loads becomes a political and power issue. This point is particularly salient in global environmental issues where Western and non-Western scientific approaches clash. Even a regional agreement such as CLRTAP is affected by virtue of the technology issue supporting the scientific method chosen and institutional factors deciding what model will be chosen.

To conclude, the example of the critical loads approach has demonstrated that science plays an important role in agreement-making by providing a knowledge base, but that this knowledge base is not value-neutral. In general, it is evident that both the role of science in agreement-making and its analysis are centred on the concept of institutional effectiveness which means that feasibility as compared to necessity reigns in the actual agreement-making process.

Regulatory structures

The subject of regulatory structures lies at the centre of institutional effectiveness since it is directly concerned with institutional design. However, it is also directly relevant to the study of environmental change. The most ardent proponent arguing that 'regime design matters' is Mitchell:

> Regime design matters. International treaties and regimes have value if and only if they cause people to do things they would not otherwise do. Governments spend considerable resources and effort drafting and refining treaty language with the (at least nominal) aim of making treaty compliance and effectiveness more likely ... This article demonstrates that whether a treaty elicits compliance or other desired behavioural changes depends upon identifiable characteristics of the regime's compliance systems.
>
> (Mitchell, 1994: 425)

This view underlines regime theory's basic tenet that cooperation and international organisation are a function of will and therefore it is possible to achieve cooperation/compliance/effectiveness if the contents of the regime reflect a common basis. The flaws of this argument have already been discussed extensively. The basic focus of Mitchell's argument is on power (overt and covert), probability of success and leadership – hence the emphasis is on change in actor behaviour, not the condition/problem to be regulated.

Jacobson and Brown Weiss also regard the agreement itself as a major factor for effectiveness and compliance. Their research shows that equity between members is a key feature for enlarging membership of the agreement while insistence on progress reports is not seen as helpful since most member states are overburdened with these demands (Jacobson and Brown Weiss, 1995: 140). However, the basis of this research is a concept of institutional effectiveness not incorporating environmental effectiveness. The writing of progress reports as an institutional duty may be time and resource consuming for member and future member states of the agreements but it may be leading towards greater environmental effectiveness. This aspect was not assessed by Jacobson and Brown Weiss, which is a general shortcoming of all regime theoretic approaches. Since regime theorists in general are not interested in environmental effectiveness, then 'regime design' can necessarily only be analysed in relation to its effect on levels of cooperation.

Likewise in Mitchell's study:

> Nations can design regime rules to improve compliance … even within a single-issue area, reference to design features of compliance systems surrounding particular provisions is necessary to explain observed variance in compliance. In [the case study] the same governments and corporations with the same interests during the same time period complied far more frequently with rules requiring installation of expensive equipment than they did with rules limiting total discharges of oil. Where theories of hegemonic power and economic interests fail to explain this variance, differences in the subregime's compliance systems readily explain why the former subregime led powerful actors to comply with it while the latter did not.
>
> (Mitchell, 1994: 456)

Mitchell noted in his study that equipment standards on oil tankers elicited higher compliance rates than tanker discharge restrictions despite higher costs. However, equipment standards are more transparent and can be more easily checked and controlled compared to discharges in the open sea. Thus, Mitchell's argument is that despite the higher cost the equipment standards regime design invites greater compliance because it can be more easily applied and controlled.

This debate takes place without reference to environmental benefits. An agreement that is complied with is obviously more environmentally effective than one that is not if this agreement has an environmental benefit. Nevertheless, a complied-with agreement that is of little or doubtful environmental benefit cannot be called environmentally effective. Thus focusing on compliance means ignoring vital preconditions that have to be met first. Hence, the debate does not take place at the heart of the issue. In addition, it fails to place its case studies into a wider context which could also provide explanations for changes in actor behaviour. Thus the causal link argued by Mitchell may only be coincidence as it is not placed in context.

In fact, there are several issues even within the institutional context which are not properly distinguished and accentuated. These are issues about the actual formulation of the agreement, the administrative organisation and possible reporting or review mechanisms.

The legal perspective

Since the issue of compliance is a legal matter, it is useful and necessary to review the international law perspective and feed the knowledge gained into the debate. It is one of the main occupations of international law analysts to study the contents, structures and mechanisms of international law, and international environmental law is no exception.

A well-known study by Sand (1990) is the most authoritative source for investigation. Sand primarily deals with problem issues that persist in treaty-making, such as the lowest common denominator, compromise-building by leaving loopholes, or the convoy travelling at the speed of its slowest boat. For example, the deliberate planting of loopholes in an agreement will lead to wider acceptance and a higher common denominator as parties that would not have otherwise signed the agreement are now prepared to do so.

This issue has also been the object of study of other writers. Brown Weiss (1992: 253) also points out that

> those who draft international legal instruments also have to be concerned increasingly with designing the instruments and implementation mechanisms with sufficient flexibility so that parties can adapt to changes in scientific understanding.

In a similar vein, Susskind (1994: 7) laments the lack of effective monitoring and enforcement mechanisms that are actually implemented. However, he focuses on conventional legal structures and their effectiveness in general and argues that there are fundamental flaws in the Convention–Protocol approach.

The Convention–Protocol approach means that a framework convention outlines the basic intentions and concerns of the parties concerned while concrete policies or regulatory approaches are treated in separate protocols. Generally, this means that the convention is cloaked in very vague terms, the specifics being left to be treated in protocols. Susskind's main criticism of the Convention–Protocol system is that the process is long and drawn-out and leads to lowest-common-denominator compromises. Susskind further argues that the Convention–Protocol approach leads to a decreased importance for scientific knowledge as not all recommendations are incorporated. In addition, the terms of a convention can limit the scope of following protocols, thus neglecting new research results. This is exacerbated by the fact that negotiations are often dominated by powerful states.

It is not clear why Susskind blames the Convention–Protocol approach for the above problems as they seem to be applicable to international environmental agreements in general. Most agreements are based on the Convention–Protocol approach but, for example, EC law is not and the above criticisms can also be applied to many pieces of EC legislation which is also subject to the lowest-common-denominator problem. A notable exception to the Convention-plus-Protocol approach is MARPOL 73/78, which is based on an annex system, fulfilling a similar function to protocols.

The study of international environmental law literature in general does not offer systematic treatment of the question if, and how, provisions and review procedures matter for the effectiveness of an international environmental agreement, be it in the restricted institutional or environmental sense. It depends on what aspect a particular author considers to be the most important factor in effectiveness: large membership, ongoing debates, higher standards than the lowest common denominator. There is no agreement on what aspect is the most important, thus leading to conflicting ideas of what constitutes effectiveness. The concept of environmental effectiveness is ignored. In fact, the existing literature can be described rather flippantly as following the 'what's your variable?' approach.

The policy-maker's perspective

The next step in this review will be the analysis of a policy-maker's view on the subject of regulatory structures. The essence of an article by Feldman (1992: 43–58) will be used to summarise the policy-makers' priorities. The aim of Feldman's work is to find out how treaties managing global climate change can be made 'implementable', and he isolates four characteristics that need to be present for a (global) agreement to be effective (pp. 43–44):

- A balanced number of participants, i.e. a sufficiently high number to offer legitimacy to the negotiating process but not so many as to complicate negotiations and agreement on institutional provisions.
- Compliance mechanisms that 'do not point the finger' but achieve their aim through confidence-building.
- The text of the agreements needs to be formulated clearly and precisely but there needs to be a discretionary margin for the participants.
- Negotiations need to be open to change and problems encountered. This openness needs to be encouraged and supported by the inclusion of NGOs in the negotiating process.

Feldman fundamentally argues that the structure of an agreement does matter but that this structure should not be too tight because this would act as a deterrent to both membership in the agreement and implementation. The deduction is that ambitious structures that need a lot of input will not be accepted and implemented by participants in the agreement. Consequently, an agreement can be little more than a 'talking shop' since measures going beyond the lowest common denominator will not be put into practice. This leaves two options: either have an agreement on the lowest common denominator with little or no effect on the environment, or have an agreement that ambitiously tries to achieve environmental change but with little or no chance of success.

This is a fatalistic view. First, it denies that actors' negotiating positions are guided by anything but power and economic interest. Second, it sees the environment as an economic resource and environmental agreements as resource cooperation without taking into consideration the irreversible nature of environmental degradation. Third, it sees a set of negotiations as an issue isolated from other policy issues and from the structures within which international cooperation takes place. Therefore it can only come to a limited interpretation and conclusion. Again, this is a methodological constraint. Analysis is limited to a narrow aspect of institutional mechanisms because the methodology chosen cannot adequately deal with the issue area within broader social structures. The structures reflect the state of environmental awareness, knowledge and priorities of the member states and thus the lack of effectiveness is caused by lack of good structure but lack of good structure is caused by lack of cooperative will and enthusiasm. In that respect regime theorists are right: good 'regimes' are a function of will. However, not in the sense regime theorists use the term. At present, environmental quality is not a function of will but of luck, i.e. when it is considered important by all members and when all members agree on what constitutes environmental quality.

The context in which such structures evolve

The provisions of an agreement are basically a reflection of the negotiating process and the input from various domestic agencies and political cultures but also the scientific and economic context of the problem to be regulated. Concepts of time are hardly reflected in the provisions of an agreement with the exception of stringent target years for agreements that are considered urgent (such as the Montreal Protocol). Therefore the process that leads to the establishment of an agreement needs to be studied in order to see how concepts of environmental effectiveness evolve. This point is quite case-specific and is illustrated with the examples of the Convention on Long-Range Transboundary Air Pollution and the Mediterranean Action Plan.

The neorealist school of thought considers power and economic interests as the driving forces behind the formation of negotiating positions. Other approaches incorporate this and elaborate into game theoretic and rational choice-oriented interpretations of negotiation processes. The legal school of thought does not look at motivation at all. Clearly, the neorealist school does not take a holistic view of the negotiating process, nor does it account for structural conditions or change.[11] Such an analysis of the negotiation process would involve defining the motivations for the individual actors' negotiating stances, the bureaucratic conditions underlying the stances, ideological viewpoints and the structures of the system in which negotiations take place. For a holistic analysis incorporating the object of study, the environment, the relation between the negotiating process and the environmental problem in question also have to be incorporated. Thus the limited focus on institutional effectiveness of current studies is not appropriate for studying the role of international environmental agreements in environmental degradation.

Review mechanisms in international environmental agreements are also a reflection of environmental awareness and of the accepted institutionalisation of the agreement. In CLRTAP, for example, the review mechanisms are a definite sign that the convention and its protocols have become a bureaucratic process that is considered to be long-term and part of the participators' policy programmes. Therefore, review mechanisms are not controversial but generally accepted as part of the process. In contrast, MAP does not contain any review mechanisms but MAP has not resulted in an institutionalisation of the environmental policies recommended.

This point will be illustrated with the examples of CLRTAP and MAP. The holistic approach will be used, integrating the institutional approach into a wider concept of environmental effectiveness.

The Convention on Long-Range Transboundary Air Pollution and protocols have undergone quite an evolution during their lifetime. Since the earlier stages have been amply documented elsewhere (Boehmer-Christiansen and Skea, 1991), there will be an emphasis on the developments since 1990. However, it is not the aim of this section to explain the evolution of CLRTAP but to use it to illustrate the points made. CLRTAP evolved not so much out of environmental pressure or awareness but as an initiative to increase East–West cooperation with the pleasant side-effect of placating the Scandinavian countries (hard hit by acid rain) which had been pressing for international measures on this subject for many years (Chossudovsky, 1989). Accordingly, the first sulphur protocol was not a reflection of environmental awareness or a distilled consensus of negotiating positions but rather a combination of many factors. The trend in CLRTAP has been that science and research have increased their influence over time and also that certain political developments, i.e. the breakdown of the Warsaw Pact isolation, have helped to solidify CLRTAP. However, this last event only supported an already existing trend, i.e. the institutionalisation of CLRTAP was well on its way when the Iron Curtain was removed.

In this section, we will concentrate on the second sulphur protocol and the new protocols under negotiation. Starting from the position of the national actor, it cannot be assumed that the actor has a unitary negotiating position. Usually, several ministries are involved in formulating the negotiating position and this position has to be recoordinated 'at home' after each negotiating session. A detailed discussion of this can be found in 'the logic of two-level games', which, however, is limited to game-theoretic interpretations (Putnam, 1988: 427–460). Each actor is dependent on the bureaucratic system 'at home' and subjected to a particular form of political culture. Therefore, actor motivations and behaviour are case-specific. For example, in the new sulphur protocol, the German delegation was initially against the use of critical loads and advocated the use of the concept of Best Available Technology (BAT) since this came closest to the concept of the precautionary principle anchored in German Federal law.[12] The British delegation, on the other hand, sees cost and feasibility in policy terms as the prime issues determining its negotiating stance and thus advocated an effects-based approach.[13] Equally, the Swedish delegation backed an effects-based approach because it was regarded as having direct reference to environmental criteria.[14] The Eastern European countries regarded the use of the critical loads concept as a fair and equitable method and therefore backed it.[15]

These empirical reference points demonstrate that the formulation of a national negotiating position is extremely case-specific. Different issues are prioritised by different actors, which can be a result of the following:

bureaucratic structures (e.g. environment ministry answerable to finance ministry); political culture; particular social, political, economic or environmental conditions; even varying degrees of environmental 'objectification' in environmental consciousness (i.e. economistic approaches in varying shades); varying concerns for human health or environmental damage or the cost of damage limitation. Clearly, a neorealist or neoliberal institutionalist analysis cannot fully capture this wide gamut of policy bases as it reduces policy motivation to power or economic interest.

However, to explain how these varying negotiating positions are amalgamated and formed into a protocol can only be explained by looking at the structures of the system in which these negotiations take place. In addition, different starting positions do not mean that the negotiating stances are not similar or identical. For example, two states may want the same outcome in the negotiations but may differ on the technical method of how this outcome can be achieved. Also, some countries relate their negotiating position to what they think they are able to implement whereas others go along quite happily with the trend but then fail to implement what they have signed. This diversity of strategy is also apparent in CLRTAP. In communications with policy-makers during the UNECE working group on strategies meeting in Geneva between 19 and 23 February 1996 it was gleaned that some member states will only sign an agreement if they can be sure that they can fulfil its requirements. These states are very active negotiators and take commitments seriously, trying to change emission limit requirements if they feel they cannot fulfil them. Other states are less concerned about the actual agreement and will sign regardless of whether they will be able to achieve the target.

In order to have a clear view of the structures surrounding CLRTAP, these have to be defined. There are the bureaucratic systems of the UNECE, of international law and custom in general, of the international environmental policy process, of East–West relations etiquette (in the 1980s), the ideological structures of what values underlie the process, what is desirable and what the human relationship to the environment is as well as the environmental structures of what constitutes the environment or environmental quality. In CLRTAP, there seems to be a tacit consent, or at least a position that is tacitly accepted as a compromise, on what values are regarded as the basis. This is also confirmed by the increasing reliance on a science base, which is generally accepted. This science base and common values did not exist at the beginning of the process but have developed incrementally over time.

The Mediterranean Action Plan, on the other hand, has not undergone a similar evolution. It is a process that has not been subjected to many changes since its inception, leaving aside the new convention of 1995. However, even the new convention and the new biodiversity protocol follow the same trend of carefully worded, 'full of good intention but vague in content' approach.

This lack of commitment has not been commented on in the literature analysed because most writers focus on the phenomenon of cooperation given the diversity of actors of the Mediterranean region. Interviewed on this, MAP's legal adviser attributed this domination of 'soft law' to a culture of distrust, a political culture of commitment angst, worries about potential economic disadvantages in marine exploitation and a general vagueness as a chronic developing countries' disease.[16]

There is no information on how national negotiating positions are arrived at because this process is kept opaque in many countries. However, since the protocols are not concrete or strict, the negotiating positions do not need to be fed from so many channels as would be the case with more stringent agreements.

The structures within which MAP operates are those of UNEP, existing international law and custom, the North–South divide on the bureaucratic side and the ideological structures of what such a regional agreement actually means. It seems that environmental structures are only beginning to be formulated now with the incorporation of the Rio process in the new convention. Again, there is an inherent acceptance of the value base that such an agreement on a regional level should not impose any restrictions on the members but safeguard sovereignty. This is also demonstrated by the complete lack of review mechanisms.

From the evidence available, it is clear that the lack of tight provisions in MAP can be attributed to a lack of environmental structures in the process, the political culture of the region with strong emphasis on sovereignty and a belief system that sees MAP as an agreement of a non-restrictive nature. This explains the limitations of MAP. Although the new convention of 1995 takes on board the idea of sustainable development and Agenda 21, it is not very likely that it will change the general direction of MAP since it has been relegated to the same position of non-restrictive agreement by its member states. In addition, it is doubtful whether the idea of sustainable development will have any effect on environmental quality.

The illustrative consideration of the issues at stake has helped to highlight what place the provisions and structures take in the policy-making process. To recapitulate, national negotiating positions are formed with reference to various subactors, political culture, bureaucratic structure, environmental consciousness, ideological preference, values, etc. These characteristics and their mix are case-specific and therefore it is not possible to assume that a negotiating position is guided primarily by, for instance, economic advantage. The individual case needs to be studied and this explains why neorealist or rational choice approaches often fail to explain negotiating behaviour.

Conclusion and the need for a wider context

This chapter has made a heuristic distinction between institutional and environmental effectiveness. This enables us to contextualise the limitations of the effectiveness debate and to demonstrate that a concept based solely on institutional effectiveness is artificial. Existing analyses of the concept of effectiveness focus on the performance of an international environmental agreement in institutional terms rather than relate effectiveness to the environmental concerns that triggered its formation. Therefore, it is argued that a methodologically useful concept of effectiveness has to embrace a holistic definition of effectiveness, here called environmental effectiveness.

One of the main failures of regime theoretical analysis is that analysis is focused on actor behaviour within the regime and leading towards regime formation, as well as actor interests, motivating behaviour. This approach neglects the social environment in which the 'regime' is formed and of which it is part. The basis for this neglect is that regime analysis is based on the belief that international order is a function of will, which implies that effective international order is also a function of will. However, this is clearly not the case in relation to the effectiveness (in whatever sense) of international environmental agreements.

The analysis of the existing literature has shown that, to date, the main concern of theorists has been the performance of the institution behind an agreement. The main focus of inquiry was how institutions cooperate and how this cooperation can best be put into practice or what factors can be singled out that affect performance. All this concentrates on the role of actors in institution-building but is removed from the actual problem inciting the cooperative attempt. This means that analysis takes place on the level of what is here called institutional effectiveness, and the idea of what I refer to as environmental effectiveness has been neglected.

Thus a new concept has been developed that defines effectiveness (called environmental effectiveness to distinguish it from the methodologically limited institutional effectiveness) in a more holistic sense. An agreement can be called effective if the degrading or polluting processes it aims to regulate are actually arrested or reversed. This implies an effective agreement text *and* the putting into practice of policies. The main improvement of this new approach is that it goes beyond treating an agreement as a closed institutional or social unit and re-embeds the agreement in its social and environmental structures.

These four determinants are considered to provide the basis for an analysis of environmental effectiveness. The liberation of the concept of institutional effectiveness from the methodological constraints of current analysis has opened up possibilities of a new, open, inclusive concept of environmental effectiveness. This chapter forms the basis of the new definition of effectiveness by demonstrating the width of the concept through the analytical distinction of environmental and institutional effectiveness. Part II will demonstrate the consequences of ignoring the concept of environmental effectiveness with reference to the Mediterranean Action Plan and the Convention on Long-Range Transboundary Air Pollution.

Part II
Empirical studies

In Part I an analytical distinction was made between the concepts of institutional and environmental effectiveness which demonstrated that the conventional study of international environmental agreements and their effectiveness is firmly grounded in a methodology that tends to be restricted to the consideration of institutional mechanisms. In Chapters 5 and 6 the consequences of ignoring environmental effectiveness will be discussed. Since such consequences are by definition case-dependent, the two empirical studies of the Mediterranean Action Plan and the Convention on Long-Range Transboundary Air Pollution will serve as an example.

This section of the book is necessarily descriptive to a certain extent as detailed knowledge of the two empirical studies is necessary in order to understand their effectiveness. However, the description of the two agreements will be used to analyse their institutional and environmental effectiveness in a critical form.

The pollution of the Mediterranean Sea is an important environmental problem for the following reasons. The pollution of the Mediterranean Sea interrupts the food chain because the fauna and flora living in the sea become unfit for consumption either by other animals or by humans. Ignorance or the lack of other food sources lead to the passing on of the pollutants which then cause disease or malformation in humans of the region or other areas to which seafood is exported. The pollution of the Mediterranean Sea also leads to the death or extinction of certain species with the result that food sources for other species vanish and the natural balance of the waters is overturned. Therefore, vast areas in certain regions are declared 'dead', i.e. are lacking in sufficient oxygen to host life. For example, the disappearance of the *posidonia* sea grass in the western Mediterranean has fundamental consequences for all social and biological activity in the region. They are considered to be the 'lungs' of the Mediterranean Sea and are choked to death by heavy metal and insecticide run-offs, oil spills and fishing, as well as tourism (Luke, 1991: 11).

There are two consequences of marine pollution in entropic terms. On the one hand, the 'poisoning' of the food chain leads to a break-up of the food chain and to health consequences for the participants in the food chain. Therefore their use and transformation of energy is minimised. On the other hand, marine pollution leads to the creation of marine wastelands which can no longer fulfil their entropic role, i.e. they have reached the limits of the finite entropic ecosystem.

The environmental problem in the case of acid-rain question is the use of fossil fuel, i.e. finite fossilised organic material that is part of a natural cycle, the extraction of which from the natural cycle creates energy for industrial society. This extraction and processing results in the release of air pollutants into the environment. The cyclical phenomenon of growth and decay, and the subsequent use as fertiliser of the decaying organic matter, is disturbed by the extraction and burning of the fossil fuels. First, large vacuums are left underground, which do not occur naturally. Second, the burning of these fossil fuels produces CO_2 and air pollutants, which are not part of normal organic processes and therefore 'surplus', or waste. This surplus upsets the careful rhythm of natural processes and, in the case of CO_2, leads to global warming. In the case of air pollutants it leads to the phenomenon of acid rain which manifests itself through the death of forests, lakes and health problems in humans, apart from damage to human monuments.

The damage caused by acid rain is not thought to be irreversible, therefore it is assumed that time frames lack the sense of urgency related to, for example, biodiversity. If air pollutants are filtered out and are no longer released into the environment, ecosystems will slowly recover and return to their pre-acidification state after many years. However, this assumption disregards notions of change. It is not possible to return to a previous state because of the irreversibility of time. It may be possible to return to a non-acidification state but not the pre-acidification state. For example, loss of biodiversity may have occurred, or soil erosion due to the death of forests, and will have irreversibly changed the ecosystem in question.

The occurrence of acidification damage can be directly related to the beginning and advancement of the industrial age and the ever-increasing burning of fossil fuels. The twentieth century, with its exponential growth in energy consumption, led to the excesses in acidification experienced from the 1970s onwards. Between 1860 and 1990, global carbon dioxide emissions increased by 5.8 billion metric tonnes of carbon from around 0.1 billion tonnes to about 5.9 billion tonnes. (Porter and Brown, 1996: 7). The relations between these environmental problems and the institutional arrangements to regulate their effects will be discussed in the following two chapters.

5 The consequences of ignoring environmental effectiveness (I)

The Mediterranean Action Plan

The Mediterranean Action Plan (MAP) has achieved quite a difficult task by initiating and maintaining a process for more than 20 years in a region traditionally hostile to cooperation. Its structures reflect this need for diplomacy and care. It was developed following a series of conferences and meetings by UN agencies and Mediterranean governments on the state of pollution in the sea, and as a reaction to the 1972 Stockholm UN Conference on the Human Environment (Raftopoulos, 1993). MAP was created in 1975 at an inter-ministerial conference and its legal framework, which is the Barcelona Convention, was established in 1976 simultaneously with the first two protocols. At this time, little was known about the nature, origins and pathways of pollution in the Mediterranean Sea and this was reflected in its structure. The Barcelona Convention forms the legal part of MAP and is complemented by a research component (MEDPOL), policy-planning programmes (Blue Plan and Priority Actions Programme) and financial/institutional arrangements, covered by UNEP.

The four components will first be described and an analysis of MAP will then be given, highlighting central issues and concerns. Since MAP has a complex structure and its components interact, the best approach is to separate the four components for descriptive and analytical purposes. However, this analytical separation does not mean that the components are not interconnected.

The structure of MAP is based on a three-pronged approach: to research the origins of pollution, to take common action in the form of legal agreements and to try to deal with problems of development and their impact on the environment in the policy-planning programme. The different levels were clearly intended to interact and feed each other. However, in practice this has not happened to the extent envisaged and indeed necessary. This may be related to the compartmentalisation of MAP as compared to other agreements but there are many other indicators (e.g. overall lack of enthusiasm *vis-à-vis* concrete action, lack of financial support, lack of environmental awareness) which make it impossible to determine the significance of this compartmentalised structure of MAP.

In institutional terms, the three-pronged approach of MAP aims to make the agreement transparent and thus have maximum participation, following the idea of functionalism. This means that cooperation in so-called uncontential issue areas will spill over into more fundamental policy-making. It also addresses the different capacity problem of the membership and the lack of scientific capability in some of the member states. However, this could also have been achieved with a more conventional structure.

The Barcelona Convention, its protocols and the new Convention

The original Barcelona Convention consists of five protocols:

1 Dumping from Ships and Aircraft (1976)
2 Cooperation in Combating Pollution by Oil and Other Harmful Substances in Cases of Emergency (1976)
3 Pollution from Land-Based Sources (1980)
4 Specially Protected Areas (1982)
5 Pollution Resulting from Offshore Activities (1994).

In 1995, the Convention was replaced by a new, amended version which takes direct account of the recommendations of the 1992 Rio Conference on the Environment and Development. In addition, the protocol on Specially Protected Areas was replaced by a protocol on Biodiversity.

The original framework convention was signed together with the first two protocols in 1976 and came into force in 1978. All Mediterranean states and the EC/EU are parties to the Convention and the first two protocols. It was a provision of the Convention that at least one protocol had to be signed at the same time as the Convention for a state to become a signatory. This provision was intended to increase participation.

The Convention defines key terms such as the exact area of the Mediterranean Sea and lists the key pollution issues to be addressed. However, these issues are not treated in detail and there is no mechanism for the administration and implementation of the Convention. It is noteworthy that internal waters of the contracting parties are not included in the convention and that in the Eastern Mediterranean, the 'demarcation line' is the southern limits of the Straits of the Dardanelles between Mehmetcik and Kumkale lighthouses, i.e. the sea of Marmara, the Bosphorus and the Black Sea are excluded.

The areas in which the contracting parties will take measures are pollution caused by dumping from ships and aircraft, pollution from ships, pollution resulting from exploration and exploitation of the continental shelf and the seabed and its subsoil, as well as pollution from land-based sources. Pollution is defined in article 2(a) as

> the introduction by man, directly or indirectly, of substances or energy into the marine environment resulting in such deleterious effects such as harm to living resources, hazards to human health, hindrance to marine activities

including fishing, impairment of quality for use of sea-water and reduction of amenities.

The protocol for the prevention of pollution of the Mediterranean Sea by dumping from ships and aircraft was signed in 1976 and came into force in 1978. It prohibits the dumping of substances such as organohalogen or organosilicon compounds, mercury, cadmium, persistent plastic, hydrocarbons, radioactive materials and acid compounds and requires the issuing of a permit by the competent national authority for substances listed such as heavy metals, cyanides, pesticides and synthetic organic chemicals. All other dumping of wastes requires a general permit from the national authorities. This protocol applies to ships and aircraft of each respective signatory state as well as ships and aircraft in its territory but it does not apply to ships and aircraft owned or operated by a state party and used only on government non-commercial service.

Likewise, the protocol on cooperation in combating pollution by oil and other harmful substances in cases of emergency was signed in 1976 and came into force in 1978. It prescribes cooperation in the Mediterranean region in case of oil or other emergencies in order to reduce or eliminate any damage caused by an incident. Any other state likely to be affected by such an incident must be informed, and UNEP must also be notified in case of an emergency caused by an oil spill. In addition, a regional activity centre to deal with such emergencies (REMPEC) has been established in Malta.

Cooperation on oil pollution includes actions such as salvage or recovery, the dissemination of information about new ways in which pollution can be avoided, the dissemination of reports, and the instructions to ship-masters and aircraft pilots to report accidents and take all practicable measures available to avoid or reduce the effects of pollution. Assistance can be requested from other signatory states or from the regional activity centre and will be given in the form of expert advice and supply of products, equipment and facilities.

These three legal documents form the beginning of the Barcelona Convention and reflect the immediate and principal concerns of the time when MAP was being set up. Although pollution from land-based sources, the development dimension, and pollution resulting from offshore activities are mentioned in the Convention, these issues were thought to be insufficiently researched to be put on the agenda for the first protocols (Boxer, 1983). Therefore, the emphasis was on hydrocarbon pollution and on mobile sources.

Before discussing the next protocol, which was signed three years later, it is useful to review the context in which the Barcelona Convention was developed. The choice of the two protocols is arbitrary. On the one hand, there is existing international law on the subject, in the form of the 1972 London Dumping Convention and the International Convention for the Prevention of Pollution from Ships 1973, as amended in 1978 (Marpol 73/78), which regulates all forms of marine pollution except dumping and even gives the Mediterranean special area status, i.e. *no* tanker or non-tanker vessel discharges are permitted. However, not all Mediterranean states are parties to the London Dumping Convention or

Marpol.[1] Marpol was not reproduced in a Barcelona Convention protocol because it is directed at the shipping community whereas the Barcelona Convention is directed at its member states.[2] However, a number of Mediterranean states are also important actors in the shipping community. After all, the second protocol on combating emergency spills and the need for cooperation does not contain any provisions on the permissibility of discharges, so only accidents are covered.

Since the first protocol deals with dumping, it seems that both accidents and discharges are covered. However, this is not the case. There is a difference between dumping and discharging. In the case of oil, discharges occur routinely as part of the loading or unloading procedure. This requires special tanker equipment and port reception facilities to avoid or reduce the amount of petroleum released into the sea. Since oil pollution was the main concern of MAP's designers in the 1970s, it is an omission with consequences for the effectiveness of these protocols. Although the reproduction of Marpol in a Mediterranean context was not necessary, because Marpol is directed at the shipping nations while MAP is directed at its member states, this still does not explain the omission of discharge regulations. A regime theoretical approach would not detect the absence of discharge regulations because it does not place its focus on the broader marine pollution 'regimes' and their relationship with marine pollution. This point highlights the fact that an analysis concentrating on participation or composition of the member states, or the provisions of the agreement, will neglect the omission of sources of pollutants because it does not focus on environmental benefit.

To summarise, the shortcomings of the first two protocols of the Barcelona Convention are the lack of a consistent approach to discharges into the marine environment from mobile sources. This is also a definitional problem. The lack of clearly defined time limits relating to implementation of the measures prescribed in the protocols is also an effectiveness deficit. However, the most severe problem with the first two protocols of the Barcelona Convention is that they do not tackle the problem of mobile source pollution convincingly. The inclusion and exclusion of substances and special inventories of pollutants, as well as the proviso that special national licences to pollute may be granted, show that there is no determined effort to abolish the introduction of deleterious substances into the marine environment.

The protocol for the Protection of the Mediterranean Sea against Pollution from Land-Based Sources was signed in 1980 and came into force in 1983. Some states only acceded in the 1990s.[3] The protocol tackles the problem of discharges from direct or coastal outfalls and from rivers or other watercourses or run-offs and of atmospheric pollution. Again, substances in the annexes should be either eliminated or strictly limited. There are no emission limits but the provision is that parties should progressively adopt guidelines on emission limits. In addition, paragraph 4 of article 5 reads that the standards and the timetables for the implementation of the programmes and measures aimed at eliminating pollution from land-based sources shall be fixed by the Parties and periodically reviewed, if necessary every two years, for each of the substances listed in annex I, in accordance with the provisions of article 15 of this protocol.

Substances in annex I, i.e. those to be eliminated, are selected on the basis of their toxicity, persistence and bioaccumulation. They include organohalogen compounds, organophosphorous compounds, organotin compounds, mercury compounds, cadmium compounds, used lubricating oils, persistent synthetic materials, radioactive substances and substances that have carcinogenic, terato-genic or mutagenic effects. Substances in annex II, which are to be strictly limited, include various heavy metals, biocides, organosilicon compounds, crude oils, cyanides, non-biodegradable detergents, pathogenic micro-organisms, thermal discharges, etc. No time limits are imposed.

The list of substances in annexes I and II is based on EC legislation and on similar regulations issued by the Paris Commission for the Northeast Atlantic (Pastor, 1991: 114). The signatory states commit themselves to develop standards or criteria progressively to deal with pipeline outfall specifications, coastal water quality, the control/replacement of installations causing substantial pollution and emission standards for substances in annexes I and II. Although the protocol contains lists of substances that are to be controlled, as to how and when this will be done and how much control is necessary is not addressed. Equally, although a review mechanism is suggested to tighten up this protocol, this has not resulted in any amendments to the protocol. According to Greenpeace's Xavier Pastor, the protocol was scheduled to come into full effect by 1995 when 50 different measures for pollution control would have to be set. Only eight of these had actually been set by 1990 and there has been widespread reluctance to provide information on sources of pollution, discharge permits issued or amounts discharged. No standards were included in the 1995 reprint of the protocol. However, MAP's technical report series has published copious material on this subject. Emission standards are to be imposed on blacklisted chemicals (annex I) while greylisted substances (annex II) will be dealt with by ambient standards. Although both are quantitative limit values, ambient standards measure the pres-ence of substances in the environment while emission standards measure their concentration in the actual waste stream entering the sea. Ambient standards cannot control the introduction of pollutants into the environment and are not an instrument of abatement. The source of a pollutant is difficult to trace when using ambient standards and when direct connection can be made between pollutant and polluter; it is, therefore, not an effective pollution control method due to a lack of linkage. Again, these loopholes are considered to be positive measures by institutional methodologies although their environmental benefit is non-existent. They do not even improve effectiveness by increasing membership because the increased membership does not commit itself to any measure ameliorating the degradation of the marine environment.

This protocol completes the inventory of pollutant sources. Both mobile and land-based sources of pollution are now covered. However, no standards of a clearly defined or binding nature have been imposed. Again, an arbitrary list of substances has been devised instead of a ban on all deleterious substances.

The protocol concerning Mediterranean Specially Protected Areas was signed in 1982 and came into force in 1986. The protocol is special in the sense that there are no provisions for it in the framework convention unlike the other protocols. It encourages parties to establish protected areas and to work on their restoration. This provision applies not only to areas of environmental importance but also to historical and archaeological sites. A regional activity centre specialising in protected areas was set up in Tunis in 1985. Jurisdictional zones are defined in accordance with international law. The following measures are to be taken progressively: a planning and management system; a ban on dumping or discharge of waste; regulation of ship traffic, fishing and hunting and economic activities related to the fauna and flora; and regulation of archaeological activities.

It is unclear why this essentially unilateral or bilateral process of setting up a specially protected area needs to be regulated by an international agreement. Clearly, the aim of the protocol is to encourage as many Mediterranean states as possible to think about special areas, but since the protocol does not necessitate but only encourages their establishment, the choice of tackling this issue in protocol form is puzzling. It is rather an issue to be treated in a declaration or to be recommended by policy action programmes.

Although the protocol for the Protection of the Mediterranean Sea against Pollution resulting from Offshore Activities was signed in October 1994 by nine members to the Convention, it has not yet been ratified. The protocol requires offshore activities to be authorised by the competent national authorities and be accompanied by a study on its effects. However, an environmental impact assessment will only be necessary if the proposed activity definitely has harmful effects on the environment. The planned installations should be monitored for safety and environmental effect so that data are available should they be needed. In case of an emergency, cooperation should be encouraged and national contingency plans developed. However, operators are subject to strict and limited liability. The protocol includes lists of noxious substances and materials the disposal of which is either prohibited or subject to a special permit in the protocol area. In addition, the disposal of sewage, hazardous waste, oily substances and rubbish from offshore installations is prohibited.

Apparently, the aim of this protocol is to strike a balance between development and environment, possibly with a view to sustainable development (Sersic, 1989: 164). The balance, however, seems to be heavily weighted in favour of industrial development. Although this protocol regulates the discharges emanating from offshore installations quite strictly, it does not prescribe stringent measures on the operation of offshore installations. It provides the relevant authorities with a list of criteria, which are very general and non-committing.

The fact that this protocol took so long to negotiate (nearly ten years) is a clear indication that the subject of the protocol is a delicate matter. The oil industry was heavily involved in the negotiations, which may be the cause of the delay. However, again, a protocol has emerged that neither introduces clearly defined standards nor makes an organised effort to regulate offshore activities. Therefore it is of no significant environmental benefit although it introduces concepts such as environmental impact assessment. These environmental concepts, however, are not applied in a context where they could lead to environmental improvement.

The new convention and protocols

In 1995, the Barcelona Convention was amended to reflect the developments that had taken place on the global level since the 1992 Rio UN Conference on Environment and Development (UNCED) and renamed Convention for the Protection of the Marine Environment and the Coastal Region of the Mediterranean Sea against Pollution and its protocols. In addition, the protocol for prevention of pollution of the Mediterranean Sea by dumping from ships and aircraft was amended to include incineration at sea. The protocol concerning Mediterranean Specially Protected Areas was replaced by the protocol concerning Specially Protected Areas and Biological Diversity in the Mediterranean. This new version takes account of the UNCED Biodiversity protocol.

The new amended Barcelona Convention for the Protection of the Marine Environment and the Coastal Region of the Mediterranean includes provisions for the precautionary principle, the polluter pays principle and environmental impact assessment. It also advises the introduction of time limits on environmental regulation. In general, it lists priority fields of activities for the environment and development in the Mediterranean Basin, which are based on the recommendations of Agenda 21. The new protocol concerning Specially Protected Areas and Biological Diversity in the Mediterranean has extended its legal reach to include the high seas rather than territorial seas only. It includes a list of specially protected areas of Mediterranean interest (SPAMI) (Scovazzi, 1996: 95–98).

There are two comments to be made on these changes. On the one hand, the Barcelona Convention had exhausted its capacities and these changes can inject new life into it and keep up the regional environmental effort in the Mediterranean area. On the other, the establishment of a new convention and protocols is a lengthy administrative process and it will take years before it will be ratified and implemented. If the energy of this effort had been spent on the implementation of policy programmes such as the Genoa Declaration (see p. 74), this would have been more environmentally effective given the time dimensions involved. Moreover, the recommendations of the Rio process are vague and are not likely to lead to any concrete policy action in the Mediterranean region. Therefore the environmental benefit of the adoption of the new convention and sustainable development action plan is negligible, at least in the short term.

However, such points are not addressed by institutional thinkers such as the regime theorists. In their view, a new agreement confirms institutional commitments and the will to achieve order. The focus is not on environmental benefit – and the introduction of a new convention system rather than an improvement of policy measures within the MAP system shows that environmental concern is not the driving force behind these institutions.

MEDPOL

MEDPOL is the scientific component of MAP. When the Mediterranean Sea problem became institutionalised in the 1970s, there was practically no marine science base in the region and the aim to develop scientific capabilities, especially in the south, was a fundamental aspect of the institution. Haas (1989) provides data on the distribution of the various marine science disciplines in the Mediterranean region. The science base that did exist, or was being developed, needed to be standardised in order to use the same measurement techniques and develop a compatible system of analysis throughout the region.

Boxer (1983: 274) argues that lack of trust in scientific decisions often leads to declining public confidence in scientific solutions to environmental problems. However, he argues, this is not the case in the Mediterranean. There was much physical evidence of the degradation of the sea in the form of debris, oil films, sewage or smell but no scientific consensus was established on the source of the pollution or on what to do about it. One of the first tasks of MAP, therefore, was to develop and unite the scientific community and organise some form of consensus.

Aims of MEDPOL

For the first ten years of its existence, the targets of MEDPOL, the scientific component of MAP, were as follows:

* to formulate and carry out a coordinated pollution monitoring and research programme, taking into account the goals of the Mediterranean Action Plan and the capabilities of the Mediterranean Research Centres to participate in it;
* to assist national research centres in developing their capabilities to participate in the programme;
* to analyse the sources, amounts, levels, pathways, trends and effects of pollutants relevant to the Mediterranean Sea;
* to promote the scientific/technical information needed by the Governments of the Mediterranean States and the EC for the negotiation and implementation of the Convention for the protection of the Mediterranean Sea and its related protocols;

- to build up consistent time-series of data on the sources, pathways, levels and effects of pollutants in the Mediterranean Sea and thus to contribute to the scientific knowledge of the Mediterranean Sea.

(Jeftic and Saliba, 1987: 199)

MEDPOL is the assessment component of MAP and was agreed upon in 1975 when MAP was established. Its purpose is to generate data on the state of the marine environment as so little was known in the early stages of MAP. At first it was funded solely by UNEP and other UN agencies. One of the problems in the beginning was the lack of a scientific base in the southern countries with neither expertise nor equipment to carry out monitoring activities. So, one of the benefits for southern MEDPOL participants was the establishment of scientific facilities by UNEP. For the usefulness of the monitoring activity this had the following effect:

> ... [G]aps and weaknesses in the scientific outcome of the research projects were inevitable, given the widely differing levels of competence and experience of the cooperating centres and the difficulties inherent to the programme. The concern in the first place was the validity and comparability of the data, and also their geographical coverage, as well as the fact that the programme was scattered over too many projects.

(Jeftic, 1990: 68)

This critique was made in general and is meant to apply to the two phases of MEDPOL that were either under way or completed.

MEDPOL phase I

Phase I (1976–1980) was mainly concerned with the setting up of centres and the training of scientists although research projects were also carried out. By 1976, 13 projects had been agreed on but only two of these were actually completed (Haas, 1990: 100). Haas argues that none of the studies on biogeochemistry of selected pollutants in the open sea, on the role of sedimentation, on atmospheric pathways and on marine modelling were completed because

> France blocked funding for studies that would generate data that might undercut its position at ongoing meetings on the Land-Based Sources Protocol regarding which pollutants should be covered and the pathways by which they are transmitted.

(Haas, 1990: 101)

This important point will be developed further below in the discussion of phase I. As regards the LBS protocol, a study of land-based sources of pollution (Med X) was concluded in time for the LBS protocol as part of the initial phase I projects and showed some interesting findings. Data are inter-calibrated between different national institutions. Haas (1990: 102) summarises the results of this project well:

> ... It demonstrates that industrial and municipal wastes exceeded oil pollution as the principal problems in the Mediterranean; 85 per cent of all pollutants in the Mediterranean were found to originate on land, 80–85 per cent of land-based pollutants were transmitted to the Mediterranean by rivers; and over 80 per cent of all municipal sewage entering the Mediterranean was untreated. In fact, it was discovered that much of the oil in the Mediterranean comes from automobile owners who drain their oil pans into municipal sewers.

There are several points to be made on the Med X report. On the one hand, Med X can be taken as an indicator as to what sort of policy priorities MAP should have. It illustrates sources and quantity of discharges in the Mediterranean region. Its data provisions are based on collection of figures and the decision on what substances should be covered by Med X was made by a body composed of different UN organisations, which meant that the political and economic influence of the member states on substance choice was limited. However, political and economic influence on the scientific base of MAP was exerted in other ways.

According to Boxer's findings, UNEP suspected from the outset that land-based pollution in the form of industrial discharges, sewage and agricultural run-offs was one of the major contributors to the degradation of the Mediterranean Sea (Boxer, 1983: 293). However, since no concrete data were available, these had to be acquired first.

Boxer argues that the effort to establish objective scientific information was continuously frustrated. The industrialised northern states were active in avoiding UNEP studies on the effect and pathways of pollutants in coastal waters by reducing the MEDPOL budget and taking funding out of existing projects. Since half the funds come from MAP members and primarily from north-western states, this was an effective bar to many activities. Another reason for reservations is the presence of international researchers in territorial waters where there are possible sea-bed and continental shelf resources. This worry is shared by all the Mediterranean states. Moreover, Boxer (1983: 298) maintains that many states might not be interested in the scope of environmental degradation on their coasts and certainly do not want the data to become public because of tourism and image implications.

While it is not possible to confirm Boxer's argument concerning the funding, or withholding of funding, of MEDPOL projects as data are no longer accessible due to time lag, it is possible to retrace the developed countries' negotiating positions and reservations *vis-à-vis* the LBS protocol. There is no record of French reservations to the contents of the LBS protocol; however, the Italian negotiating party did indeed criticise the inclusion of atmospheric pathways of pollution:

> The question of pollution transferred by the atmosphere is still under study both by scientists and by organisations such as UNEP and OECD, and for that reason we do not have sufficient data for embarking on a study of that type of pollution ... In particular, scientific knowledge does not make it possible to discern the sources of pollution carried by the atmosphere.[4]

We can therefore assume that there was some reluctance by Italy to the inclusion of atmospheric pathways of pollution but the MAP Scientific Adviser vehemently denied that the practice of withholding funding – as suspected by Boxer and Haas – to avoid particular studies ever took place,[5] and given the bureaucratic processes through which funding has to be authorised, this seems plausible. The individual member states' contributions to MAP have to be authorised through parliamentary proceedings in many member states despite the fact that they are routine expenditure.

To summarise, MEDPOL phase I had the task to more or less establish an inventory of pollution problems in the Mediterranean Sea. However, the completion of this task was subjected to political considerations and these had to be accommodated with scientific concerns. The experiences of phase II have to be considered in order to judge the policy impact of MEDPOL.

MEDPOL phase II

This was a long-term phase that ran from 1981 to 1995 and aimed to provide further information on possible reviews and implementation of existing protocols and on future ones as well as to provide regular assessments on sea-water quality. There are 11 study areas with more than a hundred institutions involved. Jeftic and Saliba (1987: 204) list the 11 areas as:

- the development of sampling and reporting standards,
- the development of a scientific basis for emission standards,
- epidemiological studies,
- criteria for application of the LBS protocol,
- research on oceanographic processes,
- research on properties of the substances covered by the LBS protocol,
- research on eutrophication,
- research on ecosystem change,
- research on the effects of thermal discharges,
- research on biogeochemical cycles of specific pollutants, and
- research on pollutant transfer processes.

This research agenda seems to indicate that UNEP is active in improving the protocol on land-based sources and also prioritising the standardisation of research projects as well as the LBS protocol. However, this can only happen with the cooperation of the member states and better links between scientists and policy-makers. Very often the objectivity of scientists as policy advisers is doubted in science policy studies but this does not seem to be a major issue in MEDPOL. Science by MEDPOL delivers results which are not acted on regardless of the status of the findings.

This point applies to phases I and II of MEDPOL. It is relatively meaningless how well MEDPOL fulfils its aims and how politicised it is, since it does not really make an impact at the policy level. Therefore it can be argued that an analysis that concentrates on the content of MEDPOL and neglects its actual role in policy-making cannot capture its role in achieving effectiveness. In order to improve the environmental effectiveness of MAP, MEDPOL needs to target its research towards improving environmental effectiveness *and* enhance its influence at the policy level. At the moment it is closer to performing the former role rather than the latter, despite the political influences in scientific agenda-setting.

The purpose of MEDPOL

In this context the functionalist argument has to be discussed which supposes that environmental consciousness can only develop with the establishment of a scientific base and this scientific base can only develop through a monitoring programme as a training stage. According to Mee, development of scientific capacity can only be achieved through the building of monitoring bases (Jeftic, 1990: 69). This will be the beginning of environmental research and will lead to the training of scientists. Once this research capacity has been established, routine work will be done by junior members of staff and senior scientists can focus on more innovative research. Jeftic uses Mee for arguing that this is the only way research activity in scientifically developing states can begin and UNEP follows this line by funding the establishment of monitoring stations in developing Mediterranean states. The stronger the scientific basis, the more likely it is to have an impact on policy-making, following the epistemic community approach. Unfortunately, practice does not seem to confirm this view.

Although research projects tended to be completed in phase II and a lot of monitoring technology was transferred to scientifically less developed states, this may have resulted in publications and technical reports (92 by 1995 according to Skjaerseth, 1996b) but not in any action in policy terms and certainly not in prioritising environmental issues on the policy agenda or relating them to development issues. In fact, originally, MEDPOL had several aims: first and foremost the production of scientific knowledge for other components of MAP, but *inter alia* also the putting on the agenda of the environmental issue and the establishment of a definite environmental policy. Since MEDPOL was not connected to the other components in any useful way, it is difficult to assess the validity and relevance of its findings and this would also be fruitless. The focus has to be on institutional failure. There is no way the internal failings of MEDPOL can be discovered as it was never put to the test. On the other hand, it can be argued that the neglect of MEDPOL led to the institutional failure of MAP. Although the UNEP/MAP Coordinating Unit is very eager, it has failed to establish a well-working institutional framework, presumably due to the lack of interest of its members. However, an analytical approach focusing on institutional effectiveness would not detect this institutional failure as it would be outside its remit. This institutional failure has direct bearing on environmental performance since the institution is not equipped with the tools to deal with environmental degradation.

Policy-planning

The policy-planning component of MAP was established in 1977 after two years of negotiations on the shape it should take. Its scope goes beyond marine pollution issues and extends to regional development and environmental issues in general.

In the planning stages, there were disagreements between the member states as to the form a policy-planning programme should take. It was generally accepted that the state of the marine environment could not be improved merely by studying individual emission sources but that issues of social and economic planning were directly related to the problem. A two-pronged approach was chosen to deal with the prevailing necessities: a study-oriented programme and an action programme (Raftopoulos, 1993: 22). The policy action programme is designed for immediate action but also for the implementation of the findings of the study plan (the Blue Plan). Therefore they are meant to complement each other.

Moreover, several policy-oriented conferences have taken place that highlight policy priority issues. The Genoa Declaration, which is an issue of coastal management, was adopted at the Fourth Ordinary Meeting of the Contracting Parties in 1985. It lists ten priority targets for the decade 1985–1995. According to *The Siren News* (30/1986: 34) these are:

- establishment of reception facilities for ship discharges;
- sewage plants for all cities (more than 100,000 inhabitants) and appropriate treatment plants for all towns with over 10,000 inhabitants;
- environmental impact assessment for all new activities;
- cooperation on environmental safety of maritime traffic;
- protection of endangered marine species;
- concrete measures on pollution reduction;
- identification and protection of at least 100 coastal historic sites of common interest;
- as well as 50 new marine and coastal sites of Mediterranean interest;
- effective measures on soil erosion, forest fires and desertification; and
- substantial reduction in air pollution.

These policy recommendations have been much quoted but have not been incorporated into the legal, or applied, component of MAP. Likewise, the 1990 Nicosia Charter on Euro–Mediterranean cooperation is based on policy recommendations. It brings together the Commission of the European Communities and 12 MAP member states, based on the idea of involving the World Bank and the European Investment Bank as sponsors for a Mediterranean sustainable development programme. The aims of the Charter are:

- give managerial and financial autonomy to appropriate environmental institutions;
- integrate environmental management into socio-economic development;
- establish an integrated legislative and regulatory framework;
- implement environmental impact assessment;
- adopt economic and fiscal strategies as environmental policy measures;
- control population growth in the coastal regions;
- speed up the completion of the protocol on offshore installations.

In addition, the coastal zones to be protected were to be designated by 1993; 10 million inhabitants be connected to sewage plants; 25 controlled waste dumps for industrial products created and 20 ports equipped with reception facilities for dirty ballast waters by 1993.

The Nicosia Charter is an attempt to achieve policy targets by bypassing conventional channels of action and involving outside funding agencies. The advantages of this approach will be discussed after studying the two components of MAP's policy action programmes.

The Blue Plan

The Blue Plan was endorsed in 1977 and is a comprehensive study of the economic activities in the Mediterranean Basin and their effect on the environment. It is a collection of data of social and economic trends which are used as scenarios for future developments. This is supposed to give an idea of future trends and acts as indicator for long-term planning. For example, a good illustration of what the Blue Plan does is its study of the agro-food sector: the Blue Plan looks at food dependency, the fragility of natural resources, availability of water resources and trends, fertiliser use and effects, demand trends, potential produce shift, constraints on the growth of the sector and it models the agro-food sector in the light of the scenarios (Grenon and Batisse, 1989).

One of the main criticisms is the limited usefulness of modelling and scenarios. Modelling as a method of research usually disregards wider social, political and economic factors and creates 'laboratory condition' predictions which may mean nothing in 'the real world'. This is certainly true, but in this case the Blue Plan is still extremely valuable despite the potential futility of its findings. Its predictions are based on developments in the past 30 years and they have been used for computer trend analysis for the next 30 years. Although the actual data predictions should be treated with caution, general trends are important for policy-making. After all, it may not be possible or even that important to know the exact number of tonnes of fertiliser run-offs for the year 2010, but on the policy level it is important to know about the rising trend and its potential effect on health and soil or sea contamination. Policies can be adopted on a preventive basis and without the Blue Plan such data would not have been avail-able as such socio-economic research is not very likely to be on the top of the research agenda in the southern Mediterranean countries. In addition, the economic and development focus gives the Blue Plan more credibility with policy-makers than a study with a highly environmentalist attitude would have had.

The Priority Actions Programme

The Priority Actions Programme (PAP) was also agreed upon in 1977 with a perspective to act immediately in demonstration and pilot projects (Raftopoulos, 1993: 27). It started late because of problems in establishing the institutional framework, disagreement about content and financial problems. PAP's first aim is not the targeting of environmental degradation but 'contribution to the reduc-tion of existing socio-economic inequalities among Mediterranean states' (Chircop, 1992: 23). The areas targeted are

- integrated planning and management of coastal zones;
- aqua culture;
- rehabilitation and reconstruction of historic sites;
- water resources development for islands and isolated coastal areas;
- land-use planning in earthquake zones.

Although these priority areas were identified, there was no clear idea as to what exactly should be done and where the funding should come from. The UNDP offered its support but only with the financial help of some member states that had specific programmes in mind did a project plan come into being in 1981. The Coastal Area Management Programmes (CAMPs) have designated several local areas for detailed study.

Since funding was a problem, one strategy was to attract outside funding, such as from the Environmental Program for the Mediterranean by the World Bank.[6] However, this programme was only started in the late 1980s, which makes the name *Priority* Action Programme a misnomer with the priority actions not happening until 16 years after their conception. In addition, an alliance with the World Bank may be financially promising but it also means that choice of projects will be limited to those that meet World Bank specifications (see Nicosia Charter above).

Given the environmental record of the World Bank (Rich, 1990), this is a disturbing thought. For example, in the early phase of MAP, a list of World Bank projects in the Mediterranean region was established and their details published. Most projects were either related to sewage works construction or port extension facilities.[7] Typical terms were loans for about 20 years at an annual interest rate of between 7 and 8 per cent. These projects are among those that led to the Latin American debtor crisis in the early 1980s, which should come as no surprise given the conditions of the loans. Although these loans provide help towards sanitation projects, they also lead the recipient state into a debt trap. Therefore World Bank involvement in the Mediterranean Action Plan has two sides to it.

To conclude, the policy action programmes of MAP seem to suffer a fate similar to that of MEDPOL. There is a lot of disagreement on research agendas, and administrative and financial obstruction. Although the Genoa Declaration is a brainchild of PAP, it has to be concluded that, again, there are communication difficulties between research and application. There are also communication problems within the policy research component which result in delays of research projects but these lack significance at the moment since the research findings are not used anyway. Still, again it can be deduced that UNEP seems to be the most active actor in this component. This raises questions about the *raison d'être* of MAP if there is no commitment from its member states or no willingness to cooperate. The Genoa Declaration and the Nicosia Charter can be regarded as efforts to overcome these problems but it is unclear how this fits in with the 1995 amendments to MAP. Moreover, in a personal communication with the MAP Scientific Coordinator, it was conceded that MAP–World Bank cooperation only began in earnest in 1995.[8]

Another policy programme is the introduction of Coastal Area Management Programmes (CAMPs). This scheme was launched in 1989 and consists of MAP providing financial help for member states that plan to develop ecologically sensitive coastal areas (Lempert and Farnsworth, 1994: 116). Host states apply for funding for a specific project which then needs to be approved by MAP officials. The four existing CAMPs are Izmir Bay in Turkey, the island of Rhodes in Greece, Kastela Bay in Croatia and a project on the Syrian coast.

The 1995 amendments to MAP have resulted in an espousal of the policy recommendations of Agenda 21. Again, these are not formulated in the terminology of concrete policy proposals but rather present a set of guidelines for general direction of action. This is a general problem of Agenda 21 and the concept of sustainable development that has not been improved upon by transplanting it on the regional level.

Since the problem of funding seems to be chronic with MAP, the last component regarding financial and institutional arrangements needs to be looked at in order to find out why these financial difficulties persist and why they were not dealt with and perceived when MAP was established in 1975. After all, it is one of the most recurrent issues in international environmental cooperation.

Financial and institutional arrangements

Originally MAP was administered by the UNEP Regional Seas Office in Geneva. When the Regional Seas Programme increased its number of projects, a special coordinating unit for the Mediterranean was set up in 1979, which moved to Athens in 1982. Also, a Mediterranean Trust Fund was established which relied on the contributions of Mediterranean states as UNEP resources had to be distributed between an increasing number of regional programmes.

The states involved paid, or were supposed to pay, amounts proportional to their overall UN schedules, which left France with a bill of 48 per cent of overall government contributions (Haas, 1990: 125). Before the Trust was set up in 1979, MAP was exclusively funded by UNEP but with the Trust individual states were directly responsible for the funding of MAP.

This resulted in the usual late payments and a permanent cash crisis for MAP. Although UNEP continued to channel resources into the MEDPOL programme, policy programmes and Regional Activity Centres ran on an extremely low budget. The late payment of members' contributions is a chronic and recurrent problem. For example, by October 1979, 13 countries and the EC had not paid their annual contributions to the Trust Fund while four members had effected partial payment. Only one country, Greece, had paid all its dues.[9] The figures available for 1995 show that about a third of all Mediterranean Trust Fund contributions were not expected to have been paid by 31 December 1995.[10]

The resources available are administered through the UNEP/MAP coordinating unit in Athens. Although there are regular meetings by various committees composed of national delegates which take financial and administrative decisions, the routine running of MAP and the routine allocation of resources are still done by UNEP via the coordinating unit.

The consequences for MAP are, first, that this bureaucratic layering and use of the coordinating unit leads to a time-lag in deciding on a project and the money becoming available. Second, it also means that UNEP remains the driving power behind MAP. Seeing the quibbles and disinterest of the member states in MEDPOL and the policy-planning component, this strong presence can be seen as an advantage. However, UNEP and, especially, the Coordinating Unit are not independent actors since they are composed of individuals of the member states. This could lead to doubts over MAP's neutrality in allocating project funds but, in practice, this problem has not arisen.

There is definitely a bias in favour of funding MEDPOL projects over PAP but it is difficult to explain why, except that scientific research was seen as more neutral and less threatening to individual states than PAP research. Moreover, MEDPOL projects do not necessitate concrete policy action whereas PAPs do. Also, it is perhaps revealing that the main failure of MAP – namely, the missing coordination between MEDPOL and the legal and policy-planning components – is exactly the area where UNEP initiative could not be useful.

Institutional and financial arrangements are extremely important and they are actually the facility that holds together a functioning institution. Since MAP is not a well-functioning institution, the institutional framework has to be taken as the point for failure. However, apart from the cash crisis, it does not seem that the coordinating unit has failed in an extreme way. Rather, the relationship between MAP and its member states needs to be investigated. After all, if your member states are not interested in supporting you, then your success will inherently be very limited. The various consequences of this will be discussed below.

The lack of Haas, Keohane and Levy's '3 Cs' (concern, contractual environment and capacity) in the case of the Mediterranean Action Plan proves that these are *conditions* and not *sources* of effectiveness. Since the conditions for their type of effectiveness do not exist, there cannot be an effective agreement. This lack proves that it is analytically more appropriate to define determinants of effectiveness. In this case, the economic and production structures are so dominant that they do not incorporate environmental concerns. There are no time frames in which to solve environmental problems and no awareness of the effect of social onto environmental rhythms. Although there is no political economy of science in which economics determines scientific expertise, science has been 'imported' and the regional science base is dislocated. Clearly, this all demonstrates that the instititutional structures of MAP are not geared to solving the problem of Mediterranean pollution.

The main issues of MAP

During the 1970s, in the early stages of MAP, immediate action concentrated on the most visible and aesthetically disturbing pollutant, i.e. oil. It was recognised that little was known about the actual state of pollution in the Mediterranean and therefore the emphasis was placed on knowledge generation in MAP, both with MEDPOL and with policy-planning.

The effect of oil pollution was clearly visible even to the layperson. Tar balls were found on beaches and in the open sea, having clearly visible and tangible effects on human and livestock health. Since the Mediterranean Sea is one of the busiest oil shipping areas in the world proportionally (20 per cent of oil transit is through the Mediterranean Sea), the origins of oil pollution were also assumed to be clear. This explains the focus on oil pollution in the first two protocols of the Barcelona Convention. However, the ignorance about the origins of pollution had to be researched and this process was initiated with the setting up of MEDPOL.

The structure of MAP is designed to research the origins of pollution, take common action in the form of legal agreements and try to deal with problems of development and their impact on the environment in the policy-planning programmes. In short, it tackles the issue of regional marine pollution on three levels: the generation of knowledge, legal commitment and socio-economic trend observation. It was planned that these different levels interact and complement each other, especially the research component feeding into the policy-planning and legal components and policy-planning feeding into the legal component. However, in practice this does not seem to have happened to the extent envisaged and necessary. This point has so far eluded the effectiveness researchers as it is outside their concept of effectiveness.

As the section on MEDPOL explained, funding was not adequate and also the linkage between research and research application was not well developed. The literature suggests several reasons for this shortage. Jeftic (1990: 68) argues that the development of a scientific basis in the region is a precondition for its research to have any impact on policy-making. MEDPOL did contribute substantially to the development of marine scientific capabilities in areas without prior experience but this does not seem to have led to major successes. On the other hand, Haas (1990: 101) sees the issue to be more closely connected to agenda-setting and funding, using the example of France blocking research funding for studies that might reveal the importance of other pollutants than those tabled by France during the negotiations of the protocol on land-based sources. Boxer (1983: 298), in contrast, argues that marine pollution is just not a high priority issue and therefore there is no interest in generating data that will then have to be acted on with huge financial implications in order to keep the tourist, fisheries and related industries in business. All three viewpoints suggest that financial considerations play a large part in MEDPOL's achievements or lack of achievement.

Another point emerges very clearly here: MAP certainly does not follow the linear model of scientific research leading to policy action despite one of its aims being to establish the science underlying Mediterranean pollution. The establishment of a science base in the Mediterranean region has clearly not led to the establishment of science-based policy action. Thus the choice of the first protocols under MAP is also not science-driven but based on knowledge gained from other regions or international pollution control efforts. Only from the 1980 protocol on land-based sources of pollution onwards can a scientific community be partially located in the Mediterranean region. Still, this does not mean that science did not influence the contents of the first two protocols and of the convention but that the scientific base was not directed at the Mediterranean but imported from elsewhere. Thus debates about science and power apply only partially since the power base of the imported science is not related to power issues in the Mediterranean region.

The Barcelona Convention lists a number of issues that it aims to regulate and these are essentially those that are then treated by its protocols. It was developed on the recommendation of various UN agencies that had experience with regional marine pollution. Basically only the Land-Based Sources (LBS) protocol has a concrete, overt scientific base whereas the other protocols are not directly linked to scientific problems. Even the LBS protocol mostly incorporates measures and lists of substances from other, earlier, regional marine pollution agreements such as the Oslo Convention. Even the latest (1995) developments of bringing MAP into a post-Rio format are based on outside influences, so there is no direct link between MAP policy and its scientific component. This lack of communication has been cited in other sections of this book and been listed as one reason for the lack of effectiveness of MAP. It means that the relationship between MAP and the environmental problems of the region is lost.

However, presupposing that this problem could be fixed, this does not mean that MAP would suddenly become effective. In order to achieve this, the science base would have to be vetted to find out if it is targeted towards environmental effectiveness or towards institutional effectiveness. At the moment it is not targeted for policy-makers as this example on the atmospheric transport of pollutants demonstrates:

The Working Group discussed how to approach the assessment of the contribution of atmospheric transport to the total contaminant load of the Mediterranean Sea … Measurements in the Mediterranean region have already shown some evidence for long-range atmospheric transport of metals from diverse sources. Any strategy for abating contamination in the Mediterranean region must take into account this contribution.

… For coordinating the research and monitoring and reviewing the results of these studies, the establishment of an *ad hoc* group of experts from the participating countries is recommended.[11]

The only message this report has for policy-makers is that more research is needed and that the phenomenon of atmospheric transport of contaminants needs to be treated. As to how this should be done, there is silence.

The same applies to the policy-planning programmes. On the one hand, funding is a major problem, on the other, lack of funding seems to be related to low priority status and agenda-setting.

Since the MAP of the 1980s and 1990s is mainly funded by its member states, albeit indirectly, the lack of funding mirrors its perceived lack of importance, and since only information gathered by MEDPOL and PAP can change that perception there seems to be a vicious circle. Bringing in outside funding is an option to break this circle and this is what is happening with EC and World Bank initiatives. However, these are recent phenomena and there are other problems related to this.

The Mediterranean Action Plan operates on the basis of an enabling and awareness-raising agreement. It operates with basically no concept of temporal dimensions, neither at the institutional nor at the environmental level. Although the LBS protocol imposes time limits for the phasing out of the emission into the marine environment of a list of pollutants, this does not even come close to the achievement of feasibility-related effectiveness since, overall, the MAP policy-making community does not use time and deadlines as policy tools. Emphasis is laid on cooperation and the achievement of a consensus rather than a concrete deadline by which targets have to be achieved. On the one hand, this does not matter as the above discussion shows, since concrete time plans would still be based on administrative concerns and thus not address environmental necessities. On the other hand, the integration and institutionalisation of environmental policy-making by at least making it part of concrete administrative structures shows that a process of environmental awareness has taken place, although still at the infancy stage.

In 1995, MAP celebrated its twentieth anniversary and this has led to a number of revaluations. The main argument is that after 20 years MAP should be well on track for achieving its target. The Barcelona Convention has fulfilled its aim by covering its targets with relevant protocols and both MEDPOL and the policy programmes are working. However, there is general dissatisfaction with the overall achievements in terms of quality and this was brought to the open at the recent meetings of the contracting parties.[12]

Although lack of quality in MAP was bemoaned, the policy-making community still decided to revive MAP with a new amended convention rather than a revising and tightening of the existing protocols. This move characterises and summarises the dilemma of MAP. There is a willingness among member states to agree on good intentions but a refusal to be committed to any clearly defined policy measures. Thus MAP cannot even achieve a state of institutional effectiveness, let alone an environmentally beneficial framework, i.e. the consequences of ignoring environmental effectiveness as opposed to institutional effectiveness do not seem to matter because not even institutional effectiveness has been achieved.[13]

6   The consequences of ignoring environmental effectiveness (II)

The Convention on Long-Range Transboundary Air Pollution

Acid rain has been a prominent issue in Scandinavia since the late 1960s. Although the term 'acid rain' was coined as early as 1872 when the British chemist Robert Angus Smith reported in his book *The Beginnings of a Chemical Climatology* that sulphuric acid levels are related to coal burning, the actual phenomenon of acid rain did not receive attention until the acidification of Scandinavian lakes became apparent in the 1960s. The issue was raised at the 1972 Stockholm Conference. An OECD study commissioned in the early 1970s in response to the Stockholm Conference showed that industrial air pollution from Western and Central Europe travelled in the atmosphere and was deposited in Scandinavia as well as other places.[1] However, Scandinavian appeals for international regulation were resisted because Western states were asking for more evidence. An unrelated initiative by Leonid Brezhnev in the CSCE conference round in 1976, requesting more East–West cooperation in a low politics area, led to the choice of transboundary air pollution as an issue for this occasion (Chossudovsky, 1989). The United Nations Economic Commission for Europe was chosen as the organisation under whose auspices the agreement should be placed since the CSCE has no organisational infrastructure that could have been used (Levy, 1993b: 81).

The Convention was signed on 13 November 1979 in Geneva by 34 member states of the UN Economic Commission for Europe. It was the first multilateral agreement on air pollution and the first international environmental agreement involving nations of both East and West Europe as well as North America. There are seven protocols to the Convention:

1   Long-term financing of cooperative programme for monitoring and evaluation of the long-range transmission of air pollution in Europe (EMEP protocol, 1984).
2   The reduction of sulphur emissions or their transboundary fluxes by at least 30 per cent (sulphur protocol, 1985).
3   The control of emissions of nitrogen oxides or their transboundary fluxes (NOx protocol, 1988).
4   The control of emissions of volatile organic compounds or their transboundary fluxes (VOC protocol, 1991).

5   Further reduction of sulphur emissions (new sulphur protocol, 1994).
6   Heavy metals (Aarhus protocol on heavy metals, 1998).
7   Persistent organic pollutants (POPs protocol, 1998).

The provisions of the Convention are as follows: article 2 of the Convention states that

[t]he Contracting Parties ... shall endeavour to limit and, as far as possible, gradually reduce and prevent air pollution including long-range trans-boundary air pollution.

In order to achieve this aim, article 3 states:

[t]he Contracting Parties, within the framework of the present Convention, shall by means of exchanges of information, consultation, research and monitoring, develop without undue delay policies and strategies which shall serve as a means of combating the discharge of air pollutants, taking into account efforts already made at national and international levels.

Further, the European Monitoring and Evaluation Programme (EMEP), a research network, was created in order to facilitate the exchange of information on policies, scientific and technological activities and to promote cooperation between researchers. EMEP organises the research of different national teams and publishes the results. In particular it is concerned with the need to use comparable or standardised procedures, the desirability of basing the monitoring programme on the framework of both national and international programmes, the need to exchange data, the willingness to continue the exchange and periodic updating of national data, the need to provide meteorological and physical-chemical data and the desirability of extending the national EMEP networks to make them operational for control and surveillance purposes. An Executive Body comprising representatives of the contracting parties and meeting at least annually was set up to review the implementation of the Convention.

The main virtue of the Convention was its inclusion of most Eastern European states (with the exception of Albania) which would not have been possible under other forms of international cooperation. However, the shortcomings of the Convention nearly outweigh this achievement.

Since it merely provides for the sharing of information and continued monitoring and research, it contains no attempt at common action. The wording 'endeavour to limit', 'as far as possible gradually reduce' or 'the best available technology economically feasible' is so vague that it is left completely to the signatories' discretion to take, or not to take, any necessary measures (Rosencranz, 1981).

In order to alleviate some of these shortcomings, a protocol system has evolved. These protocols differ from the Convention in that they are legally binding by setting specific goals and outlining responsibilities for signatories. This separation of a vaguely worded Convention and specific protocols may seem a recipe for inaction but it can also be argued that this is one of the strengths of the agreement as the flexibility of the protocol system makes it easier to react to new scientific findings and technological innovations. On the other hand, not all 34 member states (of which only 31 have ratified the convention) have signed the respective protocols.

The protocol on Long-Term Financing of Cooperative Programme for Monitoring and Evaluation of the Long-Range Transmission of Air Pollution in Europe (EMEP), which was signed in September 1984 and came into force in January 1988 was ratified by 30 member states. It is concerned with the long-term financing of the regional monitoring programme. These programmes, and their budgets, are under the supervision of the EMEP Steering Body and are approved by the Convention's Executive Body during the annual meetings (Sand, 1990: 254).

The aim of the protocol, especially given the silence of the Convention on the question of funding, is to place the funding of EMEP on a long-term and secure footing. The protocol stipulates that EMEP is to be funded by a mixture of mandatory and voluntary contributions. Voluntary contributions may be used either for reducing mandatory contributions or for financing specific activities within the scope of EMEP.

The protocol on the Reduction of Sulphur Emissions or their Transboundary Fluxes by at least 30 Per Cent (sulphur protocol) was initiated by the Nordic countries which wanted to put some flesh on the bones of the Convention and introduce specific emission reductions and time limits. It was adopted in July 1985 and came into force in September 1987. Twenty member states signed and ratified or acceded to it. The basic provisions stated in article 2 are that

> [t]he Parties shall reduce their national annual sulphur emissions or their transboundary fluxes by at least 30 per cent as soon as possible and at the latest by 1993, using 1980 levels as the basis for calculation of reductions.

Pressure for the drafting of this protocol was exerted from the first meeting of the executive body in June 1983. However, a consensus could only be achieved on the phrase that it was necessary to 'effectively reduce the total annual emissions or their transboundary fluxes by 1993/95 with 1980 as the base year for the calculations'.[2] More substantial progress was achieved during the Munich Conference in June 1984 which was organised jointly by the German Federal Government and the UN Economic Commission for Europe. During this conference, 18 states declared their preparedness to reduce their annual sulphur emissions or their transboundary fluxes by at least 30 per cent by 1993. The Working Group which was subsequently put into place by the Executive Body presented a draft protocol during the Third Conference on the ministerial level in July 1985 in Helsinki, which was subsequently signed by 21 states.

Although a laudable achievement, a 30 per cent reduction is very arbitrary without any scientific evidence to support this figure. In addition, a percentage reduction does not take into account regional fluctuations in intensity of SO_2

emissions, nor does it specifically target sources that are more likely to be responsible for transboundary air pollution. Second, the use of a baseline year does not make for equal starting positions for individual signatory states as states that have already started to take action will be put at a disadvantage financially. The United Kingdom, for example, refused to join the '30 Per Cent Club' for exactly these reasons. Third, the sulphur protocol does not take into account synergistic reactions with other pollutants and it might be better, from a scientific point of view, to tackle several pollutants together in one agreement.

The protocol concerning the Control of Emissions of Nitrogen Oxides or their Transboundary Fluxes (NOx protocol) was signed in November 1988 by 26 countries (ratified by 17) and came into force on 14 February 1991. It committed signatories to restrict emissions of nitrogen oxides to their 1987 levels by the year 1994. In addition, national emission standards were to be applied to major new stationary sources based on the best available technologies that were economically feasible. Article 3 regulated the facilitation of technology transfer, which was particularly relevant for less developed countries in order to reduce NOx emissions. This not only provided help for the poorer countries to obtain environmentally friendlier technologies but also gave a trade advantage to the richer ones and perpetuated the divide between the developed West European and 'developing' East European countries.

Negotiations for the NOx protocol lasted well over three years (Fraenkel, 1989: 472). There were several obstacles in the way of the agreement according to information gained by Tessa Robertson (WWF) during talks with Working Group delegates at the February 1988 meeting.[3] One of the biggest problems was the USA–Canadian disagreement on a 'credit clause' on which the United States insisted in order to obtain a credit for already having taken action to reduce NOx emissions. The Canadian government objected to the US argument in favour of a credit clause on the basis that it would lead to an increase in NOx pollution in North America and also insisted that countries wanting to go further than the lowest common denominator should have the choice to do so. Switzerland, too, was opposed to a protocol that sanctions an effective increase in emissions and would have preferred to bring forward the freeze date and introduce a percentage reduction proposal. The Federal Republic of Germany had a slightly different stance. The delegate attached importance to the agreement on a protocol and was willing to make concessions in order to achieve this aim. Although he acknowledged that there were problem states such as Spain, Italy and Ireland, their emissions were mostly not of a transboundary nature and therefore it was not imperative that they signed the protocol. In the final draft these differences were overcome by giving a choice of base year and by providing an additional declaration for states that wanted to go further than the NOx protocol proposals.

It is more difficult to achieve reductions in NOx than SO_2 since most emissions stem from mobile sources and the state of the art technology is not as well developed, which means that reductions are primarily achieved by lowering output. Although the protocol was a compromise solution, 12 of the European signatory states went a step further and signed an additional declaration committing themselves to a 30 per cent reduction in emissions by the year 1998. This protocol-plus-declaration formula helped to overcome the dilemma of bargaining between states with different priorities and levels of development: it ensures a wide membership to the protocol but does not 'slow down the convoy to the speed of the slowest boat' (Sand, 1990: 5).

The protocol concerning the Control of Emissions of Volatile Organic Compounds or their Transboundary Fluxes (VOC protocol) was concluded in November 1991, signed by 23 countries, and came into force in 1997. The aim of this protocol was to reduce VOC levels by at least 30 per cent by the end of the century, using 1988 or any year between 1984 and 1990 as the baseline. Volatile organic compounds react with NOx to form tropospheric ozone, which is a health hazard. Because of the role of NOx in its formation, it is considered to be a transboundary air pollution issue. An important aspect of the protocol seems to be that it gave countries in different stages of economic development the chance to meet the protocol's requirements in different ways. For example, it was possible for signatories to choose a base year between 1984 and 1990 for the 30 per cent reduction. In addition, states could determine the geographical areas which cause transboundary air pollution and reduce emissions only in these regions.

The protocol on the further reduction of sulphur emissions was signed in June 1994 by 30 member states and came into force in August 1998. Its main provision was that the member states

> control and reduce their sulphur emissions in order to protect human health and the environment from adverse effects, in particular acidifying effects, and to ensure, as far as possible, without entailing excessive costs, that depositions of oxidised sulphur compounds in the long term do not exceed critical loads for sulphur given, in annex I, as critical sulphur depositions, in accordance with present scientific knowledge.

Emissions are to be reduced by the figures listed in annex II of the protocol. There is a choice of year ranging from 2000, 2005 to 2010 and a state's commitment is dependent on its domestic situation and critical loads data in annex I. The individual commitments can be found in annex II. A detailed description of the critical loads approach can be found in Chapter 4 in the science section.

The other annexes contain control technology details for sulphur emissions from stationary sources, general options for the reduction of sulphur emissions from combustion, and emission and sulphur content limit values. This protocol is based on detailed calculations, based on scientific research and financial feasibilities, which prescribe individual emission reduction targets for each state. An overall 60 per cent reduction of sulphur emissions as compared to 1980 figures is envisaged. However, despite the target being based on scientific calculations and critical loads, this is not the figure needed for comprehensive ecosystem protection (*Acid News*).

Two new protocols were signed in 1998, one on heavy metals and one on persistent organic pollutants. Another new protocol, concerning a new multi-substance approach to NOx, was under negotiation in the second half of 1999. Again, these protocols will be based on a type of critical loads approach. The 'heavy metal' protocol targets cadmium, lead and mercury emissions which need to be reduced below the levels of the base year of choice. The 'persistent organic pollutants' protocol bans the production of some chemicals and stipulates the phase-out of others.

The central issues of CLRTAP

The beginnings of CLRTAP were partly fortuitous rather than planned or needs-driven. The transboundary nature of air pollution and the problem that polluting states did not equal polluted states (until the advent of *Waldsterben*, or forest death, in Germany in the early 1980s) were the underlying reasons for lack of consensus on international action.

Air pollutants are not confined to areas within national borders but travel extensively into other states' territories. This became a serious problem after the Second World War when industrialisation had reached such a high level that transboundary air pollution became an important contributor to air pollution in general. The main culprits are the products of the combustion of fossil fuels, i.e. fuels derived from coal, oil and, to a certain extent, gas. The sulphur content of the fuels forms sulphur dioxide (SO_2) when it comes into contact with oxygen during the combustion process (Tollan, 1985: 615). A similar reaction occurs when nitrogen and oxygen form nitrogen oxide (NOx). SO_2 and NOx are the principal contents of 'acid rain'. Sulphur compounds are responsible for approximately 70 per cent of the activity in acid precipitation (Tollan, 1985: 615). Research has shown that acid rain, or deposition, has caused widespread damage. More than six million hectares of forest land in Europe have been affected and about one million hectares of these are severely damaged. Other serious environmental effects are the acidification of lakes and rivers and the death of fish and other forms of life in thousands of freshwater lakes in Norway, Sweden and also parts of the United States and Canada. Another aspect of acid deposition is the damage caused to buildings, especially to monuments that are part of the cultural heritage.

Factors of institutional effectiveness

Although CLRTAP lacks the non-legal components of MAP, it still has financial/institutional arrangements and a research network; however, these are regulated through the Convention and the EMEP protocol. Thus CLRTAP has a singular structure with interactive components.

Since CLRTAP has existed for more than 20 years, it is difficult to make generally valid comments on its environmental effectiveness as the situation changes over time. However, the attraction of CLRTAP as an empirical study is that it serves as an example of a case where communication and cross-fertilisation of ideas between scientists and policy-makers actually takes place. This point has been noted by researchers and is well documented in the case of the first sulphur protocol (Jackson, 1990; Tollan, 1985).

In CLRTAP, there are several bodies that interact in policy-making. The Executive Body is the ultimate decision-maker but basically just confirms the work of the Working Group on Strategies, where the work of the other working groups is brought together. The other groups are the Working Group on (air pollution) Effects, the EMEP Steering Body, the Working Group on Technology as well as Working Group on Strategies task forces on assessment modelling, emission projections and economic aspects. All these working groups report to the Working Group on Strategies and membership substantially overlaps. Therefore communication is good and knowledge about other aspects of regulation within the subject area is easily available to all participants.

At the national level, scientific institutions entrusted with research or monitoring duties under CLRTAP are in direct contact with national environmental authorities and provide them with data. Most of the reporting and scientific references in UNECE's published literature on CLRTAP relate to monitoring and impact assessment. Since the SO_2 protocol is well documented already and also quite dated, it has been excluded in this study.

The NOx protocol

The reason why NOx was targeted as an area for emission reduction is not quite clear, and the literature is vague:

> In 1977, EMEP focused mainly on measurement of sulphur compounds and assessment of their transport, transformation and deposition. During the third phase, 1984 to 1986, nitrogen compounds were included in measurements and to some extent also in modelling activities.[4]

No reason is mentioned why nitrogen oxides were targeted in addition to sulphur compounds. However, during that time period several international scientific workshops took place with the cooperation of other agencies such as WHO and WMO, and the focus on nitrogen oxides has to be seen in conjunction with these workshops. This means that what is being targeted is not necessarily a decision from within.

There is a strong economic component in CLRTAP, which tries to combine economic feasibility with ecological requirements. Therefore, the actual emission reduction path chosen will have been subjected to economic analysis and a favourable option will be 'pushed'. As the Executive Body notes:

> A characteristic feature of many national modelling efforts is that they address the issue of 'uncertainty' in a systematic and consistent way. The models are expected to yield significant insights for decision-makers, even at

a relatively simplified level of analysis, provided care is taken to present the results and their limitations. The Executive Body for the Convention has expressly recognised the usefulness of such models, both for direct policy measures and for indicating where further research efforts would be most valuable.[5]

This comment proves again that economic and scientific considerations are not separate but connected. Particularly interesting is the notion that 'uncertainty' is incorporated in environmental modelling and the silence as to exactly what this means. Another opaque phrase is the allusion to care being taken 'to present the results and their limitations'. The type of care and why care has to be taken is unclear. It might refer to scientific uncertainty. However, since uncertainty is incorporated into the models, there is no need for special care. This point remains obscure.

The working group on nitrogen oxides clearly had problems with incorporating scientific uncertainty in its models and found it difficult to make the member states accept this, as shown by an excerpt from a report on a meeting:

> Other delegations noted that the proposal concerning a 30 per cent reduction of the NOx emissions could not be accepted because it lacked the necessary scientific, ecological, geophysical and economic substantiation since the critical loads concept was not sufficiently developed and there was not yet sufficient data on source-receptor relationships. The first stage of the NOx protocol should therefore be used effectively not only to prevent higher NOx emissions in the majority of countries, but also to develop scientifically substantiated values for the necessary reductions, making it possible in an economically optimal way to resolve the problem of preventing damage to the environment from NOx emissions and their transboundary fluxes.[6]

This clearly demonstrates that member states did not agree on the state of scientific knowledge and its interpretation only a few months before the protocol was signed. The 30 per cent emission reduction target was eventually abandoned in any case, and only 12 member states committed themselves to this target in a special declaration attached to the protocol. Of these 12, only half will be able to meet this commitment.[7]

It also shows that the CLRTAP scientific community has not wholly identified the sources of NOx emissions and is therefore not able to give detailed guidelines. Even as late as 1996 there still was not sufficient knowledge to devise critical loads maps for nitrogen oxide. There seems to be an agreement that NOx emissions in conjunction with SO_2 emissions contribute to acid deposition, but what this means in the applied context of the European region is not quite clear. Therefore the protocol refers to NOx emissions and does not target specific sectors such as transport or large combustion plants. However, various suggestions for different economic sectors are given in the annex to the protocol. This emission-based focus is a characteristic of the whole Convention, not just the

NOx protocol. However, the EC/EU, which is party to CLRTAP, has developed an alternative approach and targets specific sectors such as combustion plants or vehicles.

From the VOC protocol onwards

The VOC protocol, on the other hand, gives member states a detailed inventory of measures that will reduce VOC emissions. Volatile organic compounds were chosen as substances to be regulated although they are not of a transboundary nature. Nitrogen oxide concentrations increase with high local VOC levels, thus VOCs have an indirect impact on transboundary air pollution. The decision to include a VOC protocol leads to questions on who chooses the substances to be regulated. The decision of what will form the subject of the next protocol will be taken by the Executive Body but obviously its members act on advice. However, the advisers will know the financial constraints within which they operate and streamline their policy advice accordingly. Hence the popularity of the critical loads approach.

The critical loads approach is a perfect example of how science can be used as a smoke screen. Computer models provide data on the policies that have to be taken. However, the input data are economically cleansed beforehand so the output data will never require policy action that is 'entailing excessive cost'. The decision is made beforehand. For example, the critical loads maps for the new sulphur protocol will protect 95 per cent of all ecosystems once they are implemented. This figure of 95 per cent, and the 60 per cent gap closure scenario, are highly arbitrary and have been decided on economic grounds. There was a huge amount of luck involved in that such a high figure of ecosystem protection could be achieved within an acceptable financial framework. In addition, member states with high cost burdens are the ones who are willing to afford it. This high figure gives the critical loads approach the semblance of a scientific solution that was taken up by policy-makers – a type of science-policy linear interaction which is fair and equitable because it is scientific. That the data used are not scientific but economic, and that the whole model is full of values that are applied, is secondary.

The new sulphur protocol will replace the 1985 Helsinki protocol, which expired in 1993. The Helsinki protocol came into force in 1987 with the basic provision that a 30 per cent reduction in sulphur emissions or their transboundary fluxes from 1980 levels had to be achieved by 1993 at the latest. This was quite an achievement at a time where scientific uncertainty on the origins of acid rain was still strong. For example, the United Kingdom found the commitment too strong and although it refused to sign the protocol it did achieve the target. A target of 30 per cent is very arbitrary and the figure had no scientific justification (Anon., 1995b: 18). This has since been amended. The new protocol now has a partly scientific basis and does not expect less affected states to achieve the same percentage reductions as highly sensitive states. However, since the issue is transboundary air pollution, this can also be deceptive, especially in relation to economic interests.

Another advantage of a successor protocol is that the problem at stake is already well known, with monitoring mechanisms and regulation policies well established. In other words, there already exists knowledge on which to build, which makes regulation slightly cheaper than the regulation of a new substance. The teething troubles of the first protocol do not have to be overcome again. However, it remains to be seen if this will speed up ratification and implementation. Along similar lines, the European Community/Union has imposed legislation (the LCP directive) which also regulates sulphur depositions and which also influences the behaviour of its member states at the conference table.[8] The future of CLRTAP will also be modelling-based. Thus, in this case we can argue that a true marriage between science, politics and economics has taken place.

The Convention on Long-Range Transboundary Air Pollution is different from other international environmental agreements in the sense that its protocols deal with various substances and also take on board new policy measures or formulation techniques. This means that it takes into account the latest developments in science and technology such as measuring techniques or research on the effects of certain substances in different quantities. While the first sulphur protocol was based on a uniform 30 per cent reduction target, the NOx protocol had a special declaration of one group of states setting higher aims than the lowest common denominator and the VOC protocol was flexible in base year and also introduced the concept of TOMAs – Tropospheric Ozone Management Areas. On the one hand, these new formulation techniques can be seen as progress in the sense that these techniques mean that more states can be persuaded to sign the protocols. On the other hand, however, standards remain low for those countries that are not very committed states while only those states that would have adhered to high standards even without an international agreement actually commit themselves to higher reductions.

An evaluation of CLRTAP

Although CLRTAP started off as a rather low priority convention, it has developed into a very active forum with many innovative initiatives and attempts to keep the process in motion. Its institutional structures are very strong and thus continuous upgrading takes place and progress is constant. However, this efficient institutionalisation also has its drawbacks as a veritable political economy of science has taken over that has transformed air pollution regulation into an economic sector. Environmental considerations are subject to economic and technological feasibilities and are mostly referred to in percentage terms. In addition, environmental needs are classed in terms of resource and health management. This means that not environmental benefit but economic feasibility drives the agreement.

This point is especially evident on two levels. First, scientific discovery does not drive the agreement but is immediately 'diluted' by cost analysis. Second, institutional rhythms and time dimensions determine the time frames and details of the agreement, not ecosystemic rhythms, which means that environmental necessities take second place to institutional planning. This is a common problem of all bureaucracies but it is especially apparent in CLRTAP.

The Convention and its protocols are vague on actual measures but rely on national emission reduction reports, leaving its member states to determine how to achieve emission reductions. Since knowledge on emissions is scarce in many countries, this approach is not as beneficial as a sector-based emission reduction plan such as the EC directives, which regulate power stations, vehicle emissions, gas turbines, etc. However, in other respects the CLRTAP approach is more useful. For example, tropospheric ozone emissions are composed differently in different countries. In Finland it is inefficient to reduce VOCs to achieve a reduction in tropospheric ozone levels and emphasis has to be placed on NOx emissions. In Belgium, however, only a reduction in both NOx and VOCs will result in a reduction of tropospheric ozone levels (Jäger, 1996). Thus these two countries clearly need individual strategies and a uniform agreement is ineffective. Only a more flexible approach can reflect the complexities of chemical reactions in different regions and their consequences. This point illustrates the importance of incorporating the requirements of environmental rhythms in policy-making.

CLRTAP is very much based on concepts of Best Available Technology (BAT). This concept is intimately related to the concept of green technology. However, there is no clear definition of green technology; it is used synonymously with the terms 'environmental technology' or 'clean technology' and can be said to refer to technologies that aim to have little impact on the environment. The OECD makes a distinction between two types of green technology: end-of-pipe and clean technology (OECD, 1985). CLRTAP uses both concepts. The first category covers technology that complements existing technology in order to minimise deleterious effects. It is added to an installation and prevents the pollutant from being emitted. It is often forgotten, however, that the pollutants are only collected in this manner – they still have to be disposed of. Therefore, a problem shift occurs since the pollutants still exist and are often emitted elsewhere in a different form. Thus, this method is of limited environmental benefit in a holistic sense.

The second type of technology refers to preventive systems, i.e. technology that replaces existing methods and is characterised by lower emission values or consumption in comparison to the technology it replaces. Such clean technology is supposed to be more environmentally friendly on two levels: first, it emits fewer pollutants and, second, it burns less energy and is thus more cost-efficient. Examples of clean technology are the lean-burn engine, energy-saving light bulbs, new types of power stations or solar panels. Although these measures are more directly related to the origins of environmental degradation – namely, excessive fossil fuel consumption – they in no way question the existence of this mode of production.

The study of CLRTAP has demonstrated that the consequences of ignoring environmental effectiveness may not be immediately obvious. CLRTAP is an institutionally well-functioning agreement with progressive emission limits, albeit based on economic feasibility rather than environmental necessity. From an economistic/scientistic point of view, the agreement can even be called environmentally effective. However, this is clearly not the case since the agreement is only partially directed at ameliorating environmental degradation. Why this constitutes a failure in terms of environmental effectiveness will become clearer in Chapters 7 and 8 when the problem is discussed in relation to the interaction between nature and society.

Conclusion

Two very different pictures emerge from the empirical studies. On the one hand, MAP provides a comprehensive framework that has a high theoretical potential because of its complex framework. However, in practice, the lack of interest of its member states and the breakdown of communication between policy advice and policy-making has led to an agreement that is neither institutionally nor environmentally effective. On the other hand, CLRTAP has been very successful in keeping its members together and achieving a common basis for policy-making. Although this has led to institutional effectiveness, environmental concerns have been sidelined in order to keep up the level of cooperation.

Again, this shows that the history and circumstances of an international environmental agreement are very case-specific and no general rules can be set up. In many cases, 'outside' scientific knowledge is adapted and thus the actual science has no direct political or economic content as it has been taken from a different 'political economy of science'. In that case the regulatory structures of an agreement are more interesting than the science aspect. In other cases the science is home-made and thus more directly influenced by the interplay between science, politics and economics. In either case the relationship between science and environmental effectiveness is fortuitous because of the interrelated nature of science and institutional factors.

The relationship between policy-makers and scientists is such that it is very difficult to determine whether science is made for policy or policy is made for science (to borrow Jasanoff's terminology) because the two interrelate so much that their ideas become cross-fertilised. Scientists have a fair idea of the margins in which they operate when they undertake their research, and this is reflected in their research results. This is especially the case with the various protocols in CLRTAP and with the critical loads approach. The budgetary constraints of policy solutions are already incorporated into the critical load models, thus the science used here is not separate from economic and political considerations.

An interesting point of debate is the case of outside science being brought in for use in an agreement. Clearly, it is not the direct scientific circumstances of the case that are relevant here but the wider social framework in which science was generated in that field of study. For example, in the case of MAP, the science was brought in at the early stages and thus reproduced scientific structures from other regions, setting a pattern by universalising these structures. The black and grey lists drawn up for the north-east Atlantic are reproduced in the Mediterranean,[9] thus also reproducing the reasons for including and excluding certain substances. It is an easy way of introducing standards into another region, thus avoiding discussion about legitimacy and effectiveness. This may be an efficient way of coming to an agreement quickly but it does not take account of the specific local circumstances. In the Mediterranean, this situation is aggravated by the fact that the imported science is still not translated into policy measures, and it cannot be argued that the import can act as a type of precautionary principle until local research can offer more localised regulation suggestions.

This chapter has also demonstrated that communication between scientists and policy-makers is necessary for the uptake of scientific advice on the policy level. The heeding of environment-oriented scientific advice is a precondition for the environmental effectiveness of an agreement whereas such a case as the critical loads approach is more indicative of institutional effectiveness. However, good levels of communication usually indicate that scientists are aware of institutional constraints and incorporate them in their research, thus making environmental effectiveness less of a priority. In the case of the Mediterranean Action Plan, scientific advice could be as environmentally effective as possible, but this would still not lead to an environmentally effective agreement as there is a lack of communication between the scientists and the policy-makers. All these points seem to indicate that science is more environmentally oriented in the stages of identifying environmental problems long before there are institutional approaches aiming to target them. Once it becomes part of an institutional process, science is mainly part of the political economy of science and becomes institutionalised.

In the field of time and effectiveness, the issue of appropriate time frames leads to a conflict between environmental needs and institutional feasibilities. A rigorous application of the precautionary principle would be necessary to at least address this point. Another issue is the use of technological solutions for environmental problems. We have to remember the incompatibility of organic and mechanic systems, which has demonstrated how mechanic systems wreak havoc in the environment. This proves again that economic and production structures are dominant and do not adequately incorporate environmental concerns.

This feasibility–necessity dichotomy is reproduced throughout the effectiveness debate. Regulatory structures are concerned with feasibility, not necessity. However, looking at effectiveness from the time perspective makes it especially clear that effective (in the environmental sense) agreement-making cannot be achieved within the dimensions in which policy-makers operate at the moment.

Such a process can be observed in CLRTAP. Organised along temporal lines that require the planning of air pollutant emissions and energy policy for the next 20 years, it aims to prioritise the issue of best available technology in the energy sector and thus achieve its policy aims. The question is whether this is a development in the wrong direction or the first step on a long path towards environmental awareness.

In academic terms, there is no drive towards a holistic rather than an economistic and scientistic form of policy-making. Academic disciplines such as politics, sociology, economics and IR are anthropocentric by definition and even when phenomena focusing on the whole planet such as time are the focus of analysis, they are still considered from a point of view of social benefit and feasibility instead of taking into account the link and interaction between environment and society. A case in point is the effectiveness debate in the regime theoretical wing of IR. The time debate illustrates the shortcomings and limitations of this approach more clearly and strongly than other debates. However, the whole regime theory/institutional bargaining school of thought shows us how dominant and embedded conventional behavioural and policy analysis is and how the policy-makers themselves are driven by the notions focused on in this school of thought. Therefore it cannot be expected that fundamental changes will occur in the policy-making process in the near future.

It can be concluded from this that the environmental effectiveness of international environmental agreements can only be achieved if the policies proposed transcend approaches that are based on human rhythmicity and reintegrate social (including political and economic) rhythms into natural rhythms rather than dominate them. International environmental policy-making is dominated by economistic values and perspectives and is so institutionalised that it cannot transcend these values. This means that by definition environmental effectiveness will not be achieved through an institutionalised agreement-making system, i.e. international environmental agreements cannot be effective by their very nature.

The chapters in Part II have demonstrated two issues that make the connection between the effectiveness debate and the placing into context of the concept of environmental effectiveness, which will follow in the next chapter. First, it has become obvious that the narrow focus on institutional effectiveness of the effectiveness discourse cannot adequately capture the meaning of effectiveness in an applied context. Second, this point leads to the realisation that effectiveness, or indeed environmental agreements, cannot be studied in a rigid, limited methodological context but have to be placed in a wider social, political and economic context in order to be understood and analysed in a meaningful way.

Part III

Environment, society and international relations

7 Social and structural origins of environmental degradation

An analysis of the environment–society link will show systematically why society and social actions cannot be studied without understanding the natural environment in which they operate and why the introduction of this issue area into IR is so important. The discussion here refers almost exclusively to industrial society, not only as the society propelling international environmental agreements but also as the society mostly affected by environmental degradation.

The environment has only recently started to be the subject of social scientific analysis. The use of natural resources for the production process and the abuse of the natural environment as a 'waste bin' or sink had not been seen as a problem until the 1960s and was not taken seriously as a problem until the 1980s. This is hardly surprising since, after all, social scientists are concerned with the study of society, not the study of the environment. The work of Dickens (1992, 1996) has traced and analysed this phenomenon with reference to the history of social thought, which provides a useful background for tracing the social and structural origins of environmental degradation. However, the focus here is to study the (missing) link between society and environment, although the two are obviously related.

At this point it is timely to insert a brief introduction to the terms 'nature' and 'environment' in order to clarify their meanings and to shed light on the environment–society debate. Very often, the terms environment and nature are used interchangeably. However, their meanings do not overlap entirely. Nature defines a pristine, not humanly interfered with environment, i.e. the original state as compared to the socially constructed and built environment we live in. This is not a static concept since nature itself changes constantly. Of course, in the late twentieth century there is no aspect of nature that has not been influenced by human actions and therefore it is not pristine. Thus, the distinction between nature and environment is indeterminate and for the twentieth century only the term environment should be used.

However, in this book, the term nature is used in the context of the nature–society link based on Dickens's terminology (Dickens, 1992). This means that the term is used in an atemporal sense and does not refer to specific types of environment in particular time spans but to the relationship between humans/human 'designs' and nature/subjected nature (i.e. environment). It goes beyond the relationship of society with a particular environment but is concerned with how society transforms nature into environment and what the consequences of this transformation are. Therefore it crosses time barriers and the use of the term nature is justified although it is actually the relationship between society and its particular temporal and spatial environment that is studied.

Environment refers to nature that has been transformed by society. Therefore the term is used in a very specific context and refers to an environment that is clearly defined temporally and spatially. For example, if one refers to the global environment, e.g. the concept of global environmental change, then the term clearly applies to the changes that occur at the global level in the late twentieth century.

One of the complications of seeing the environment as transformed nature is that it could be argued that since there is no such thing as a 'natural' environment, there is consequently no great difference between the urban environment and non-occupied or agriculturally used land, and especially no difference in social/environmental value. This argument is used against claims that nature and/or the environment should be safeguarded because it is intrinsically more valuable than humanly transformed environments. Both types of environment are produced by social relations and economic forms of organisation (Dobson, 1995: 175). Therefore, the environment does not fulfil a superior function as compared to humanly constructed environments.

However, this view disregards the dependence of society on either nature or environment as a provider of the functions of life. It ignores the fact that both nature and environment function according to intrinsic rhythms and mechanisms and that the imposition of social or societal rhythms can and indeed do alter natural/environmental rhythms, which lead to environmental degradation. Therefore there *is* a difference between the urban and 'natural' environment and the natural environment does indeed fulfil a superior function as it is a 'rhythm setter'. However, this function tends to be disregarded by social agents.

The relationship between nature and society can be studied from a historical angle and ecological economists such as Daly trace the origins of environmental degradation to the beginnings of the industrial revolution and the resulting unbalancing of the state of entropy (Daly, 1992). Ponting (1991), on the other hand, finds that mankind irreversibly changed the face of the globe even at the hunting and gathering stage of human evolution through converting land for agricultural purposes, hunting to extinction of animals and overexploitation in general. It is undeniable that the phenomena of pollution and degradation existed before industrialisation but these were rather localised and did not affect the general equilibrium of the global ecosystem. Therefore the industrial revolution with the consequential changes in economic, political and social organisation has to be seen as the main social origin of environmental degradation in historical terms.

This leads to the question of economic modes and their relationship with environmental degradation. The environmental literature traditionally makes a connection between the capitalist mode of production and environmental degradation. An exception is the environmental sociologist Sing Chew who argues that it is the mode of *accumulation* rather than the mode of *production* that leads to environmental degradation (Chew, 1997, 1998). He studied the economic systems of the past 5000 years and concluded that widespread environmental degradation existed in all societies that trade widely. Therefore the developments associated with the industrial revolution, changing modes of production and the Protestant ethic, which are considered the triggers of capitalism, only aggravate the scale of environmental degradation and do not cause it – the mode of accumulation on which all trading societies are based also leads to environmental degradation.

Redclift and Woodgate (1994) give a summary of the different interpretations that exist on the relationship between nature and society. The phenomenon of coevolution sees society as part of the physical processes occurring in nature, i.e. sees society as part of nature. Coevolution can be described as an interactive process between society and nature while nature changes through evolution and society changes through processes of structuration. With historical changes, industrial society has increasingly taken over the role of nature as changes in agriculture demonstrate. Aspects of nature have been integrated in the production process and placed under scientific control. Thus increasingly large parts of nature are under the control of society.

Regardless of whether the origins of environmental degradation lie in capitalist modes of production or accumulation, it can be argued that the scientific and technological advances that coincided with what is termed the rise of capitalism have led to a substantial increase of environmental degradation as compared to previous forms of social organisation. We cannot establish whether this is due to the specific nature of capitalism or advances in science and technology and although resolution of this point is important, it is not vital for studying the social and structural origins of environmental degradation.

Time, society and environmental degradation

One aspect of the social and structural origins of environmental degradation can be found in a mismatch in temporal structures which is traced to the advent of Newtonian science and the mechanisation of society (Adam, 1998). The mismatch between the time dimensions and concepts of time used in modern society and those of nature are analysed and the consequences discussed.

So far, IR has nominally taken account of the issue of time through the use of historical approaches such as those by Cox, Braudel, Helleiner, Bernard or Wallerstein. These can be termed evolutionary approaches in the temporal sense. They are concerned with the notion of social change but mostly disregard the relationship between social change and social dependence on the environment in terms of air, water, energy, resources, etc.

An obvious starting point for the discussion of the temporal environment and society link is a definition of the concept of time. One of the classic writers on time is Norbert Elias (1984) whose starting point is to see time as a measurement. Time is measured by clocks. This means that time can be divided into units of measurement which are universal and can be compared – it is a standard. Therefore it can be argued that clocks are a tool in the coordination of social and natural processes, i.e. a type of universal standard to measure time. However, time is much more complex than the standard of clock time.

Two diametrically opposed theories of time exist, which give nature different roles. On the one hand, the concept of time as an objective criterion of natural creation suggests that time is not any different from other natural objects, except that it cannot be perceived. Newton with his concept of absolute time and absolute space was a proponent of this theory. On the other hand, time was seen as a type of 'seeing together' events that are based on the peculiarity of human consciousness/reasoning and is thus the precondition for experience. In other words, time is a form of experience humans are born with and thus a constant characteristic of human nature. Therefore it is not a natural phenomenon. These two theories see time as either an absolute concept or as an aspect of human consciousness.

Unlike Elias, Rifkin sees time as a concept that is outside human control but interwoven with social fabric in such a way that it cannot be separated. This is different from Newtonian absoluteness but does not match the idea of time as a form of human experience either. However, Rifkin does not clearly define how time can simultaneously be an independent phenomenon outside human experience but still be interwoven with social fabric in such a way that it cannot be separated from human experience.

Hohn (1984) also sees a problem here. The positivist concept of time as a given, measurable unit which forms a linear and neutral relationship with nature and society does not only dominate the natural sciences but also our perception in everyday life. The problem with this is the concept of a socially and historically universal abstraction of time as such. This presupposes that each culture has experienced time as a measurable unit, has identified past, present and future as clearly defined 'givens'. However, he argues, time as something 'disposable' that can be organised and related to the future is only the result of the social differentiation and rationalisation process that culminated with the establishment of capitalism:

> Zeit ist weder eine Eigenschaft der Natur, noch liegt sie im Bewußtsein *a priori* vor. Sie existiert nicht 'als solche', sondern als soziales Konzept, das mit den Arbeits- und Interaktionsformen von Gesellschaften konstituiert und variiert wird.[1]

Therefore, it does not make sense to see time as a measurable unit but it has to be treated both as a product of and as an aid for the specific form of communication of the human being with nature. This comes close to Rifkin's definition of time as being something that exists outside human consciousness but can be experienced as a social construct only. However, again, it does not address the issue of how natural and social aspects of time relate to each other.

Young (1988) is less concerned with the spatial placement of time but rather with its consistency and constitution. He looks into different aspects of time of which the cyclical and linear distinction and social evolution are the most interesting for the study of the society–environment link. He is mainly concerned with rhythms of time and their perception. This will be followed up below as it pertains directly to the relationship between nature, society and environmental degradation.

The preceding discussion on defining time has shown that a distinction should be made between what time is and how it can be understood. Time can only be understood socially in a constructed manner and although an absolute concept of time in nature is likely to exist, the human understanding of time can only be subjective. This predominantly social understanding of time means that it is very difficult for social actors to incorporate an understanding of ecological time frames in analysis and policy-making as the two empirical studies clearly show. Therefore, the remainder of this section will be concerned with the various forms in which time is socially constructed and how this impacts on our understanding of the environment–society relationship and environmental degradation. For this, the concepts of social evolution and the cyclical/linear dichotomy are considered to be the most relevant sections and will thus be discussed here.

Social evolution

The social evolution of concepts of time is concerned with notions of change. Young and Nowotny focus on how time changes by emphasising rhythmicity. Nowotny believes that social evolution of time perception can be studied in historical terms or by looking at cultural, class or gender issues. This point disregards the relationship between society and nature since the social evolution of time refers to the human perception of time. However, an understanding of the human perception of time is necessary to contextualise the relationship between society and nature.

Hohn (1984: 6) maintains that modern concepts of time evolved with the establishment of capitalism. This would mean that concepts of time change with the prevailing ethics and modes of production in a society, i.e. the steam engine and the Protestant ethic have changed our understanding of time and have led to the obsession with speed in modern society.

The social evolution of the understanding of time is connected to social evolution in general. The increased importance of the use of technologies has also had an influence on concepts of time. Again, this demonstrates the overarching hold of economic structures over social organisation. The relationship between the economic and the social is mutually constitutive but the importance of the relationship between society and environment is not sufficiently recognised.

The cyclical and the linear

Young distinguishes between two dimensions of time, namely the cyclical and the linear. The cyclical reproduces the past while the linear introduces novelty (Young, 1988: 4). For example, the process of life from birth to death can be seen as linear if talking about one individual; however, considering life in terms of generation after generation introduces a cyclical dimension since one birth to death process is followed by another.

In modern society, the cyclical element of time is often denied its place and history is seen as an exclusively linear process. Cyclical events such as the calendar year or the life span of a parliament lose their significance and become subordinated to a linear vision of life. Since nature is fundamentally based on cyclical rhythms, a possible conflict between social and natural rhythms is pre-programmed.

The passage of time is seen as a linear process. Time, in our perception, flows in a line as a river flows to the sea and does not circle as the earth around the sun. Time is like an arrow on which we ride towards the future. This means that the future is separate from the cycles of past experience. Our minds are forward-working, we plan the future step-by-step, in a cause and effect matter. Therefore we tend to overemphasise our linear thinking in our perception of time dimensions. This affects our understanding of nature and will obviously impact on our approach to solving environmental problems as the examples of MAP and CLRTAP show.

However, the cyclical informs the linear and vice versa. They are two complementary approaches that are not mutually exclusive but look at the same things with different perspectives:

> We fail to realise that although no present event can recur, it yet has similarities with past events and presumably with future events, and that if it did not, our sense of order could be shattered.
>
> (Young, 1988: 14)

There is a clear connection between prevailing linear concepts of time and environmental degradation. As Kümmerer (1996: 226) argues:

> It is not by chance that the start of the modern development of technology coincided with the invention of the mechanical clock that is, the human construction of time in terms of exactly recurring periodic processes.

In the case of Mediterranean pollution, this connection is expressed by the continued and increased use of the sea as a sink without taking account of its limited sink capacity and the irreversibility of damage or recovery times. For example, it takes 80 years for the waters of the Mediterranean Sea to be replaced by new water from the Atlantic, discounting the link between the Mediterranean Sea and heavily polluted Black Sea.

Rhythmicity

Rhythmicity is the development of the concept of cyclical time that has important repercussions for the study of environmental degradation. This section will deal with several aspects of rhythmicity and relate them to the relationship between society, nature and environmental degradation.

The rhythms of human beings are matched by those of their wider surroundings such as the physical environment, solar and lunar movements and the weather seasons. This creates a complex web of rhythmic behaviour of various lengths that is seemingly easily coordinated to form the machinery of nature. A common characteristic of this web is that it is exclusively cyclical at the holistic level (although still linear for the individual flower or bee). The consequences of this discovery will be discussed below. This seemingly easy web is a very complex phenomenon, which does not function according to social or scientific (i.e. constructed) logic. Therefore, scientific explanations of environmental degradation have to be treated with caution. For example, acid rain regulation and the decrease in sulphur emissions have had no measurable impact on the phenomenon of forest death. This could mean that either emissions have not been reduced sufficiently or that there might not be a connection between forest death and sulphur emissions.

If nature works according to intricate rhythms, then this seems to suggest that a concept of time exists other than our social understanding of it. Thus, time is more than a social construct. After all, the observed rhythmicity of nature is not a social construct but an observed natural phenomenon although it is observed with the socially constructed tool of science. However, even from within a social construct it is possible to acknowledge that there are temporal movements going on that are independent of the temporal concepts from within the social construct. In addition, it shows that the above definitions of the concept of time are built on anthropocentric notions and that interference can have disastrous consequences for natural phenomena resulting in widespread environmental degradation. The case of the death of the sea grass *posidonia* in the western Mediterranean is an example of this interference and its disastrous consequences.

This problem relates back to the dichotomy between the cyclical and the linear. Rhythmicity is a concept that is related to cyclical notions of time. Natural rhythms are a cyclical phenomenon. However, modern human conceptions of time are linear. Therefore, there seems to be an incompatibility between human and natural rhythms of time. Since human beings are part of nature and the larger physical environment, this clash of concepts leads to questions about the effect of an 'unnatural (i.e. social) rhythm' on the larger physical environment. However, this identification of two separate rhythmic phenomena and the isolation of human rhythms from the rhythms of the larger physical environment means that modern society has distanced itself from natural rhythms, either consciously or as an unintended consequence of other processes. Large sections of humankind in the west/north are no longer dependent on the seasons, the lunar phase, night or day or the weather but can create their own systems with recourse to electricity in order to create artificial light or heat and transport systems that bring the fruits of summer in the other hemisphere into supermarkets. Thus, sun, weather and the climatic cycles lose their relevance for human beings. Society has developed its own rhythm which is independent of the rhythms given by nature. Before the evolution of modern society, people lived according to natural rhythms (and many people still do today), which meant that, for example, food was seasonal, agriculture was dependent on weather and soil fertility, people went to bed early when it got dark in the winter, to give just a few illustrations.

With the changes that constitute modern society, this behaviour changed. With the increased use of machinery and technology, human beings became more independent of the rhythms dictated by the environment. Not only could electric light and central heating change living conditions but the use of fertilisers, refrigeration, preservatives, greenhouses and fast international transport also changed food consumption patterns. This changed the relationship between humans and nature from 'part of nature' to 'dominator of nature'.[2]

However, this aspect of rhythmicity does not occupy a central place in the existing literature on time. What has been written on rhythmicity is largely concerned with the intrinsic rhythmicity of society or the relationship between individual and society. The relationship between the rhythmicity of the physical environment on a local/regional/global level and society is less of an issue. Nevertheless, it is of central importance for the problem of environmental degradation as the examples of MAP and CLRTAP show.

The rhythmicity dichotomy

This rhythmicity dichotomy is not just a time problem. Giddens (1990) maintains that a parallel movement to the rise of linearity and the beginning of modernity is the separation of time and place/space. The coordination across time is the basis of the control of space. In premodern societies, he argues, space and place were more or less synonymous because space, or the location, refers to the physical setting of social activity, which coincided with presence or 'time'. Consequently,

> the advent of modernity increasingly tears space away from place by fostering relations between 'absent' others, locationally distant from any given situation of face-to-face interaction ... What structures the locale is not simply that which is present on the scene, the 'visible form' of the locale conceals the distanciated relations which determine its nature.
>
> (Giddens, 1990: 18)

Thus, the separation of time and space is not a linear concept but is a dialectical process which is crucial for the dynamism of modernity for three reasons. First, the time–space separation disconnects social activity from its particular social context. This leads to a break away from local cultural activities and habits and a move towards 'disembedded' institutions. Second, it provides the foundation for the rise of what Giddens calls the rationalised organisation and which Weber associated with bureaucracy. However, even more than the inertia criticised by Weber, modern rational organisations are characterised by a dynamism on the local–global level that was unthinkable in Weber's age. Third, the notion of history has changed fundamentally with the rise of the above rationalised organisations. Unitary standards of measuring time ensure a universality of history and with the universal mapping of the planet, 'time and space are recombined to form a genuinely world-historical framework of action and experience' (Giddens, 1990: 21).

In terms of rhythmicity, this means that the rhythms to which societies are subjected are no longer an evolution that finds its origin within society but are imposed on society by means of external mechanisms, i.e. we have reached another level of social organisation. The society in question cannot determine its own rhythmicity. This is one step further than the distinction between natural and social rhythms. It basically means that society is not in control of its own rhythms and therefore cannot adjust its relationship with nature. Our rhythmicity is compared by Giddens to a careering juggernaut which is out of control. The agents are no longer in control of the structures they created and can no longer dictate its rhythms.

However, Shiva does not agree that the consequences of the time–place–space distanciation are that far-reaching:

> The global in the dominant discourse is the political space in which a particular dominant local seeks global control, and frees itself of local, national and international restraints. The global does not represent the universal human interest, it represents a particular local and parochial interest which has been globalised through the scope of its reach. The seven most powerful countries, the G-7, dictate global affairs but the interests that guide them remain narrow, local and parochial.
>
> (Quoted in Adam, 1998: 115)

According to Shiva, there is no 'careering juggernaut' of lost social control but social structures are still as much dominated by the powerful as they have always been. What has changed is the nature of that control. Regardless of the exact nature of structural change of 'globalisation', the main point of the lack of a connection between environmental and social rhythms applies to both scenarios. First, it demonstrates again that regime theoretical analysis with a focus on agency cannot do justice to understanding and solving environmental problems. Second, it shows that economic and regulatory structures are 'disembedded' and not equipped, thus not able, to address environmental problems adequately. Third, it is obvious that natural rhythms are disregarded by social processes and that there is no available social mechanism to deal with this issue.

Adam (1998: 11) lists three characteristics of industrial time as evidence of the mechanisation of society: the invariable beat of the clock, the economic commodification of time and the scientific use of time as measure of abstract motion. This linear view of time clashes with the rhythmic nature of cosmological time. A linear concept stresses the movement towards a destination, making events unique while a cyclical concept stresses the occurrence of rhythms and the repetitive regularity of events. Both exist simultaneously but society sees itself predominantly as moving along a linear trajectory. This has effects on perceived rhythmicity and emphasises a distinction between natural and social rhythms.

Science and the social and structural origins of environmental degradation

The progress of science and technology since the industrial revolution has impacted deeply on the extent of environmental degradation. It is important to study science as a structural and social origin of environmental degradation because the changing role of science in society is at least partly a phenomenon that is related to modernity and simultaneous with the rise of environmental degradation. The increasing industrialisation and technologisation of society is linked to advances in scientific knowledge and, in turn, advances in scientific knowledge result from the demands of the capitalist mode of production. Thus our understanding of our surroundings is increasingly based on very scientific and technical concepts of a mechanical nature. This point is intertwined with the above discussion on time and will be discussed further below.

Science can be both knowledge and tool in the process of understanding and the remedying of environmental degradation. In policy-making, this also means that this general process is reflected in the microcosm of decision-making. A scientised view of social and environmental problems means that there must be a logical, scientific cause and a logical, scientific solution to an environmental problem.

According to Merchant (1992: 49), post-Enlightenment science is based on mechanistic principles which means that modern science applies the same principles to machines as it does to nature. As Merchant (1992: 55) summarises:

> Both order and power are integral components of the mechanical view of nature. Both the need for a new social and intellectual order and new values of human and machine power, combined with older intellectual traditions, went into the restructuring of reality around the metaphor of the machine. The new metaphor reintegrated the disparate elements of the self, society and the cosmos torn asunder by the Protestant Reformation, the rise of commercial capitalism and the early discoveries of the new science.

This view presupposes that scientific knowledge can constitute an absolute truth. However, Wynne (1994: 175) argues:

Although the reflex reaction is still to understate and, where possible, conceal scientific uncertainties in public policy issues, it is now common-place to find the inevitable limitations of scientific knowledge recognised as a fact of life which policy-makers and publics should learn to accept ... Thus scientific uncertainty is widely discussed as the cross which policy-makers have to bear, and the main obstacle to better and more consensual or authoritative policies. Yet much of this debate still assumes that if only scientific knowledge could develop enough to reduce the technical uncer-tainty, then basic social consensus would follow, assuming that people could be educated into the truth as revealed by science.

Wynne makes the point that our society and thus also the policy-making domain is indoctrinated into believing that scientific knowledge can provide all the answers to causes and effects of and remedies for environmental degrada-tion. This belief and trust in science is investigated as a structural origin of how the problem of environmental degradation is approached.

However, science is not necessarily only a negative influence in our under-standing of environmental degradation. Without science, humankind would not be able to study and attempt to understand natural phenomena and would not be able to make the connection between human activity and environmental degradation. In fact, some aspects of degradation, such as global warming or ozone depletion, are not perceptible to the human senses and can only be perceived through scientific means. This means that science provides us with a window to study our environment, but it can also prove that nature is more than a social construct. The status of nature or environment has been the subject of many academic debates. Many social scientific approaches, as Dickens has argued, tend to internalise nature/environment in their studies of the relation-ship between nature and society. However, nature/environment exists independently from society and needs to be studied in an integrated approach, not as an internalised construct but also not as an object of research as the natural sciences do. As Litfin (1994: 26) says with regard to the relativist–objectivist debate:

> The failure to respect the fundamental distinction between ontology, which studies the nature of existence, and epistemology, which studies the nature of knowledge, has been a major source of misunderstanding between objec-tivists and relativists. As they talk past one another, the former seem to claim that knowledge faithfully reflects reality, and the latter seem to say that all knowledge is arbitrary. A more balanced view is that objects and events actually exist and that our knowledge has something to do with them. This is the basis of an ontological realism and a hermeneutical, yet pragmatic, epistemology.

There is a difference between the nature of knowledge about nature and the nature of existence of nature. The nature of our knowledge is necessarily constrained by the social structures in which knowledge evolved and which provide the prism through which knowledge can be studied, analysed or processed. However, natural processes are not affected by how they are understood – it does not influence them. What affects them is how social, political and economic processes change them and thus irrevocably influence some processes and imbalance others. The creation of imbalances is what leads to large-scale environmental change such as climate change, ozone depletion, the existence of endocrine disrupters. Irrevocable change can also be of a smaller scale such as local marine pollution or desertification. The pollution of the Mediterranean Sea is an example of regional change. The case of acid rain in Europe, on the other hand, was supposed to be a regional issue for many decades but now research has emerged demonstrating that acidifying pollutants may travel to Europe from destinations as far as the United States (Agren, 1994: 14).

To summarise, the social and structural changes related to the rise of capitalism have also led to a new rationality underlying social organisation that is based on the same mechanistic principles that can be found in the temporal organisation of society. This means that the relationship between environment and society is studied by a set of tools that treat the environment as a mechanistic system rather than a connected whole. As Wynne argues, such a world-view is ill informed as the nature of knowledge is not absolute. Therefore our scientific tools for studying environmental degradation have an inbuilt bias which leads to mechanistic solutions for holistic problems.

Economic structures and the society–environment relationship

As the two preceding sections in this chapter show, economic structures are not just another layer of social organisation. Rather, they are the determining layer of social organisation and there are very strong arguments for the case that all our social and structural relations can be traced to the rise of capitalism in one way or another. The capitalist form of economic and social organisation is fundamentally based on the subjection of nature to mechanistic principles. Perhaps the best way to describe how economic organisation affects the environment is to have recourse to the idea of Daly's steady-state economy. He describes the two visions of the economy, that of standard (capitalist) economics and that of the steady-state economy:

> For standard economics ... the economy is an isolated system in which exchange value circulates between firms and households. Nothing enters from the environment, nothing exits to the environment. It does not matter how big the economy is relative to its environment. For all practical purposes an isolated system has no environment. For steady-state economics, the preanalytic vision is that the economy is an open subsystem of a finite and non-growing ecosystem (the environment). The economy lives by importing low-entropy matter-energy (raw materials) – and exporting high-entropy

matter-energy (waste). Any subsystem of a finite non-growing system must itself at some point also become non-growing.

(Daly, 1992: xiii)

The implication of the steady-state economy approach is that it is physically impossible to continue extracting resources and creating waste while expecting unlimited economic growth. However, this is exactly what is happening. Economic organisation of society does not take account of the finite nature of the environment but treats it as a static, abundantly available 'given'. In addition, economic organisation of industrial society disregards the first two laws of thermodynamics which determine the existence of energy on the planet. The first law states that the amount of existing energy and matter is constant on earth, i.e. cannot be changed. The second law of thermodynamics argues that the state and quality of existing energy can change. For example, the heat of boiling water transforms itself to steam, the steam will settle somewhere in the form of condensation and will be transformed back into water. What has happened in industrial society is that existing energy gets transformed into 'waste', i.e. a form of energy that cannot be reused.

The underlying idea of environmental economics suggests that the environment is a resource that has so far been taken for granted and exploited as a free good.[3] However, it has become clear that the environment is not an infinite free good but that natural resources (used here as a concept going beyond economically viable resources such as fossil fuels or wood and including sinks such as fresh air or water) are limited. Once they have been transformed into waste products, they are filling up the planet with 'untappable' energy that becomes surplus and disrupts the balance of energy flows. This results in disturbed rhythmicity. In order to use natural resources wisely, or 'sustainably', environmental economists argue that a value needs to be attached to them to reflect their true cost. The environmental economics approach is therefore not a new form of economic organisation but merely a reorganisation of the existing economy by assigning a value to a component that was treated previously as a free and unlimited resource. This can happen through an externally imposed levy such as, for example, taxation, through the polluter pays principle or through other mechanisms on other levels.

Writers such as Martinez-Alier and Daly have developed an alternative view of environmental economics which is referred to as ecological economics and looks at structural or systemic origins of the relationship between economic organisation and the environment rather than finding solutions within the mechanism of the existing system. Their argument is that conventional economics neglects the moral side of environmental exploitation:

The recognition that there are problems of political economy that have no technical solution but do have a moral solution goes very much against the grain of modern economic theory.

(Daly, 1992: 2)

The difference between these two strands of economics is that environmental economists such as Pearce *et al.* (1989) believe in a technical solution to environmental degradation that requires reform but no change of the economic system (technological fix, increasing cost of scarce resource will lead to use of alternatives) but ecological economists such as Daly do not see this as a realistic option. Their argument is that environmental problems started with the advent of the industrial revolution when energy use moved out of an equal input/equal output situation to the burning of fossil fuel which was not replenished in energy terms, equalling negative entropy.[4] An environmentally benign, 'steady-state' economy requires a system

> with constant stocks of people and artefacts, maintained at some desired, sufficient levels by low rates of maintenance 'throughput', that is, by the lowest feasible flows of matter and energy from the first stage of production (depletion of low-entropy materials from the environment) to the last stage of consumption (pollution of the environment with high-entropy wastes and toxic materials).
>
> (Daly, 1992: 17)

However, economic structures, by providing employment, distribution and production of goods necessary for survival, are such priority structures in social organisation that society finds it impossible to override them and restructure economic organisation despite the overriding logic and warnings of ecologists and ecological economists. All modern social organisation is dependent on economic organisation and the current form of economic organisation finds it impossible to change the relationship between environment and economic organisation as the whole rationale of the economic system is built on the premise that the rhythms of nature can be overridden and that the resources propelling the capitalist mode of production are inexhaustible. Therefore there is a fundamental flaw in the relationship between nature and society.

Consequences for IR

With the rise of capitalism a change in the awareness of the relationship between society and its surrounding environment took place. Because of the scientific and technological achievements of this era, the fact that humankind and its activities are part of a larger whole on which humans are dependent was largely ignored. Society's environment and the resources it provided for survival were regarded as having been mastered and dominated by the human achievements of the industrial revolution and the scientific discoveries of this period. This view persists today with the attitude that problems of environmental degradation only necessitate a correction or improvement of these exploitative processes rather than a rethinking of the attitude towards environmental degradation.

There are three counts on which the nature–society relationship is disturbed:

changed rhythmicity by the imposition of mechanical onto ecological rhythms, a Newtonian rationality based on studying parts rather than wholes, and disregard for the concept of entropy. All three points can be found in the temporal and economic organisation of society as well as in the scientific paradigm in which society operates.

This brings us back to Chew's argument made in the introduction to this chapter that there is ambiguity as to whether the capitalist mode of production or the capitalist mode of accumulation is the trigger of environmental degradation. The above argument suggests that it is the capitalist mode of production rather than accumulation that is responsible for widespread environmental degradation because of paradigmatic changes in the perception of the relationship between environment and society. It can be argued that, as a consequence of trading (Chew, 1998), cases of environmental degradation observed as early as the Bronze Age were physically localised and the result of a disregard of the entropic principle. It was not time–space–place distanciated. The type of environmental degradation experienced since the rise of capitalism is of a different scale than that experienced in the Bronze Age in terms of geographical impact (although the scale was probably quite comparable in terms of social worlds as the geographical size of trading areas was much smaller in the Bronze Age).

Relating the social and structural origins of environmental degradation back to the effectiveness of international environmental agreements and IR, it shows that the regulation of environmental degradation necessitates an approach that can take account of these structural constraints underlying the nature–society relationship. First of all, social and economic organisation and therefore also regulatory organisation lack an appreciation of the dependence of social systems on ecological systems. This problem is manifested both in theory and in practice. In practice, this means that policy-making, whether national or international, is focused on making environmental regulation fit in with existing social structures. Such an approach is based on feasibility in terms of existing structures but not on actual problem resolution. The origins of this approach can be found in the application of mechanistic principles and the scientific rationale that parts of the ecosystem can be treated individually and need not be seen as part of a bigger whole.

In theory, this means that most IR theory is focused on the study of social systems, be it state systems and their motivations for going to war or historical or systems theory approaches and their focus on economic factors. These approaches have not located their analysis of social systems on the fact that these social systems/society are dependent on well-functioning ecological systems for survival. Such an omission is particularly problematic in the study of the effectiveness of international environmental agreements. Since the traditional focus of such analysis has been on treating international environmental agreements as closed systems, this subject has been fully in the domain of a Newtonian part–whole distinction and the ensuing neglect of issues of entropy and rhythmicity. However, as this chapter has very clearly demonstrated, environmental degradation cannot be understood without studying its social and structural origins and without making the environment–society linkage more explicit.

Therefore a conceptual approach to the study of the effectiveness of international environmental agreements has to take account of the social and structural origins of the problem giving rise to the international environmental agreement. This point will be explored further in an applied context in the next chapter.

8 The social origins and context of acid rain and pollution of the Mediterranean Sea

This chapter traces the social and structural origins of the environmental degradation giving rise to the conclusion of CLRTAP and MAP. The missing link between environment and society is discussed in the applied context of acid rain and pollution of the Mediterranean Sea. The chapter demonstrates that these agreements have developed irrespective of the social and structural context of acid rain or Mediterranean pollution respectively and that these agreements, therefore, do not adequately address the origin of environmental degradation. In order to establish the missing link between the origin of degradation and the agreement in question, particular attention is paid to the economic, temporal and scientific structures underlying degradation and regulation.

It is deemed most viable to undertake this analysis by dealing with the two illustrative studies individually. First, a temporal and spatial analysis will be used as an introduction to the analysis. Then the political economy of acid rain will be discussed, followed by the Mediterranean problem. Again, analysis will take account of institutional set-ups as well as social, political, economic, technological and environmental structures. This will be followed by a general discussion and conclusion.

A temporal and spatial analysis

So far, the study of the provisions of international environmental agreements has led us to investigate the existing literature, which looked at international environmental agreements as closed units, and to apply an international political economy approach, which demonstrated that international environmental agreements need to be studied in their wider environment in order to be understood. The aim of this section is to superimpose a temporal and spatial dimension on the issue.

At the policy level, environmental problems are evaluated within the framework of the policy-maker's institutional margins, which means that the solutions necessary are not considered but only the solutions feasible. Hence, the problem of institutional and environmental effectiveness, and the feasibility –necessity dichotomy. Another effect of this practice is that the policy-maker only sees part of the problem and process and thus does not really

understand what their own role in this process is. For example, the British delegate at CLRTAP Working Group on Strategies meetings for the planned
protocol on Nitrogen Oxides and Related Substances, when asked, did not know
what the proposed ammonia reduction figures meant in real terms and what
measures were necessary to achieve them.[1] He considered that the government
scientists should assess the figures, and that other policy-makers, also cooperating
with the government scientists, should implement the necessary measures. The
government scientist responsible, on the other hand, relied on information from
policy-makers on cost and feasibility and was thus not fully informed about his
work either. This phenomenon can be found in most policy-making environments, both in CLRTAP and MAP. There is a division of labour between the
members of the policy-making community that results in a distanciation of the
object of the policy-making process.

The meaning of this phenomenon has wide-reaching consequences. It means
that in the policy-making process, the process is not directed intentionally but is a
composition of myriad micro-levels which are not coordinated to form a macro-
level, and the outcome is partly one of coincidence. Conventional theories are
able to explain actor behaviour because they work on the same limited principle
as the actor/policy-maker. These theories use as their basis the same type of
information available to the policy-maker and thus also operate on this closed-
system limitation.

Beck (1986, 1995) has taken up this phenomenon of the society fragmented
in its knowledge structures and has highlighted the major features of what he
terms the risk society – risk society being in effect the result of distanciated
policy-making. He distinguishes between risks that were created in active and
conscious decisions, and which can thus be controlled, and risks that have
avoided social control mechanisms. The structure of decisions taken in industrial
society and their global consequences are not harmonised. These decisions are
taken at the national or firm level but the risks involved affect all members of the
world risk society. As Beck argues,

> Mit dem ökologischen Diskurs wird das Ende der 'Außenpolitik', das Ende
> der 'inneren Angelegenheiten eines anderen Landes', das Ende des
> Nationalstaates alltäglich erfahrbar.[2]

The question that follows as a logical conclusion to Beck's argument is how
national policy-makers with their limited expertise and accountability can legiti-
mately deal with the problems of the 'ecological world risk society'. They do not
understand and by their profession are not required to understand the structures
of the world risk society and the way it has evolved and is evolving, and still they
have to decide how it is regulated with their narrow concept of institutional
feasibility.

Beck (1995: 19) sees, as a solution to this problem, an increased awareness
demonstrated not only by the rise in international environmental agreements but

also by action taken by non-industrial actors as well as by the so-called green industry, which evolved as an antithesis to the risk industries.

As this book demonstrates, Beck's argument that the proliferation of international environmental agreements in the past 20–30 years witnesses a development that counteracts the evolution of the risk society is not a persuasive argument for several reasons. First, these agreements are not related to processes outside the negotiating process and are thus unaware of their role as ascribed by Beck. Second, the participants in the negotiating process are not aware of the structures of the risk society because social structures are outside their expertise and horizon. Third, and most important, the assumption that international environmental agreements control environmental risks is wrong.

Part of the specialisation of policy-makers can be explained with bureaucratic theories, bureaucracies taking on a life of their own and justifying their existence by constantly inflating themselves. CLRTAP is definitely a process that is aided by its bureaucratic institutionalisation, which leaves its *raison d'être* beyond reasonable doubt.

However, the main problem is that bureaucratic institutions, and especially policy-makers, get their motivation from the inside and thus their interests are also guided from the inside. Since environmental degradation is an externality, it is outside bureaucratic processes, but this does not mean that bureaucratic processes are hermetically sealed against outside influences. So, factors such as public opinion, scientific expertise from non-governmental sources, NGOs, etc., can still influence the policy-making process, although filtered through bureaucratic channels. This means that evolution and change of processes are necessarily long-term phenomena, while environmental degradation is a problem that necessitates swift reactions. There is, therefore, an incompatibility.

Acid rain

The institutional structure of CLRTAP has been discussed in preceding chapters. We will now consider how this institution forms part of a much wider institutional web and will then place CLRTAP within the wider social, political, economic, technological, scientific, temporal, environmental and even historical-industrial structures surrounding it. This will lead us to understand better the social and structural origins of acid rain.

Integration

The UNECE Convention on Long-Range Transboundary Air Pollution is just one institution in a whole web of other relations. Primarily, it is part of the whole European integration project. It started its existence as a *rapprochement* measure in the last stages of the Cold War (Chossudovsky, 1989), which explains the presence of states that are not really affected by or interested in transboundary air pollution. However, because they 'integrate' in other spheres such as defence or economic integration, they cannot exclude themselves in the acid rain case without jeopardising the whole integration process, but the importance they attach to this specific policy process depends on their values and priorities and may indeed be low, thus leading to sluggish policy-making. A case in point is the disagreement between the United Kingdom and the north-west European states during the mid-1980s. The United Kingdom suffers from acidification damage but has a tradition of inciting industry to take voluntary action rather than impose regulatory measures. In addition, there is no traditional use of the precautionary principle but rather a tendency to wait until a definite cause–effect relationship has been established. The Germanic–continental tradition is not compatible with this approach, and this has resulted in a lot of debate and tension, not just in CLRTAP but also in other policy-making domains (Boehmer-Christiansen and Skea, 1991). These traditions also affect corporate climates and industry's policy-making behaviour (Dosi *et al.*, 1991; Fagerberg, 1988). The emphasis on innovative research is quite different in various parts of Europe, or the world for that matter. For example, the Anglo-Saxon tradition believes that regulation hinders innovation while the Germanic tradition assumes that regulation will lead to innovation.

Other factors for differing priorities given to CLRTAP include environmental awareness within a population and the importance of public perception/opinion in the particular state's policy-making mechanism. In Germany, for example, public awareness about acidification, among other matters, led to the representation of the Green Party in the Bundestag, which in turn led to the espousal of environmental awareness and subsequent policies by the mainstream parties. In the United Kingdom, on the other hand, such a process could never take place because of the bipartisan nature of the electoral system with its first-past-the-post principle. This also relates to historical factors influencing values, culture and priorities. Some nations have embedded concepts in their culture, which lead to values being prioritised that may not attract sympathy in other parts of the world. Cases in point are parts of Germany and forests or Britain and animal welfare.

These concepts are part of national and regional traditions and thus form part of the structures within which societies operate and in which diplomacy takes place. The different layers of structures (institutional, political, economic, social, temporal, scientific and technological) pertaining to CLRTAP's institutional effectiveness are: integration, diplomacy, bureaucracy, market, energy, transport, knowledge, security (at early stages of the Convention) related to the East–West divide, and the economy/environment dichotomy. Some of these have already been discussed in previous chapters. These structures will be discussed before this cobweb of social structures is put into context in relation to environmental structures.

Economic and market structures

Market structures are manifold and reach from the structures of the world economy to more local structures. Global structures include the competitive market structure, emphasis on free trade, liberal hegemony, the GATT/WTO regime and the post-war economic order in general. It also includes the European Community and the Common Market. It goes beyond the scope of this book to discuss these structures in detail and there is a wealth of literature that fulfils this task admirably. However, suffice to say that market structures predetermine the range of economic policy instruments available and their importance in relation to non-economic policy measures.

For example, CLRTAP is subject to GATT rules and cannot override them. In the final stages of the 1994 negotiations for the new sulphur protocol, a potential conflict arose when Spain wanted a clause inserted to allow it to continue to use indigenous coal and have the negotiated provision relating to the use of best available technology only apply to imported coal. The Spanish government felt it was not able to afford the import of low sulphur coal and close down its own coal industries. However, Canada and the United States objected to this special option for Spain because it contravened GATT rules, stipulating that indigenous products are not allowed to receive preferential treatment over imported products. The problem was then finally solved by a change in phrasing which is not entirely acceptable in GATT terms but was allowed to pass.[3] This demonstrates that there are many obstacles to environmental policy-making that are not openly perceivable but determine what is feasible and what is not. This example is a case of an overt clash. However, a much more important aspect of the predominance of market structures is already incorporated in agenda-setting, relating to Lukes' (1974) third dimension of power. Translated to environmental policy-making, this means that, owing to the nature of the structures in which a debate is conducted, certain topics are included or excluded *per se*. In this case it means that the nature of the economic system and its detrimental effect in terms of acid rain are not questioned. The competitive nature of the economic system, based on growth and innovation, leads to options such as best available technology being favoured rather than concepts of energy efficiency or alternative, non-growth-based economics.

The political economy of energy (national and international) is structured heavily in favour of fossil fuels. Their predominance is not questioned despite constant warnings that fossil fuel supplies are finite and seriously tax the capacity of planetary sinks. Petrochemical companies are very big conglomerates and so diversified that they penetrate the majority of sectors in international and domestic markets. Alternative energy forms are not cost-competitive at the moment, partly because they do not have the same type of support network as petrochemical companies. In addition, fossil fuels externalise environmental and health cost, which means that their price does not reflect their true cost. Alternative renewable energy forms do not externalise cost and are thus realistically priced, but this difference between the two forms of energy is not reflected on the market. These structures obviously influence international environmental policy-making and at no time was the predominance of fossil fuels questioned in CLRTAP. Even more so, the latest negotiations are moving away from controlling fossil fuel-based emissions with technological means to controlling rather insignificant sectors such as ammonia emissions from livestock farming.

Likewise, the transport sector is neglected in CLRTAP. Although road transport is responsible for the lion's share of NOx and VOC emissions, there is no direct attempt to target the transport sector. In addition, there is no account of the increasing proportional rise of transport emissions in the overall total. Again, the petrochemical firms (fuel) and car manufacturers are major European industries and the link between road transport and transboundary air pollution is not made explicit in CLRTAP. Fossil-fuel-based transport and the use of individual transport have become very embedded in Western societies and elsewhere and thus it is assumed that this privilege can be extended to an unlimited extent and is a corollary to development. This assumption has never been officially questioned and is another example of how existing structures, also thought structures, constrain and channel debate.

This brief summary of institutional economic structures demonstrates that policy-making within CLRTAP is constrained on several levels. First, existing industrial structures, and thus traditional protection of certain industries, means that the role of fossil-fuel-based production sectors is never questioned. This is especially apparent *vis-à-vis* the transport sector. It is less true of the coal industry, but then the decline of the coal industry cannot be reduced to environmental concerns. In fact, environmental factors play only a subordinate role in the coal debate.

Second, the industry-based nature of the European economic system means that the emphasis in CLRTAP is on technology-based solutions to the problem of acid rain with the aim of leaving the fundamental structures in place. Thus, catalytic converters or end-of-pipe solutions are preferred policy options while a change in production and funding patterns resulting in the subsidy of alternative fuels is not. Boehmer-Christiansen and Skea (1991) give a good account of how continental, and especially German, industry used the acid rain scare to establish a vital market for end-of-pipe technologies and how international acid rain policy-making was used as a forum for pushing and securing markets for specific technologies.

Third, the nature of the economic structures sets the agenda and dictates the policy options that are desirable or undesirable. Therefore a change of modes of production cannot even enter the agenda as a policy option because it is outside the ruling economic paradigm. This explains why the dependence on fossil fuels of our society is not questioned.

Security and diplomacy

Security and the East–West divide were important structures in the early stages of CLRTAP when the bipolar security structure was still in place. In the minds of the policy-makers, bipolarity was a very real concept and therefore it will be treated as such here, although it is conceded that in IR terms bipolarity is not an uncontested concept. Literature in the traditional realist field dealing with various concepts of balance of power is prolific. Most of this literature deals with high politics and especially the Cold War. As was mentioned above, security considerations were in fact partly responsible for the negotiation of CLRTAP. Obviously, with more research and increasing evidence of the damage done by acid rain, the Convention developed more of an individual life. However, in the late 1970s and early to mid-1980s, confidence-building was a priority and the process was quite successful. This conclusion can be reached since now there is a general consensus that trust exists between the Eastern and Western member states. The security aspect of CLRTAP has been widely discussed in the early literature and need not be reiterated here. The East–West divide is more of an economic nature now, although this affects mostly negotiating behaviour since Eastern states cannot afford the technological solutions suggested by Western states. Although this is also an issue of economic structures influencing the agreement, it manifests itself mainly at the negotiation level.

Diplomatic structures, again, are related to security and to integration since all aspects of communication between states involve some degree of diplomacy. They correspond quite closely to traditional regime theory foci of agreement analysis. Diplomacy is a code of behaviour and there are certain conventions surrounding the making of agreements and also environmental agreements. There are several consequences. First, states tend to be content with their usual allies and play certain 'games'. For example, the Soviet delegation threatened repeatedly to walk out in the negotiations in the 1980s because the West German delegation comprised a member from the Federal Environment Office (Umweltbundesamt as opposed to the Bundesumweltministerium, which is located in Bonn) situated in Berlin.[4] According to the Quadripartite Agreement on Berlin, the city had special status and no functionaries from Berlin were authorised to participate in international diplomatic meetings. The fact that the Soviet delegation was prepared to walk out of the negotiations because of this matter demonstrates that diplomatic rules can take precedence over the importance of the issue under negotiation. Second, another diplomatic rule is that of consensus-seeking. Finding a common basis is seen as more important than finding an effective solution. Third, 'finger-pointing' is avoided as a rule. Therefore the inadequacy or deliberate stalling of a negotiating party cannot be publicly denounced but has to be condoned. Thus diplomatic structures influence policy-making by providing a code of behaviour that has to be followed. This can have a positive impact by providing a generally acceptable framework, but it can also hinder the agreement-making process.

Science and knowledge structures

Knowledge structures have been discussed to a large extent in preceding chapters. It needs to be added that other structures, especially economic and industrial structures, heavily influence the type of knowledge that is requested in CLRTAP. Thus the policy-making process is already limited from the outset. The example of the critical loads approach in the preceding chapters is a case in point. As Wynne (1994) argues, society is led to believe that scientific research can provide clear-cut true answers to all questions relating to environmental problems. However, the structures within which scientific knowledge relating to acid rain policy is produced, predetermine what type of knowledge is required. As demonstrated above, the economic and industrial structures underlying the European region mean that scientific research is limited to technological fixes. The nature of a fossil-fuel-based energy production system is not questioned, neither from inside the production system nor from the scientific base. Thus, knowledge production operates in confined structures.

Human production systems, time concepts and policy frameworks are all geared towards efficiently administering society, but they fail to take account of the limited capacity of the environment in its function as resource provider and sink. There is a tendency in industrial societies that are environmentally aware to integrate waste into the economic process and thus avoid externalisation:

> Prioritäres Ziel ist, Umweltgifte gar nicht erst entstehen zu lassen. Dies ist in aller Regel der bessere, auch wirtschaftlichere Weg. Das Ziel eines integrierten Umweltschutzes erfordert auch die Einbeziehung der festen Abfall- und Reststoffe sowie des Abwassers.[5]

This recommendation of the German Ministry for Research and Technology with reference to the coal industry, demonstrates that although awareness exists that the environment is used as a sink, this issue is still treated solely from an economic angle. If waste matter is integrated into the production process and not externalised and released into the environment, it will still have to be released as an end product at some stage. Again, the nature of the production process is not questioned but taken for granted. However, it has to be admitted that the awareness that waste is being externalised and the incorporation of this notion into the policy process is a definite improvement compared to the *status quo ante*.

This brief overview shows that there are many structural and systemic constraints that influence and shape actor behaviour. However, these are constraints within social as well as economic, political, technological and scientific structures and do not take into consideration systemic constraints of the environment. This issue will be raised now.

Temporal and systemic constraints

Acid rain is a highly complex phenomenon that arises when sulphur and nitrogen oxides get released during the burning of fossil fuel. These oxides react in the air and produce acidifying substances that get transported with wind and weather patterns. These wet and dry deposits are referred to as acid rain. Some acid rain gets deposited locally or regionally but large proportions are transported over large distances. Therefore acid rain is a transboundary, regional pollution problem. It is a highly complex phenomenon whereby airborne pollutants are deposited over ecosystems and cities alike. They have a cumulative effect, i.e. build up over time. In ecosystems with high sensitivity to acidification they cause substantial damage by upsetting the normal acidity of the soil or water area. Particularly vulnerable areas are the Scandinavian lakes or central European forests where over-acidification has led to the 'death' of fauna and flora. Cultural monuments such as the Dome Cathedral in Cologne have also been affected and air pollution is the cause of respiratory diseases in humans, especially children.

It has been argued that there is a certain amount of natural acidification and that not all 'dead' lakes and forests were the victims of acid rain. This is true of a limited area of moorland but certainly does not excuse the existence of acid rain.

Acid rain primarily consists of sulphur dioxide and nitrogen oxides. Nitrogen oxides also contribute, together with VOCs, to the formation of ground-level ozone in summer, but this is another matter. Ground-level ozone is a local air pollution problem with devastating health effects for children, old people and asthmatics. However, transboundary nitrogen oxides are an agent in ground level ozone formation and therefore VOCs are also a substance regulated under CLRTAP. All these substances are produced through the burning of fossil fuels. The extraction and burning of fossil fuels upsets the careful balance of the global ecosystem because it burns something that is part of an entropic cycle, thus unbalancing it and causing the release into the atmosphere of by-products which in this case are responsible for acid rain.

The human innovation system has created technologies that can vastly reduce the release of these by-products, thus aiming to eliminate the existence of acid rain in Europe by 2010–2020.[6] The special technological circumstances in this case mean that a system that focuses on institutional factors and ignores its place within the global ecosystem can seemingly solve an environmental problem. Whether this is actually the case, only time can tell. I argue that it is not institutional effectiveness that has achieved this provisional success but mere fortuity as the basic problem – namely, the indiscriminate consumption of fossil fuels – remains untouched as an issue.

If the assumption of CLRTAP policy-makers is correct and transboundary air pollution can be eliminated by 2010–2020, then the technology-based solution effort would obviously be successful and there would be no environment–society dichotomy in the case of acid rain. Although the solution effort is based on a social, economic and technological fix, it would provide a solution that is environmentally effective. One aspect of this problem is that acid rain damage is not considered irreversible, so in temporal terms the preconditions are very favourable. This is pure fortuity. Technological solutions cannot provide permanent solutions to the acid rain problem because of their failure to take account of nature's rhythms. Thus, several faults can be determined in the policy-makers' assumption that the acid rain problem will be eradicated in the next 25 years:

- Acidifying substances will be filtered out to a large degree but they will still have to be deposited somewhere so the problem only gets shifted to another level.
- There is a failure to take account of the rise of the transport sector. Nitrogen oxides emanate mostly from mobile sources and the increase in mobility will at least partly offset emission reductions achieved. This becomes obvious when one considers the traffic-related ground-level ozone values in the 1990s as compared to the 1980s.
- Eradicating only the release of acidifying substances does not address the problem at the holistic level. Fossil fuel consumption generates problems at many levels (global warming, local and transboundary air pollution, release of carcinogenic substances, and marine oil pollution through carbon transport to name but a few) and the CLRTAP approach takes a very narrow focus. It closes its eyes to the holistic problem. The problem of entropy is ignored and the root of the problem remains untouched.

This study of the social and structural origins of acid rain demonstrates that policy-making is constrained by social, economic, political, technological, knowledge and temporal structures and the fact that these structures are in direct conflict with the environmental necessities relating to the acid rain *problématique*. These structures are geared towards organising human needs as efficiently as possible but ignore that these structures need to be in harmony with environmental structures.

Pollution of the Mediterranean Sea

Because of the different nature of Mediterranean pollution and its wider applications, the structures analysed in relation to the Mediterranean will be slightly different to CLRTAP, which only dealt with air pollution. Again, the web of institutional structures in the Mediterranean region will be discussed first, followed by a study of the social and structural origins of the environment and society delinkage in the Mediterranean region. The institutional web consists of issues of integration, bureaucracy, market, energy, transport, knowledge, security, food and infrastructure.

The Mediterranean region as a whole is treated as having the history of an integrated system but cannot be described as such today. It is segregated into subregional systems that may trade with each other but have no definite structures to keep it together. These subsystems are the European states, the Maghreb world, the Arab world and a few in-between states. MAP has to be seen very much as an effort towards integration in the region, bridging gaps over conflicts and mistrust. This role is considered more important than its environmental *raison d'être* by Mediterranean government officials, and this fact already points towards a definite delinkage between environment and society and a lack of awareness of the importance of relinking environmental and social structures.

The consciousness that a prioritising of the environment is out of the question and that questions of sovereignty and economic development take absolute priority channels the debate in such a way that the 'dos' and 'don'ts' are clearly defined and determine the structure. For example, the Greek–Turkish conflict over resources in the Aegean and the two states' differing interpretation of the Law of the Sea pertaining to this matter have stalled the finalising of the offshore protocol for many years. A draft protocol was available and ready for signature in 1987 but the protocol was not presented for signature until 1994 due to the spillover of this conflict into the negotiations.[7] Again, this demonstrates how political power struggles take precedence over the environmental issue to be regulated.

Economic and market structures

Economic and industrial structures do not affect MAP to a great extent because of its informal nature. However, they do affect the way the environment is perceived by the regional inhabitants to a large extent. Owing to the emphasis on political cooperation in MAP and the reservations of the Arab/Maghreb world towards neoliberal policies, economic structures affect MAP mostly by the prioritising of economic development and through the World Bank Environment Programme for the Mediterranean region (World Bank, 1990). The World Bank has taken over the policy recommendations put forward by the 1985 Genoa Declaration but has been criticised by the MAP Secretariat for not taking sufficient account of existing MAP research and policy recommendations.[8] In addition, the World Bank Environment Programme for the Mediterranean is no different from other World Bank policies with their emphasis on structural adjustment and the ensuing problems (Kütting, 1994; Devlin and Yap, 1994). These ideological shortcomings have been discussed elsewhere and will not be reiterated here. Suffice to say that the lack of financial support from elsewhere and the resulting dependence on World Bank and European Investment Bank assistance means that policy action in the Mediterranean takes place within the constraints of liberal economic hegemony. This does not apply to the discourse within MAP but to actual policy measures taken, especially outside the European Union member states. A condition for investment is that Western industrial structuring patterns are reproduced and that integration into the world economy is paramount. However, the world economy is organised in such a way that it serves as a vehicle for ensuring most efficient supplies for the industrialised, Western countries. For example, agricultural production patterns in developing countries reflect demand in Western states, not requirements in the producer country (Redclift, 1984: 33). Issues such as food self-sufficiency or minimum wages for labourers are therefore not on the agenda. This is just one aspect of problems with structural adjustment policies.

It is difficult to discuss the energy structure of the Mediterranean region with reference to MAP because the area is quite diverse and MAP does not really refer specifically to energy. Petroleum-extracting and refining industries are a major part of the economy of the Mediterranean, which is also the world's busiest petroleum transport route. Therefore, oil products have to be seen as part and parcel of people's livelihood, which again affects the structure within which environmental policy is made. In a region where survival and fighting for at least a subsistence wage are not uncommon among large parts of the population, there is simply no space for considering a replacement of the carbon industry with alternative or renewable energy sources. Petroleum products provide a much needed income on which these countries are very dependent, and although alternative energy might be more suitable for these countries it would deprive them of their export earnings. In many ways the Mediterranean climate is ideal for switching the energy supply to solar-powered sources and in some countries this has partially happened in the domestic sector. However, this switch requires an initial investment, which simply cannot be made. An option would be World Bank investment, but, as the above paragraph demonstrates, the organisation of the world economy foregoes this option. Realistically, there is no question of clamping down on oil but some 'peaceful coexistence' between oil and risk minimisation has to be found. The number of oil spills in the region has decreased but, as the Med X report states, the vast majority of oil residues in the Mediterranean Basin stems from land-based sources. These have to be regulated by national policies.

Similarly, the transport sector is not the direct concern of MAP but influences the options available in negotiations and policy-making. Nor can the shipping industry be separated from the Mediterranean region, and Mediterranean ports are in competition with other regions despite their geographical advantage in the case of goods arriving, for example, through the Suez Canal. This has repercussions on port reception facilities, oil tanker cleaning facilities, regulations concerning discharge, etc. The securing of port usage has vast economic consequences with many industries and services depending on it. Again, this means that these structures constrain the environmental debate in MAP. However, international efforts at regulating shipping and its degrading effects can have an influence on the Mediterranean region, which is shown through the structures of international shipping laws. Worth mentioning in this context are Marpol 73/78, the London Dumping Convention and the UN Convention on the Law of the Sea. These have introduced a global regulation of tanker standards that have influenced behaviour in the Mediterranean region.

Security

The security structure can be argued to be one of the more dominant structures in MAP. The Mediterranean region is a conflict-ridden area and, of course, this is reflected in MAP. There are the Arab–Israeli, the Turkish–Greek and the Cypriot conflicts, internal upset in Egypt and in Algeria, anti-colonial feelings towards France in the Maghreb, the Yugoslav conflict and the Libyan case. These are conflicts on a subregional level and it is only because this level is transcended within MAP that cooperation can take place. However, it is evident that this is a tense, untrusting working environment that cannot easily create a neutral, professional climate. This also means that what was said about diplomatic structures in the context of CLRTAP does not equally apply in the Mediterranean context despite the supposedly international nature of the diplomatic code of conduct. Also, environmental cooperation is mainly based on shared aims and values, which cannot occur if the members are involved in conflict with each other. Although the members share an interest in the Mediterranean Sea as a resource, there is not much agreement on environmental policy-making otherwise. This obviously influences the scope that MAP can take and limits its role to a body or institution that provides help with scientific research and policy-planning if requested to do so but does not impose any regulations. This is the basis on which MAP has functioned in the past 20 years and this is still the basis after the 1995 amendments to the Barcelona Convention. Thus the security structure is a key defining factor of the scope of MAP.

Food and infrastructure

The food structure of MAP refers to agricultural patterns, pesticide use and food markets. The southern economies are predominantly agricultural with production geared towards northern markets. This requires intensive farming methods and high use of pesticides, especially in less fertile soils, which result in damaged health in farm workers and nearby residents but the run-off also reaches the sea and thus pesticides affect all levels of the food chain. Agriculture is one sector in which developing countries can compete with industrialised states due to the low land and labour costs. Also, due to lax regulatory structures, pesticide use is not controlled to the extent that would prevent severe degradation. Even in the British context, 80 per cent of agricultural fertilisers and pesticides used on fields become straight run-offs into lakes, rivers and the sea owing to the lack of knowledge of the farmers using them (Macgarvin, 1997). Comparable figures for the Mediterranean do not exist but can be expected to be at least the same. Organic farming is not seen as a viable alternative and thus the dependence on large-scale agricultural use affects agenda-setting in environmental policy-making.

The Mediterranean infrastructure is such that the population is concentrated in coastal areas and the majority live in big cities. This trend is set to increase in the next 30 years in a disproportional trend (Grenon and Batisse, 1989). The underlying issues are rural exodus, concentration of industries and jobs in cities. This necessitates a prioritising of sanitation programmes which is not happening because it is seen as a national issue, which MAP does not deal with. Again, this necessitates a pointer to World and European Investment Bank policies.

It can be argued that the political and economic situation prevents MAP from making an environmental impact. Let us now look at how this relates to environmental degradation.

Temporal and systemic constraints

The Mediterranean Basin is highly dependent on the Mediterranean Sea for its livelihood and all the riparian states share this dependency. Because the Mediterranean Sea is semi-enclosed and only has a small opening to the Atlantic Ocean, it takes more than 80 years for the sea water to be exchanged. This means that whatever is put into the Mediterranean Sea will stay there for a long time and will not get diluted and flushed out easily. At first, it was thought that this meant pollution was a regional issue, affecting everyone across the board, whether polluter or not. However, research has shown that, ship-source pollution taken apart, pollution from land-based sources mostly stays in the vicinity of its source. This could also be a reason for the lax nature of MAP as there was no pressure on big polluters to clean up because they only harmed themselves. Equally, it could be that because of the delicate nature of MAP, research was focused on areas where pollution was known to stay locally by UNEP deciding to give out research grants in this area only. However, the MAP Scientific Adviser argues that scientific perception of the most pressing problems was the deciding factor in allocating projects.[9]

However, a problem of an international nature is that of migratory animals. They are exposed to pollution and spread it to unpolluted areas through the food chain. Migratory fish, birds and sea mammals deserve particular mention here. The Mediterranean monk seal has been decimated through contracted viral disease in the western Mediterranean and suffers from habitat destruction in the eastern Mediterranean. There are now less than 300 animals of this species left, which is not enough for survival of the species through natural breeding, and they cannot be saved through captive breeding programmes because of their reclusive nature (Johnson, 1988, 1994, 1995).

Another, albeit global, problem is that of endocrine disrupters. These chemical substances such as polychlorinated biphenyls, DDT, dioxins, dieldrin, chlordane, aldrine and related products mimic oestrogen uptake and thus affect reproduction in humans and animals. Endocrine disrupters spread on a global level and can even be found in penguins in remote regions of Antarctica. The problem is also prevalent in the Mediterranean region. The only solution is a complete phase-out of the chemicals responsible. However, the 1996 changes to the protocol on Land-Based Sources did not include a phase-out of these chemicals by 2005 'because of serious economic and social repercussions' (Scovazzi, 1996b: 574).

Another problem affecting the Mediterranean ecosystem is that of habitat destruction. The population explosion and industrialisation especially of coastal regions means that on the northern coast there is not much space left for natural systems. The South will face a similar problem in the next 30 years (Grenon and Batisse, 1989). Apart from biodiversity loss, this means problems such as soil erosion, land slides, flooding, droughts, etc. There have been many incidents in recent years, and forest fires are also a resulting problem, albeit of a secondary nature.

Localised marine pollution in or near big cities has always been a problem and there are reports of pollution even at the time of the journeys of St Paul or Alexander the Great. The sea has always served as a sewage-disposal system but the increase of population and the move to the coast has exacerbated the problem over time and imposed increased pressure on the ecosystem.

The Mediterranean region has a long history as an important trading place (e.g. the Genoese empire, the Romans, the Greeks, the Egyptians) but environmental degradation had only reached its current extent during the twentieth century when the industrial revolution and its consequences fully hit the Mediterranean region. Therefore the degradation of the Mediterranean environment can be traced back to political and economic systemic changes. Since Mediterranean environmental degradation is strictly speaking not of a transboundary nature, the justification of cooperative action is not perceived as an urgency.

Because of its limited nature, not just in environmental but also institutional terms, the MAP is not equipped to deal with the underlying systemic problems causing environmental degradation in the Mediterranean Basin.

Review

This chapter has outlined the institutional social and structural constraints in which MAP and CLRTAP are located and thus contributed to an understanding of the social and structural origins of environmental degradation. These findings were then related to the environment–society dichotomy.

In IR terms, this analysis has once again demonstrated that conventional methods of studying effectiveness are too methodologically limited to fully capture the complexity of aspects of environmental degradation. It is especially shown by the acid rain case that actor-centric analysis is concerned with explaining the behaviour of a certain actor, or group of actors, in a particular negotiation process. The aim of this type of analysis is to find out what motivates actor behaviour which helps to understand bargaining processes by predicting individual positions. Therefore, the study of actor behaviour does not go beyond explaining why certain actors behave in a certain way in a certain situation. It does not explain (a) why some forms of cooperation are more successful than others, (b) why cooperation is made possible in the first place, (c) why evolution in cooperation takes place, or (d) how the cooperative process can be improved upon. Regime theorists would argue that this is not the aim of their research. However, I argue that the aim of research must be to further knowledge on social change and thus find out about mechanisms that explain change. Explaining an actor's behaviour in a certain situation cannot explain social change.

Structural/systemic approaches look at underlying patterns and relationships, thus trying to answer some of the above questions. Depending on how far the analytical net is cast, analysis over time and across systems deepens the analysis. It is fairly obvious that systemic/structural analysis offers a deeper insight than actor-centric analysis.

Introducing the society–environment dichotomy has helped to explain the limitations of conventional analysis by dissecting the social and structural origins of degradation and by analysing the relationship between environment and society. Thus, the relationship between pollution and social (including economic, political, technological, scientific) activity can be analysed in a systemic fashion.

However, the most salient feature about systemic/structural analysis is that it can incorporate non-social systems. Since the regulation of an environmental problem essentially deals with the degradation of a non-social system, it is necessary for a holistic approach and complete analysis to take on board the object of study, namely the environment. Thus it is not a question of studying either agency or structure but for the inclusion of a non-social system, analysis needs to include a substantial amount of structural analysis.

This is also the only way the concept of environmental effectiveness can be incorporated in analysis because actor-centric analysis alone cannot go beyond the confines of the human/social systems within which it operates and even systemic/structural analysis is usually centred on social phenomena unless it makes a conscious effort to incorporate the environment in its analysis. Even for studying the institutional side of effectiveness, a method that includes the study of both structure and agency is necessary; however, agency analysis cannot incorporate the society–environment dichotomy.

Both studies show that the inclusion of the environmental dimension is vital to the understanding of the relationship between an environmental problem and its regulation. The CLRTAP case demonstrates that policy-making takes place within the confines of human expectations and economic necessities but not with a view to environmental requirements. The belief that acid deposition and acidification – and the environmental damage arising therefrom – are only temporary and can be repaired with the availability of 'technological fixes', make it possible that the ecology may recover if there is full cooperation in CLRTAP. However, this is not due to an incorporation of the consideration of ecological processes but to sheer coincidence if this belief should prove to be correct. However, as outlined above, it is to be expected that this attitude will prove to be a fallacy.

In MAP no understanding or attempt to understand ecological processes has taken place. Although protocols to the Barcelona Convention correspond to the ecological worries of the situation in the Mediterranean Basin,[10] these are not taken far enough to attempt to tackle the problem seriously. In MAP, substantial amounts of research on ecological processes are carried out, but this is not transformed at the policy level and it is most certainly not taken up by bureaucrats or policy-makers.

Therefore, it has to be concluded from the evidence of both CLRTAP and MAP that international environmental agreements cannot be effective unless they are able to overcome their narrow concerns and ensure that they have an understanding of their own systemic constraints and of their societies' relationship with the ecological processes suffering from degradation. In addition, there is a fundamental incompatibility between social organisation and its impact on environmental processes. As concluded in the previous chapter, there is a fundamental feasibility–necessity dichotomy as society is unable to reorganise or restructure itself in the face of environmental degradation. However, only such restructuring could lead to environmentally effective policy-making.

9   Conclusion

This book has led to the conclusion that the social and structural origins of environmental degradation need to be studied in order to understand, on the one hand, the constraints under which policy-making operates and, on the other, the complexity that underlies the study of effectiveness. In order to reach this conclusion, this book has investigated the concept and actuality of the effectiveness of international environmental agreements with special reference to the Mediterranean Action Plan (MAP) and the Convention on Long-Range Transboundary Air Pollution (CLRTAP). This has been done by examining the shortcomings of the existing literature and analysis in order to develop and use a comprehensive concept of effectiveness. A heuristic distinction was then imposed between institutional and environmental effectiveness and the consequences of ignoring environmental effectiveness was discussed.

The concept of effectiveness

In the existing literature, the motivations for studying effectiveness are generally not directed at studying the environmental impact but rather at the effect of an agreement. The institutional school of thought sees effectiveness as mainly relating to the issue of institutional importance. These writers are mostly regime theorists of various persuasions and, as such, believe in the vital importance of international institutions/agreements – or regimes as they call it – as a form of international order. They use what I call institutional effectiveness as a standard of regime strength or weakness and thus an effective regime must necessarily be one with a high level of cooperation. The issue of how adequately this cooperation deals with the problem in question takes a secondary position, i.e. cooperation is the focus of study, not the capacity of the agreement to deal with the problem giving rise to it. Only a few authors looking at environmental effectiveness (the Norwegian regime theorists and some international environmental law specialists) are concerned with the environmental problem necessitating the agreement. However, these concerns are still cast within the mould of regime theory and are therefore limited to the regime as the unit of analysis. This limitation results in environmental degradation being considered from an angle focusing on institutional constraints *vis-à-vis* environmental degradation, rather than degradation itself, as the starting point.

This problem is based on a methodological constraint. A regime theorist assumes that a significant and cooperative institution will incite change. This change will lead to an improvement compared to the pre-institutional state of being (Haas *et al.*, 1993). Some regime theorists who use rational choice frameworks have adopted the concept of 'goal attainment' to describe effectiveness, but use this term in an institutional sense only equivalent to the term change (Bernauer, 1995). However, change might, for example, only result in a rise of awareness, but for the regime theorist this is a success since an improvement on the pre-regime situation has occurred. The standard by which effectiveness is measured is not set in relation to the problem to be regulated by the regime but by its ability to bring about change. However, I argue that this standard is inappropriate because change by itself is no measurement of effectiveness and does not provide evidence for a well-functioning institution or for environmental improvement. There is not even evidence that change is attributable to the institution in question. Again, this issue highlights the methodological constraints of regime theoretical assumptions.

The work in this book on the underlying foci in the study of effectiveness has demonstrated quite clearly that, even from a regime theoretical perspective, there has to be some reference to the environmental problem giving rise to the agreement. In addition, one or several standards against which effectiveness can be measured need to be set to define the *raison d'être* of the agreement. This research focus still disregards social and environmental dimensions, especially time dimensions, and where/how they fit in, the different stages at which effectiveness could be measured and what effect this would have on the analysis.

Therefore I argue that methodological constraints prevent regime theory from offering a useful definition of either the concept or the actuality of effectiveness. However, the lesson to be drawn from regime theory – despite its methodological constraints – is that in order to have effective environmental agreements we do need to have functioning institutions. Since institutions are the focus of regime theory, the experience of this research has to be valued, but cautiously so. It has to be placed in a different analytical framework, which is not methodologically constrained by focusing on the closed system and actor-centrism.

Thus, in summary, the analysis of existing concepts on the effectiveness of international environmental agreements has demonstrated that there are vast analytical differences on the nature of effectiveness and its evaluation. Its definition depends on the research focus that is given by a particular writer, however this is mostly related to institutional performance. None of the schools of thought discussed in this book relate effectiveness back to environmental degradation as the main focus of research.

Lessons drawn from the existing literature

Despite the methodological constraints of existing approaches, several points that have emerged in the existing literature need to be reiterated and elaborated. These points relate to analytical findings and to clarification on weaknesses in regime theoretical analysis that need to be improved.

First, existing definitions of, and approaches to, the effectiveness of international environmental agreements have been used to introduce a heuristic distinction between institutional and environmental effectiveness. Institutional effectiveness relates to the functioning of the agreement, the structural organisation of the institution in question and regulatory structures in general. Environmental effectiveness, on the other hand, relates to the way the agreement actually deals with the environmental problem in question. A concept of environmental effectiveness incorporates institutional effectiveness as part of a larger whole; therefore, the distinction between institutional and environmental effectiveness is heuristic only – for example, time frames relating to implementation and compliance of an agreement relate to both institutional and environmental effectiveness.

Second, there are certain shortcomings in the existing definitions of institutional effectiveness that need improvement. The assumption favoured by most effectiveness analysts, that the effectiveness of an agreement can be measured by comparing the achievement of the agreement with a hypothetical state of affairs in the absence of the agreement, is not feasible. Moreover, it does not follow automatically that an agreement is effective simply because environmental improvement has occurred subsequent to its inception. This is not feasible as agreements do not exist in a social vacuum and such analysis would be counterfactual. It neglects the consideration of parallel social, environmental, economic, political, technological, temporal and knowledge processes that exist at the national, regional and global levels and influence policy-making or indeed environmental phenomena in the life span of the agreement. Thus, environmental change cannot automatically be attributed to the existence of an international environmental agreement as this book has demonstrated.

Third, the regime theory school contradicts itself at a basic level by attributing major importance to exogenous factors (i.e. factors that are not directly attributable to the regime-formation process), thus implying that regime effectiveness is not a function of will (Levy, 1993; Levy *et al.*, 1994; Young, 1994). However, the basic tenet of regime formation theory is that cooperation is a function of will. I argue that the distinction between endogenous and exogenous factors is not helpful and that effectiveness has to be seen as separate from exogenous factors. Since regime theoretic analysis is limited to the regime as the unit of analysis, and therefore a closed system, the so-called exogenous factors are also part of the closed system. However, as this book argues, analysis of effectiveness has to stretch far beyond the regime as the unit of analysis and therefore the distinction between endogenous and exogenous factors is not really helpful. Rather, a distinction between social, structural and behavioural factors in the determination of effectiveness expresses more accurately the levels on which effectiveness is influenced.

Fourth, it remains unclear why existing literature only relates in a very few cases to the effectiveness of an agreement to environmental indicators – such as a high degree of correspondence between independent expert advice and the regulatory measures taken; a convergence of time frames used in regulatory proceedings and those recommended by independent experts; and the absence of a problem 'shift' to another level, to name but a few. The difficulty associated with the task of relating environmental indicators to effectiveness *per se* cannot be the cause of this as some institutional indicators used (for example, the attribution of environmental change to the regulatory efforts of an agreement) are much more difficult to measure.

Finally, these existing definitions suffer from a certain vagueness as they all operate outside a time frame, yet effectiveness should be an issue very much associated with time constraints. Environmental change is usually irreversible and thus it seems imperative that a process of degradation needs to be studied and regulated with temporal constraints in mind. In addition, issues of rhythmicity and temporality have to be considered, as was done in this book.

The new concept of environmental effectiveness

The omissions of the existing literature have been taken up and explored further in a discussion of the concepts of environmental and institutional effectiveness resulting in an analytical distinction between institutional and environmental effectiveness. This enables us to contextualise the limitations of the effectiveness debate and to demonstrate that a concept based solely on institutional effectiveness is artificial. Rather, a concept of effectiveness that is methodologically useful has to embrace a holistic definition of effectiveness.

The main problem of regime theoretical analysis is that actor behaviour and the definition of actors' interests in the negotiating situation are seen as the crucial objects of study. The agreement, or regime, is seen as a closed system that can be studied adequately without placing it in the context in which it operates. This approach neglects the social environment in which the 'regime' is formed and of which it is part. In addition, there is no reference to the capacity of the 'regime' to regulate or solve the environmental problem in question. It disregards notions of environmental effectiveness. Further, the regime theoretical method of analysis disregards the relationship between environment and society – a point that will be dealt with below.

The analysis of existing concerns with effectiveness has shown the preoccupation of theorists with the performance of the institutional body behind an agreement. How institutions cooperate, or which variables can be singled out that affect performance, are the focus of analysis. This approach concentrates on the role of actors in institution-building but is removed from the actual problem inciting the cooperative attempt. This means that analysis takes place on the level of institutional effectiveness and agreement implementation only, i.e. the structures and constraints underlying the agreement-making process and the idea of environmental effectiveness have been neglected.

This book has overcome these shortcomings and developed a new framework for analysis by introducing macro-level analysis and linking the concepts of society and environment. In order to contextualise the effectiveness debate, a heuristic distinction between institutional and environmental effectiveness was made with environmental effectiveness being a holistic concept. This refocusing overcomes one of the major omissions of traditional effectiveness debates: the failure to use the environmental problem and its social and structural origins as a standard against which to pitch effectiveness. The other major problem so far – the limitation to the closed system – has also been overcome by placing the agreement in question in its social, political, economic, technological, scientific and temporal context. This goes substantially further than conventional approaches that only distinguish between agreement negotiating and agreement implementation as levels of analysis. It does not treat the agreement as a closed system.

A definition of environmental effectiveness (both the concept and the actuality) has to see the agreement in a wider social context. This book demonstrates that an agreement cannot be studied as a closed unit but has to be seen in relation to the society and the environment in which it is operating. For this, the role of some actors such as the scientific community or the bureaucrats and their limitations or position in society have been studied. However, all actor analysis in this book has taken account of structural constraints of both actors and institutions, thus going fundamentally beyond regime theoretical foci.

The resulting liberation of the concept of effectiveness from previous methodological constraints has covered new ground in the study of effectiveness. Chapters 3 and 4 have been fundamental in this respect as the study forms the basis of the new definition of effectiveness by demonstrating the width of the concept through the analytical distinction of environmental and institutional effectiveness.

The four determinants of effectiveness

Four determinants of the effectiveness of international environmental agreements have been established that are directly relevant to defining and determining effectiveness. These are economic structures, time, science, and regulatory structures.

The two case studies illustrate the shortcomings of conventional analysis and the importance of the four determinants, although two very different pictures emerge. Again, this shows that the history and circumstances of an international environmental agreement are very case-specific and that it is necessary to study the particular social and structural origins rather than try to establish ground rules on environmental 'regime' formation.

Economic structures

Economic structures are strong determinants of both the contents of an agreement and the social environment in which it is negotiated. Economic factors, as regime theorists have also recognised, are decisive in shaping an international environmental agreement because environmental regulation usually imposes a cost on society and economic activity. Both MAP and CLRTAP are heavily influenced by economic factors. This influence refers to the institutional level.

On a wider social level, economic structures determine the composition of society and therefore are the underlying organisational principle of the relationship between environment and society. This relationship ignores the finite nature of energy sources on the planet and how they are used in a non-entropic way in current forms of economic organisation. This means that energy used is transformed into matter that cannot be reused, thus slowly using up the energy matter available on the planet. Only if the mode of production can be changed to incorporate knowledge about the nature of environmental systems will the harmony between environment and society be restored.

Time

In the field of time and effectiveness, the issue of appropriate time frames leads to a conflict between environmental needs and institutional feasibilities. At least a rigorous application of the precautionary principle would be necessary to address this point.

The disturbed rhythmic interaction between organic and mechanical systems needs to be stressed. This incompatibility has resulted in mechanical systems wreaking havoc in the environment. The gap between environmental and economic rhythms seems to be unbridgeable at this moment in time. After all, our whole society is organised along mechanistic principles, making rhythmicity a problem of economic and social organisation.

Science

Quite often 'outside' scientific knowledge that evolved in a context not directly related to the agreement in question is adapted, and thus the actual science used in the agreement has no directly pertinent political and economic content as it has been taken from a different 'political economy of science'. In these circumstances, it is more informative to study the regulatory structures of the agreement rather than the science aspect informing the policy-making process. In other circumstances the science is indigenous and thus more directly influenced by the relevant interplay between science, politics and economics. In either case the relationship between science and environmental effectiveness is fortuitous in institutional terms. This means that scientific research is not carried out with the sole aim of relieving environmental degradation but operates within very clear boundaries defining feasibilities in policy terms.

The relationship between policy-makers and scientists makes it difficult to determine whether, in Jasanoff's words, science is made for policy or policy is made for science because the two interrelate so much and their ideas have become cross-fertilised. Scientists are aware of the margins within which they operate while undertaking their research, and this is reflected in their research results. This point has been clearly demonstrated with respect to the various protocols in CLRTAP and the critical loads approach. The science used is not separate from economic and political considerations since the budgetary constraints of policy solutions are already incorporated in the critical load models.

Another major point in relation to science and effectiveness is the necessity of communication between scientists and policy-makers to facilitate the uptake of scientific advice on the policy level. The heeding of environment-oriented scientific advice is a precondition for the environmental effectiveness of an agreement while the example of the critical loads approach is more indicative of the achievement of institutional effectiveness. However, good levels of communication indicate that scientists are briefed on institutional constraints and base their research within the structures given, thus not making environmental effectiveness a priority. The lack of communication between policy-makers and scientists in the case of the Mediterranean Action Plan illustrates that scientific advice could theoretically be environmentally effective but this would still not lead to an environmentally effective agreement because these recommendations will be ignored.

There is an indication that science is more environment-oriented in the stages of identifying environmental problems long before the institutional approaches aiming to target them come into existence. Once integrated in an institutional process, science is mainly part of the political economy of knowledge generation.

Regulatory structures

The main problem with regulatory structures is that, first, policy-makers operate within rigid and narrow structures with a high specialisation in the division of labour. This means that they do not have a clear picture of the whole process and are not aware of where exactly their work is leading and what impact it has. Second, policy-makers in international environmental policy-making are usually government officials and thus represent a government which, in turn, represents the people of the respective state. They do not represent the environment since their very *raison d'être* is social, not environmental.

Third, policy-making operates within administrative time frames which means that environmental rhythms have to be subordinate to administrative feasibilities. Policy-makers target policy measures that are institutionally feasible but do not relate this back to what is environmentally necessary. This feasibility–necessity dichotomy is reproduced throughout the effectiveness debate.

The environment–society divide

In academic and in policy-making terms, there is no movement towards a holistic rather than socio-centric form of policy-making that transcends the environment–society divide. Academic disciplines such as politics, sociology, economics and IR are anthropocentric by definition and even when phenomena focusing on the whole planet such as time are the focus of analysis, they are still considered from a point of view that is focused on social aspects. The example of the effectiveness debate demonstrates this very clearly. Moreover, the treatment of the issue of time illustrates the shortcomings and limitations of this approach more clearly and strongly than other debates. However, the dominance of the regime theory/institutional bargaining school of thought shows us how embedded conventional behavioural and policy analysis is and how the policy-makers themselves are driven by the notions focused on in this school of thought. Therefore it cannot be expected that fundamental changes will occur in the policy-making process in the near future.

It can be concluded from this that the environmental effectiveness of international environmental agreements can only be achieved if the policies proposed transcend approaches that are based on human rhythmicity and reintegrate social (including political and economic) rhythms to make them part of natural rhythms rather than dominate them. This implies a changed rhythmicity. International environmental policy-making is dominated by social concerns and perspectives and suffers from such a degree of institutionalisation that it cannot seriously be expected to transcend these values. This means that, by definition, environmental effectiveness will not be achieved through an institutionalised agreement-making system, i.e. international environmental agreements cannot be effective by their very nature.

Two issues create a connection between the effectiveness debate and the contextualising of the concept of effectiveness. First, it has become obvious that the narrow focus on institutional effectiveness of the effectiveness discourse cannot adequately capture the meaning of effectiveness in an applied context. Second, this leads to the realisation that effectiveness, or indeed environmental agreements, cannot be studied in a rigid, limited methodological context but have to be placed in a wider social, political and economic context in order to be understood and analysed in a meaningful way.

Temporal, economic and scientific structures form the basis of any analysis of the relationship between society and the environment and an understanding of these concepts is vital for understanding problems related to environmental degradation. The examples of MAP and CLRTAP illustrate the structural constraints of policy-making, which do not form part of conventional academic analysis of international environmental agreements. The political economy approach was used to integrate a spatial and temporal dimension. This helped to establish that negotiating processes are part of general social developments and that the decentralisation of the holding of knowledge means that policy-making processes are not conscious, driven phenomena; rather, they can happen as fortuitous consequences of a bulk of decisions.

This analysis of the policy-making process explains why only institutional and not environmental effectiveness is taken into consideration in international environmental agreement-making. However, it leads to the conclusion that the prospects for including environmental effectiveness as a concept in policy-making are bleak indeed, except as an issue highlighted by more or less integrated environmental NGOs.

The case of CLRTAP is generally seen as an effective agreement. However, analysis has clearly highlighted the extent to which the politics and economics of acid rain have been linked to the science informing the agreement. Thus, the science of acid rain used in CLRTAP is a reflection of how economic and political constraints influence the generation of knowledge and scientific recommendations made. These are woven into the policy-making process rather than forming a linear process of policy-making being based on scientific research. This makes CLRTAP institutionally very effective but not environmentally effective. In MAP, such relationships do not exist since science and policy hardly interact. Therefore, it is not really relevant whether the science produced is environmentally effective or not as it does not influence the institutional process. Because of political, social and economic structures in the Mediterranean region, the process of knowledge generation in MAP has an education role and does not inform policy as such. It could be argued that it has an enabling and not a regulatory role.

The social mechanisms directed at regulating or alleviating environmental degradation operate according to the rhythm of industrial society and are thus unable to transcend this limitation unless a reform of social and economic organisation takes place. International environmental agreements demonstrate this clearly. They are so dominated by considerations about different societies' interest, values, motivations, political systems, etc., that they cannot take on board issues such as different rhythmicities and even focusing on the problem at stake. Therefore, they cannot offer a viable solution to the problem of environmental degradation.

What these findings demonstrate is that there is a fundamental gap between social (including political, economic, technological, scientific) organisation in modern society and environmental necessities. International environmental agreements cannot be effective by their very nature because they operate under such structural constraints. A fundamental restructuring of social organisation in order to take account of historically rooted environmental ignorance is necessary to overcome this problem.

International relations and the findings of this book

The mainstream IR literature ignores the complexity of environment–society relationships by concentrating on institution-building and aspects of international cooperation. However, the environmental *problématique* shows that a fundamental rethinking has to take place in order to take account of a field of study that has been completely externalised but needs to be incorporated into academic study because it is a structural level on which all societies are dependent. Therefore it is a fatal omission to externalise it and study only its institutional aspect.

The traditional concern of study in IR has been the behaviour and/or relationships between states and other international actors. However, the case has been made in this book and elsewhere that this concern is not far-reaching enough. It is not just the actions and the behaviour of international actors trying to cooperate on an issue that needs to be studied, but even more so how they will do it. It is not sufficient to try to explain the behaviour of actors and their motivations if this does not lead to analysis of how international problems can be dealt with more effectively. This is true of social problems but becomes paramount in relation to environmental degradation.

Another issue associated with this point is the methodological limitation to the regime as the unit of analysis in traditional IR case studies. Closed-system analysis serves to explain immediate connections between motivation or cause and action but cannot capture the full web of complexities in which a particular agreement-making process or another form of cooperation is located. Trade-offs are made between different subject matters, so even in institutional terms such closed-system explanations are too limited. However, in its most obvious form the parsimonious approach with its selection of only a few key variables neglects the social and structural context in which a particular form of cooperation takes place. This has also been noted by Paterson (1996) in a slightly different context. He argues that realist, neorealist and neoliberal institutional approaches can only partially explain actor behaviour in the case of global warming but historical materialist political economy approaches are substantially more successful in explaining negotiating positions than the traditional IR approaches. However, Paterson limits himself to explaining positions rather than linking the issue directly to environmental degradation, therefore still operating within traditional IR concerns.

Empirical insights

In relation to CLRTAP, what this book has fundamentally achieved (and what traditional approaches have not captured) is that the agenda-setting process and the inclusion and exclusion of regulatory measures have been explained by placing the agreement within a social, political and economic (all in their widest sense) context which highlights the structural constraints within which the policy-making process takes place. It also demonstrates the lack of effectiveness of this approach to deal with environmental degradation through acid rain. In addition, it makes clear that acid rain is just one phenomenon of many that are related to the excessive burning of fossil fuels. However, these phenomena are all treated separately in regional or global policy-making. So, conventional IR approaches can neither fully capture the complexity of the web in which CLRTAP is placed, nor can they appreciate its environmental effect and its effectiveness. CLRTAP tries to regulate the problem of acid rain in a closed-system approach by filtering out pollutants without taking into consideration the structural origin of acid rain and other problems sharing the origin. Thus, it is also an inefficient method of regulation.

The insights generated in this book on the Mediterranean Action Plan relate to both institutional and environmental aspects of effectiveness. As an agreement, MAP suffers from a lack of scientific advice uptake, which means that the discourse on science and power does not apply. There is a fundamental lack of environmental awareness which leads to MAP's essential task being that of data collection and provision but not policy-making. In effect, this means that MAP has no role that can be seen as environmentally effective. Since it does not aim to change the state of the environment in real terms, it does not aim to be environmentally effective. It is limited to an institutional role.

Conventional approaches have not dealt with this aspect of MAP because they are methodologically limited to studying cooperation rather than the outcome and purpose of this cooperation. The Mediterranean region is caught in the web of global political economic developments; however, it plays a peripheral role, i.e. has no power to shape these developments but is rather at the receiving end. Thus it lacks the environmental awareness to work on the institutional level and is not in a position to operate on the macro-level.

Consequences for other areas in IR

The findings of this book are also applicable to non-environmental areas of IR. They are valid in other areas where the literature adopts a scientistic analysis based on rational criteria which do not address the underlying issues. Realist, neorealist and regime theoretical approaches to poverty, human rights, food aid, the North–South divide, development issues in general or property rights are a case in point.

These issues are analysed in terms that are not related to the problem giving rise to international cooperation or consultation. Therefore the problem itself is externalised from the analysis, which means that ethics, moral values and notions of responsibility or equality and equity are not addressed. In addition, the social and structural origins of a problem can be ignored in traditional actor-centric analysis which relates directly to the aforementioned point. This means that, apart from the environment–society divide, the same criticisms made in relation to the effectiveness of international environmental agreements also apply to the above issues. Therefore the findings of this book can be widely useful in the study of international or global problems in IR.

For example, traditional/orthodox IR approaches still focus on the explanation of actor behaviour and/or the consequences for world order. However, they do not focus on the solution to the problem giving rise to the cooperative effort. Thus a critical approach including this issue could substantially broaden analysis. Although there is a substantial literature looking at issues such as poverty, food aid, etc., from a critical perspective, this is not usually located within IR. The advantage a critical IR analysis can offer is that it is another move away from the scientistic approach that dominates IR due to the long 'reign' of realism.

An analysis of these cooperative efforts would involve the selection of determinants of effectiveness relating to the issue in question. These would be singled out in a study of the social and structural origins of the issue to be analysed. Therefore only the last step in this book, the linkage of environment and society, does not apply to other cooperative efforts. In the case of food aid regimes, this would mean that an analysis of the origins of famines would indicate certain key factors in global social and economic organisation that will provide the determinants of effectiveness in the case of food aid. These can then offer a starting point for remedy action, which traditional IR regime-focused analysis cannot provide due to its limited methodology focusing on the effects of food aid regime on international cooperation rather than on food distribution.

Notes

1 Introduction

1 In 1991, there were 41 global or non-regional agreements compared to 78 regional ones, excluding European Community/Union and bilateral agreements (Brown Weiss *et al.*, 1992: 7). Between 1992 and 1997, 17 new international environmental agreements were signed of which ten are global and seven are regional. These figures include the agreements of the Rio Summit (UN web site).

2 International environmental cooperation and IR: what is missing?

1 Lukes distinguishes between three types of power: overt power, i.e. A can make B do what B would not have done otherwise; covert power, i.e. A can make B do what B would not normally do because of the nature of their relationship; and structural power, i.e. the structural basis of the relationship between A and B limits B's options of actions.

3 IR theory and effectiveness

1 Compliance and implementation are very similar terms. However, compliance is a very narrow concept because it basically refers to conforming to the terms of the agreement. Implementation is concerned with the putting into practice of the agreement. Although there is substantial overlap between the two terms, implementation is a more far-reaching term because it can refer to legal implementation, i.e. a putting into domestic law of the terms of the agreement. It can also refer to policy implementation on the national, regional or local level which refers to practical implementation. Compliance is a strictly legal term.
2 An example of how misguided an excessive focus on institutional behaviour can become is given in Downs *et al.* (1996).
3 This point has been adapted from the points made by Haas *et al.* (1993) and Young (1992).

4 The four determinants of environmental effectiveness

1 Gill refines Cox's taxonomy by requiring the following criteria of critical innovation: an alternative *problématique* to the orthodoxy, a historical perspective, a comparative historical method, a rethinking of ontology and a reflection on the purpose of theory (Gill and Mittelman, 1997).
2 I am indebted to Barbara Adam for drawing my attention to this subject which has been neglected in International Relations.

3 There is no scientific basis for these protocols. However, the choice of substances to be regulated under these protocols is based on scientific decisions (UN Air Pollution Studies (1989), No. 5, *The state of transboundary air pollution*, E.89II.E.25).
4 Personal communication with MAP scientific coordinator, December 1995.
5 During phase 1 of MEDPOL, government representatives and UN agencies chose scientists on the basis of their reputation. However, in phase 2 national coordinators were appointed who chose the scientific institutions in question (personal communication with MAP scientific coordinator, December 1995).
6 He does mention some of these aspects as possible factors in a paragraph but without analysing them and their role.
7 Personal communication with MAP Scientific Coordinator, December 1995.
8 The 1996 budget for MEDPOL is US$ 615,000 (UNEP(OCA)/MED IG.5/16, Annex XIII, p 10). This includes administrative costs. As a comparison, in 1977 the first ten MEDPOL projects received funding in the region of US$ 900,000 by the UN alone (figure not adjusted) (UNEP/IG.11/3, 11 November 1977, p. 10).
9 Boehmer-Christiansen, for example, distinguishes between 10 functions of scientific expertise, many of which emphasise the politicised nature of science (1995: 195–203).
10 At the Wilton Park Conference on Securing the Marine Environment (487th Wilton Park Conference, Steyning, 13–17 January 1997) Professor Fauzi Mantoura argued that science had reached such a stage that the environmental consequences of a particular substance can be determined on all ecosystemic levels within a very short time period (16 January 1997, F. Mantoura, 'Policy-making and scientific research: how to improve interaction').
11 Even the concept of power used by the realist/neorealist tradition disregards what Lukes calls the third dimension of power, namely structural power embedded in the system within which the actors operate (Lukes, 1974).
12 Personal communication with German delegation during UNECE working group on strategies meeting in Geneva between 19 and 23 February 1996.
13 Personal communication with British delegation during UNECE working group on strategies meeting in Geneva between 19 and 23 February 1996.
14 Personal communication with Swedish delegation during UNECE working group on strategies meeting in Geneva between 19 and 23 February 1996.
15 Personal communication with Eastern European delegations during UNECE working group on strategies meeting in Geneva between 19 and 23 February 1996.
16 Personal communication in Athens on 7 December 1995.

5 The consequences of ignoring environmental effectiveness (I)

1 Non-members of the London Dumping Convention are Albania, Algeria, Cyprus, Egypt, Israel, Malta, Syria and Turkey. Marpol has not yet been signed by Albania, Algeria, Libya, Malta, Monaco, Morocco, Syria and Turkey.
2 Personal communication with MAP legal adviser, Athens, 7 December 1995.
3 Albania, Bosnia-Hercegovina, Croatia, Israel, Lebanon, Slovenia, Syria.
4 UNEP/IG. 19/4 of 20 February 1980, p. 3.
5 Personal communication, 8 December 1995, Athens.
6 For more information see *The Environmental Program for the Mediterranean* (1990) published by the World Bank, Washington D.C.
7 UNEP/IG.23/INF.25 of 5 February 1981, p. 1.
8 Personal communication, 8 December 1995, Athens.
9 UNEP/IG.18/4, annex III of 31 October 1979.
10 UNEP (OCA)/MED IG.5/16, annex XIII, p. 38. Unpaid pledge estimate: US$ 1,540,814. Mediterranean Trust Fund contribution commitments: US$ 4,406,325.

11 GESAMP – IMO/FAO/UNESCO/WMO/WHO/IAEA/UN/UNEP Joint Group
   of Experts on the Scientific Aspects of Marine Pollution. Atmospheric transport of
   contaminants into the Mediterranean Region, 1985. Rep. Stud. GESAMP (26), p. 41.
12 UNEP (OCA)/MED IG.5/16 of 8 June 1995 (report of the ninth ordinary meeting
   of the contracting parties to the convention for the protection of the Mediterranean
   Sea against pollution and its protocols).
13 This is not to mean that institutional effectiveness is a precondition for environmental
   effectiveness.

6 The consequences of ignoring environmental effectiveness (II)

1 The OECD Cooperative technical programme on long range transport of air pollutants ran from 1972 to 1977 and had 80 observer and measuring points in Western
   Europe (Mayer-Tasch, 1986).
2 Drucksachen des Deutschen Bundestags, 10/5387, Druckschrift zum Protokoll, p. 11.
3 *Mimeo*, obtained from WWF head office in Godalming, Surrey.
4 UN Air Pollution studies, No. 5, The state of transboundary air pollution, 1989,
   E.89.II.E.25, p. 19.
5 ECE/EB.AIR/5 (1985), p. xi.
6 EB.AIR/WG.3/16, of 29 February 1988, p. 3.
7 *Acid News*, No. 5, December 1996, p. 8. Sweden, Norway, Belgium, France, Finland
   and Italy cannot meet the aims of the declaration. Austria, Liechtenstein,
   Switzerland, the Netherlands, Denmark and Germany will meet their targets.
8 In fact, Peter Stief-Tauch of the European Commission argues that the second
   sulphur protocol is based on the provisions of the LCP protocol (personal communication, April 1994).
9 They constitute the annex to the protocol on land-based sources of pollution.

7 Social and structural origins of environmental degradation

1 'Time is neither a characteristic of nature nor does it exist *a priori* in our consciousness. It does not exist "as such" but as a social concept which is constituted of and
   varied by the work and interaction patterns of societies' (Hohn, 1984: 6).
2 Ponting (1991) sees this differently and points to the change from hunting to gathering society as the point in history when mankind began to dominate and
   irreversibly change the natural environment. However, it was only through the
   progress of industrialisation achieving such large-scale changes that nature was truly
   'vanquished'.
3 Orthodox approaches operate on the basis of assigning a monetary value to
   resources, goods and services. However, some environmental resources such as air, soil
   or water in their sink capacity, do not cost anything and are thus treated as 'free
   goods' and externalised in economic analyses.
4 Before the industrial revolution, energy used was fed back into the system while the
   advent of the use of fossil fuel led to the production of waste products, which break
   the cycle as they do not regenerate energy.

8 The social origins and context of acid rain and pollution of the Mediterranean Sea

1 Personal communication in Geneva, 19 February 1996.
2 'The ecological discourse makes us experience the end of "foreign policy", the end of
   "sovereignty" and the end of the nation state every day' (Beck, 1995: 16).

3 The final version reads: 'In a case where a Party, due to the high sulphur content of indigenous solid or liquid fuels, cannot meet the emission limit value set forth in column (ii), it may apply the desulphurisation rates set forth in column (iii) ...' This phrase does not explicitly state that there is a preferential treatment for indigenous fuels but it is implied. This can pass the GATT rules, although strictly speaking it is not permissible.

4 See annexes of various UNECE Working Group on Strategies meeting reports during the 1980s.

5 'The priority aim is to avoid the formation of environmental poisons. As a rule this is the better and also more economic way. The aim of integrated environmental protection also necessitates the inclusion of solid waste and rest materials as well as waste water.' Bundesministerium für Forschung und Technik (1990), *Programmreport Kohletechnik*, Bonn, p. 10.

6 This is how delegates to CLRTAP see the situation.

7 The MAP legal adviser gave Greek–Turkish disagreement as the reason for the long delay of this protocol.

8 This point transpired in personal communications in December 1995.

9 Personal communication, 8 December 1995.

10 This point is certainly true of the first three protocols to the Barcelona Convention and applies to the last two protocols and amendments with qualifications.

Bibliography

Primary sources

Commission of the European Communities (1995) Council Decision on the signature of the revised convention for the protection of the Mediterranean Sea against pollution, protocol for the prevention of pollution by dumping from ships and aircraft and protocol concerning specially protected areas. COM (95) 202 final, 29.05.1995.

FAO Legal Office Background Paper No. 8 (1975) WS/H 6138. Existing and proposed international conventions for the control of marine pollution and their relevance to the Mediterranean.

FAO/UNESCO/IOC/WHO/WMO/IAEA/UNEP (1983) Co-ordinated Mediterranean Pollution Monitoring and Research Programme (MEDPOL) – Phase I: Programme Description. UNEP Regional Seas Report and Studies No. 23.

GESAMP – IMO/FAO/UNESCO/WMO/WHO/IAEA/UN/UNEP Joint Group of Experts on the Scientific Aspects of Marine Pollution (1985) Atmospheric transport of contaminants into the Mediterranean region. Rep. Stud. GESAMP (26).

GESAMP – IMO/FAO/UNESCO/WMO/IAEA/UN/UNEP Joint Group of Experts on the Scientific Aspects of Marine Pollution (1984) Marine pollution implications of Ocean Energy Development. Reports and Studies GESAMP (20).

Greenpeace International (1994) Implementing the precautionary approach in the Mediterranean Action Plan. Discussion paper prepared by Greenpeace International, Rome.

MEDWAVES (1991–1995) News Bulletin. UNEP MAP Coordinating Unit.

Ministry of Environment, Norway (1995) Discussion paper on joint implementation under the Oslo Protocol. Oslo.

OECD (1985) *Environmental policy and technical change*. Paris.

Swedish NGO Secretariat on Acid Rain Briefing documents.

UN Air Pollution Studies (1984–1992) Nos 1–8. Geneva.

UNECE EB.AIR/24 (1990) Report of the Eighth Session of the Executive Body. Geneva.

UNECE EB.AIR/27 (1991) Strategies and policies for air pollution abatement – 1990 review. Geneva.

UNECE EB.AIR/29 (1991) Report of the Ninth Session of the Executive Body. Geneva.

UNECE EB.AIR/33 (1992) Report of the Tenth Session of the Executive Body. Geneva.

UNECE EB.AIR/36 (1993) Report of the Eleventh Session of the Executive Body. Geneva.

UNECE EB.AIR/44 (1995) Strategies and Policies for Air Pollution Abatement – 1994 review. Geneva.

UNECE EB.AIR/46 (1996) Report of the Thirteenth Session of the Executive Body. Geneva.

UNECE EB.AIR/R.62 (1991) Annual review of Strategies and Policies for Air Pollution Abatement. Geneva.

UNECE EB.AIR/R.66 (1992) Strategies and Policies for Air Pollution Abatement: 1992 review. Geneva.

UNECE EB.AIR/R.84 (1994) Draft protocol to the 1979 Convention on Long-Range Transboundary Air Pollution on further Reduction of Sulphur Emissions. Geneva.

UNECE EB.AIR/WG.3/12 (1987) Working Group on Nitrogen Oxides Report of the Sixth Session. Geneva.

UNECE EB.AIR/WG.3/14 (1987) Working Group on Nitrogen Oxides Report of the Seventh Session. Geneva.

UNECE EB.AIR/WG.3/16 (1988) Working Group on Nitrogen Oxides Report of the Eighth Session. Geneva.

UNECE EB.AIR/WG.5/22 (1993) Working Group on Strategies Report of the Eleventh Session. Geneva.

UNECE EB.AIR/WG.5/32 (1995) Working Group on Strategies Report of the Fifteenth Session. Geneva.

UNECE EB.AIR/WG.5/33 (1995) Working Group on Strategies Provisional Agenda for the Sixteenth Session. Geneva.

UNECE EB.AIR/WG.5/R.45 (1993) Integrated assessment modelling of nitrogen compounds. Geneva.

UNECE EB.AIR/WG.5/R.55 (1995) Long-term financing of effect-oriented activities. Geneva.

UNECE EB.AIR/WG.5/R.58 (1995) Working Group on Strategies Integrated Assessment Modelling. Geneva.

UNECE EB.AIR/WG.5/R.59 (1995) Working Group on Strategies Informal Planning Meeting of the Extended Bureau of the Ad Hoc Preparatory Working Group on Heavy Metals. Geneva.

UNECE EB.AIR/WG.5/R.60 (1995) Working Group on Strategies Informal Planning Meeting of the Extended Bureau of the Ad Hoc Preparatory Working Group on Persistent Organic Pollutants. Geneva.

UNECE EB.AIR/WG.5/R.61 (1995) Working Group on Strategies Possible Elements and a Structure for a Protocol on the Further Reduction of Emissions of Nitrogen Compounds and Volatile Organic Compounds. Geneva.

UNECE EB.AIR/WG.5/R.57 (1995) Joint implementation under the Oslo protocol. Geneva, Working Group on Strategies.

UNECE/HLM.1/R.1 (1979) Convention on Long-Range Transboundary Air Pollution. Geneva.

UNEP (1986) The Siren, news from UNEP's Regional Seas Programme. No 30.

UNEP (1990) Common measures adopted by the contracting parties to the Convention for the Protection of the Mediterranean Sea against Pollution. MAP Technical Reports Series No. 38, Athens.

UNEP (1995) Mediterranean Action Plan phase II and Convention for the Protection of the Marine Environment and the Coastal Region of the Mediterranean. Informal Document, Athens.

UNEP/BUR/33/4 (1988) Preliminary ideas of the Executive Director on the Refocusing of the Mediterranean Action Plan on environmentally sound integrated planning and management of the Mediterranean. Athens.

UNEP/BUR/39/Inf.4 (1991) Global Environmental Facility (GEF) – note by the Secretariat. Athens.

UNEP/BUR/44/3 (1994) Recommendations on specific issues. Meeting of the Bureau of the contracting parties to the Convention for the Protection of the Mediterranean Sea against pollution and its related protocols, Athens.

UNEP/Conf. 1/2 (1975) Conference of plenipotentiaries of the coastal states of the Mediterranean region on the protection of the Mediterranean Sea. Working Group on draft legal instruments.

UNEP/Conf.1/Inf.3 (1976) Progress report of the Executive Director on the implementation of the MAP. Geneva.

UNEP/ECE/UNIDO/FAO/UNESCO/WHO/IAEA (1984) Pollutants from land-based sources in the Mediterranean. UNEP Regional Seas Reports and Studies No. 32.

UNEP/FAO (1986) Baseline Studies and Monitoring of Metals, particularly Mercury and Cadmium in marine organisms (MEDPOL II). MAP Technical Reports Series No. 2, Athens.

UNEP/FAO (1986) Baseline Studies and Monitoring of DDT, PCBs and other chlorinated hydrocarbons in marine organisms (MEDPOL III). MAP Technical Reports Series No. 3, Athens.

UNEP/FAO (1986) Research on the effects of pollutants on marine communities and ecosystems (MEDPOL V). MAP Technical Reports Series No. 3, Athens.

UNEP/FAO/UNESCO/IOC/WHO/WMO/IAEA (1984) Coordinated Mediterranean Pollution and Monitoring Research Programme (MEDPOL) – phase 1: programme description. UNEP Regional Seas Reports and Studies No 23, Athens.

UNEP/FAO/UNESCO/WHO/WMO/IAEA/IOC (1986) Co-ordinated Mediterranean Pollution Monitoring and Research Programme (MEDPOL Phase I) Final Report 1975–1980. MAP Technical Reports Series No. 9, Athens.

UNEP/FAO/WHO (1987) Assessment of the state of pollution of the Mediterranean Sea by mercury and mercury compounds. MAP Technical Reports Series No. 18, Athens.

UNEP/IG.11/3 (1977) Report of the Executive Director on the implementation of the Mediterranean Action Plan and recommendations for follow-up actions. Geneva.

UNEP/IG.14/4/Corr.1 (1979) Report of the Executive Director on the implementation of the Mediterranean Action Plan for the period 1975 until December 1978 and recommendations for activities during the 1979–1980 biennium. Geneva.

UNEP/IG.19/4 (1980) Explanations of reservations made by experts as indicated in footnotes to preliminary draft protocol for the protection of the Mediterranean Sea against Pollution from Land-based Sources. Geneva.

UNEP/IG.23/INF.25 (1981) World Bank projects on the Mediterranean region. Geneva.

UNEP/IG.56/4 (1985) The Mediterranean Action Plan – retrospect and prospect. Note by the Executive Director of the United Nations Environment Programme. Athens.

UNEP/IG.56/5 (1985) Report of the fourth ordinary meeting of the contracting parties to the convention for the protection of the Mediterranean Sea against pollution and its related protocol. Athens.

UNEP/IG.56/Inf.3 (1985) The first ten years of the Mediterranean Action Plan – a critical review. Genoa.

UNEP/IG.6/6 (1977) Report of intergovernmental consultation concerning a draft protocol for the protection of the Mediterranean Sea against pollution from land-based sources. Geneva.

UNEP/IG.9/5 (1977) Report of the consultation concerning a draft protocol for the protection of the Mediterranean Sea against pollution from land-based sources. Geneva.

UNEP/IG.74/Inf.9 (1987) Progress report of the preparation of a draft protocol for the protection of the Mediterranean Sea against pollution resulting from exploration and exploitation of the continental shelf and the sea-bed and its subsoil. Athens.

UNEP/IOC (1986) Problems of coastal transport of pollutants (MEDPOL VI). MAP Technical Reports Series No. 6, Athens.

UNEP/IOC/WMO (1986) Baseline studies and monitoring of oil and petroleum hydrocarbons in marine waters (MEDPOL I). MAP Technical Reports Series No. 1, Athens.

UNEP/MAP (1992) The Mediterranean Action Plan – saving our common heritage. Athens.

UNEP(OCA)/MED IG.1/5 (1989) Report of the sixth ordinary meeting of the contracting parties to the Convention for the Protection of the Mediterranean Sea against Pollution and its related protocols. Athens.

UNEP(OCA)/MED IG.2/4 (1991) Report of the seventh ordinary meeting of the contracting parties to the Convention for the Protection of the Mediterranean Sea against Pollution and its related protocols. Athens.

UNEP(OCA)/MED IG.3/5 (1993) Report of the eighth ordinary meeting of the contracting parties to the Convention for the Protection of the Mediterranean Sea against Pollution and its related protocols. Athens.

UNEP(OCA)/MED IG.3/Inf.3 (1993) Report on the implementation of the Mediterranean Action Plan and other related activities. Athens.

UNEP(OCA)/MED IG.4/4 (1994) Final act and protocol of the conference of plenipotentiaries on the protocol for the protection of the Mediterranean Sea against pollution resulting from exploration and exploitation of the continental shelf and the seabed and its subsoil. Athens.

UNEP(OCA)/MED IG.5/16 (1995) Report of the ninth ordinary meeting of the contracting parties to the Convention for the Protection of the Mediterranean Sea against Pollution and its protocols. Athens.

UNEP(OCA)/MED IG.6/7 (1995) Final Act of the conference of plenipotentiaries on the amendments to the Convention for the Protection of the Mediterranean Sea against Pollution, to the protocol for the prevention of pollution of the Mediterranean Sea by dumping from ships and aircraft and on the protocol concerning specially protected areas and biological diversity in the Mediterranean. Athens.

UNEP(OCA)/MED/IG.9/4 (1996) Final Act and Protocol. Conference of plenipotentiaries on the protocol on the prevention of pollution of the Mediterranean Sea by transboundary movements of hazardous wastes and their disposal, Athens.

UNEP(OCA)/MED WG.116/4 (1996) Report of the third meeting of government-designated legal and technical experts on the preparation of a protocol on the prevention of pollution of the Mediterranean Sea area by transboundary movements of hazardous wastes and their disposal. Athens.

UNEP(OCA)/MED WG.19/4 (1991) Report of the meeting of the working group on the Mediterranean report for the 1992 United Nations Conference on Environment and Development. Athens.

UNEP(OCA)/MED WG.30/4 (1991) Report of the third meeting of the working group of experts on the draft protocol for the protection of the Mediterranean Sea against pollution resulting from exploration and exploitation of the continental shelf and the sea-bed and its sub-soil. Athens.

UNEP(OCA)/MED/WG.64/3 (1993) Report of the first meeting of Mediterranean experts on the preparation of a protocol on the prevention of pollution of the Mediterranean Sea resulting from the transboundary movement of hazardous wastes and their disposal. Athens.

UNEP(OCA)/MED WG.82/4 (1994) Report of the meeting of legal and technical experts to examine amendments to the Barcelona Convention and its related protocols and the Mediterranean Action Plan. Athens.

UNEP/WG.46/5 (1980) Draft long-term programme for pollution monitoring and research in the Mediterranean (MEDPOL phase II) – detailed programme description. Geneva.

UNEP/WHO (1986) Coastal Water Quality Control (MEDPOL VII). MAP Technical Reports Series No. 7, Athens.

United Nations (1991) Survey of existing agreements and instruments, and criteria for evaluation. United Nations General Assembly A/CONF.151/PC/WG.III/L.9, 24 August 1991.

United Nations Environment Programme (1993) Programme for the development and periodic review of environmental law for the 1990s. Nairobi.

World Bank (1990) The Environmental Program for the Mediterranean. World Bank, Washington D.C.

Secondary Sources

Abbott, K.W. (1992) *International Law and International Relations Theory: building bridges.* Asil Proceedings, 167–187.

Adam, B. (1990) *Time and social theory.* Polity Press, Cambridge.

—— (1994) 'Running out of time: global crisis and human engagement'. In: Redclift, M. and Benton, T. (eds) *Social theory and the global environment.* Routledge, London, 92–112.

—— (1998) *Timescapes of modernity; the environment and invisible hazards.* Routledge, London.

Adam, B. and Kütting, G. (1995) 'Time to reconceptualise "green technology" in the context of globalisation and international relations'. *Innovation – The European Journal of Social Sciences* 8(3), 243–259.

Adams, J. (1997) *Risk environments – risk societies.* Environmental Futures Lecture Series, Cambridge, 4-2-1997.

Adler, E. and Haas, P.M. (1992) 'Conclusion: epistemic communities, world order, and the creation of a reflective research program'. *International Organization* 46(1), 367–390.

Agren, C. (1994), 'New figures presented', *Acid News* (No. 5, December), 14.

Ahrens, G.A. *et al.* (1990) *Luftverschmutzung durch Stickstoffoxide.* Berichte 3/90 edn. Deutsches Umweltbundesamt, Erich Schmidt Verlag, Berlin.

Ahuja, K. (ed.) (1993) *Regime transformations and global realignments.* Sage Publications, London.

Akerman, N. (ed.) (1990) *Maintaining a satisfactory environment, an agenda for international environmental policy.* Westview Press, Oxford.

Albin, C. (1995) 'Rethinking issues of justice and fairness: the case of acid rain emission reductions'. *Review of International Studies* 21(2), 119–143.

Aldhous, P. (1991) 'An economic case for environmental cooperation'. *Nature* 351 (16 May), 175.

Alm, L.R. (1993) 'Regional influences and environmental policy making: a study on acid rain'. *Policy Studies Journal* 21(4), 638–650.

Altvater, E. (1993) 'Die Oekologie der neuen Welt(un)ordnung'. *Nord-Süd aktuell* 7(1), 72–84.

Andresen, S. and Oestreng, W. (eds) (1989) *International resource management*. Pinter, London.

Andresen, S. and Wettestad, J. (1995) 'International problem-solving effectiveness'. *International Environmental Affairs* 7(2), 127–149.

Anon. (1991) 'UNEP, a cleaner Mediterranean'. *Environmental Policy and Law* 21(5/6), 203–204.

—— (1994a) 'Med-nations sign protocol to protect the sea'. *Maritime Monitor* (25 October), 10.

—— (1994b) 'Long-Range Transboundary Air Pollution'. *Environmental Policy and Law* 24(6), 331–332.

—— (1995a) *Wege aus der Weltkrise – Oekobilanz '95*. Der Spiegel Special (February), 1–186.

—— (1995b) 'UN-ECE critical loads concept'. *Concawe Review* 4(1), 18–19.

Antoine, M.S. (1992) 'Case studies of land-based pollution policy'. *Marine Policy* 16(1), 51–53.

Archer, C. (1992) *International organizations*, 2nd edn. Routledge, London.

Ayres, R.U. and Simonis, U.E. (1994) *Industrial metabolism*. United Nations University Press, New York.

Bandarin, F. and Marson, A. (1995) *The impact of local environmental plans on regional seas policies: the case of the Northern Adriatic*. Conference paper, Genoa.

Barnes, B. and Edge, D. (eds) (1982) *Science in context*. The Open University Press, Milton Keynes.

Barrett, S. (1994) 'Self-enforcing international environmental agreements'. *Oxford Economic Papers – New Series* 46, 878–894.

Batisse, M. (1990) 'Probing the future of the Mediterranean Basin'. *Environment* 32(5), 4–9, 28–34.

Battarbee, R.W. (ed.) (1995) *Acid rain and its impact: the critical loads debate*. Department of Geography, University College London, London.

Beck, U. (1986) *Risikogesellschaft; auf dem Weg in eine andere Moderne*. Suhrkamp, Frankfurt/Main.

—— (1988) *Gegengifte – die organisierte Unverantwortlichkeit*. Suhrkamp, Frankfurt/Main.

—— (1995) 'Weltrisikogesellschaft, zur politischen Dynamik globaler Gefahren'. *Internationale Politik* 50(8), 13–20.

Beck, U. and Beck-Gernsheim, E. (eds) (1994) *Riskante Freiheiten*. Suhrkamp, Frankfurt/Main.

Benedick, R. (1991), *Ozone diplomacy*. Harvard University Press, Cambridge/Mass.

Bennett, G. (ed.) (1991) *Air Pollution Control in the European Community: implementation of the EC directives in the 12 member states*. Graham & Trotman, London.

—— (1992) *Dilemmas: coping with environmental problems*. Earthscan, London.

Benveniste, G. (1972) *The politics of expertise*. Croom Helm, London.

Berman, M. (1982) *All that is solid melts into air*. Verso, London.

Bernard, M. (1997) 'Ecology, political economy and the counter-movement: Karl Polanyi and the second great transformation'. In: Gill, S. and Mittelman, J. (eds) *Innovation and transformation in international studies*. Cambridge University Press, Cambridge, 75–89.

Bernauer, T. (1995) 'The effect of international environmental institutions: how we might learn more'. *International Organization* 49(2), 351–377.

Betz, J. and Hein, W. (1996) 'Globalisierung und der Weg zur Weltgesellschaft: Heraus-forderung aus dem Süden – ein Problemaufriss'. *Nord-Süd aktuell* 10(3), 466–481.

Boehmer-Christiansen, S.A. (1981) *Limits to the international control of marine pollution*. DPhil Thesis, University of Sussex, Brighton.

—— (1982) 'The scientific basis of marine pollution control'. *Marine Policy* 6(1), 2–10.

—— (1984) 'Marine pollution control in Europe: regional approaches 1972–80'. *Marine Policy* 8(1), 44–55.

—— (1988) 'Black mist and acid rain – science as fig leaf of policy'. *Political Quarterly* 59, 145–160.

—— (1990) 'Emerging international principles of environmental protection and their impact on Britain'. *The Environmentalist* 10(2), 95–113.

—— (1995) 'Reflections on scientific advice and EC transboundary pollution policy'. *Science and Public Policy* 22(3), 195–203.

Boehmer-Christiansen, S.A. and Skea, J. (1991) *Acid politics: environmental and energy politics in Britain and Germany*. Belhaven Press, London.

Bookchin, M. (1995) *Re-enchanting humanity*. Cassell, London.

Booth, K. and Smith, S. (eds) (1995) *International Relations theory today*. Polity Press, Cambridge.

Bottomore, T. (ed.) (1991) *A dictionary of Marxist thought*, 2nd edn. Blackwell, London.

Boxer, B. (1978) 'Mediterranean Action Plan: an interim evaluation'. *Science* 202 (10 Nov.), 585–591.

—— (1983) 'The Mediterranean Sea: preparing and implementing a regional action plan'. In: Kay, D. and Jacobson, H. (eds) *Environmental protection: the international dimension*. Allansheld, Osmun & Co. Publishers, Totowa/New Jersey, 267–309.

—— (1991) 'Societal contexts of ocean pollution science'. *Global Environmental Change* 1(2), 139–156.

Boyle, A.E. (1990) 'Transboundary air pollution'. *International and Comparative Law Quarterly* 39(4), 940–944.

—— (1991) 'Saving the world? Implementation and enforcement of international envi-ronmental law through international institutions'. *Journal of Environmental Law* 3(2), 229–245.

—— (1992) 'Land-based sources of marine pollution – current legal regime'. *Marine Policy* 16(1), 20–35.

Braudel, F. (1978) *The Mediterranean and the Mediterranean world in the age of Philip II*. Fontana Collins, London.

Bretherton, C. (1995) *Global environmental change: the gendered agenda*. BISA conference paper, Southampton, 18–20 December.

Brown, E.D. (1971) *The legal regime of hydrospace*. The London Institute of World Affairs, Stevens & Sons, London.

Brown Weiss, E. (1992) 'Global environmental change and international law'. *Global Envi-ronmental Change* 2(3), 250–256.

Brown Weiss, E., Szasz, P.C. and Magraw, D.B. (1992) *International environmental law, basic instruments and references*. Transnational Publishers, New York.

Bryant, C. and Jary, D. (eds) (1991) *Giddens' theory of structuration, a critical appreciation*. Routledge, London.

Bryner, G. (1996) *The role of economic theory in global environmental policy-making*. ISA Conference, San Diego.

Bull, H. (1977) *The anarchical society*. Macmillan, London.

Bullock, E. (1990) 'Acid Rain falls on the just and the unjust'. *University of Illinois Law Review* 3, 605–644.

Buzan, B. (1993) 'From international system to international society: structural realism and regime theory meet the English school'. *International Organization* 47(3), 327–352.

Caldwell, L.K. (1984) *International environmental policy, emergence and dimensions: environmental law and the UN Environment Programme*. Duke University Press, Durham/North Carolina.

—— (1990) *Between two worlds: science, the environmental movement and policy choices*. Cambridge University Press, Cambridge.

Cameron, J., Werksman, J. and Roderick, P. (eds) (1996) *Improving compliance with international environmental law*. Earthscan, London.

Carraro, C. (1994) 'Technical innovation and environmental protection – environmental policy reconsidered – the role of technological innovation'. *European Economic Review* 38(3–4), 545–554.

Carson, R. (1951) *The sea around us*. Staples, London.

—— (1958) *Silent spring*. Penguin, London.

Chatterjee, P. and Finger, M. (1994) *The earth brokers*. Routledge, London.

Chew, S.C. (1997) 'Accumulation, deforestation and word ecological degradation, 2500 BC to AD 1990'. *Advances in Human Ecology* 6, 221–255.

—— (1998) 'Nature and the Bronze Age world system', ISA Paper, Minneapolis, 17–21 March.

Chircop, A. (1992) 'The Mediterranean Sea and the quest for sustainable development'. *Ocean Development and International Law* 23(1), 17–30.

—— (1994) 'The development of a national ocean policy and institutional implications post-Rio'. *Foreign Relations Journal* 9(1), 49–62.

—— (1995) *Education and training of Mediterranean coastal and marine managers: towards a regional approach*. Conference paper, Genoa.

Chossudovsky, E.M. (1989) '"East-West" diplomacy for environment in the United Nations'. United Nations Publications UNITAR, New York.

Choucri, N. (1993) 'Political economy of the global environment'. *International Political Science Review* 14(1), 103–116.

—— (ed.) (1993) *Global accord: environmental challenges and international responses*. MIT Press, Cambridge/Mass.

Cicin-Sain, B. (1995) *Implementation of earth summit agreements: progress since Rio*. Conference paper, Genoa.

Clark, R.B. (1992) *Marine pollution*, 3rd edn. Oxford University Press, Oxford.

Conca, K., Alberty, M. and Dabelko, G. (eds) (1995) *Green planet blues*. Westview Press, Boulder/Colorado.

Conley, V.A. (1997) *Ecopolitics: the environment in poststructuralist thought*. Routledge, London.

Cox, R. (1981) 'Social forces, states and world order: beyond International Relations theory'. *Millennium Journal of International Studies* 10(2), 126–151.

—— (1987) *Production, power and world order*. Columbia University Press, New York.

—— (ed.) (1997) *The new realism: perspectives on multilateralism and world order*. Macmillan for United National University Press, London.

Cox, R.W. and Sinclair, T.J. (1996) *Approaches to world order*. Cambridge University Press, Cambridge.

Crespi, F. (1992) *Social action and power*. Blackwell, London.

Daly, H.E. (1992) *Steady-state economics*, 2nd edn. Earthscan, London.

Daly, H.E. and Cobb, J.B. (1990) *For the common good*. Green Print, London.

Daven, A. and Last, U. (1994) 'Das Seerechtsübereinkommen der Vereinten Nationen von 1982'. *Nord-Süd aktuell* 8(3), 391–395.

Demidecki-Demidowiec, M. (1984) 'United Kingdom – acid rain report and the government's reply'. *Environment* 13(3–4), 107–108.

de Senarclens, P. (1993) 'Regime theory and the study of international organisations'. *International Social Science Journal* 138, 453–462.

Dessler, D. (1989) 'What's at stake in the agent-structure debate?' *International Organization* 43(3), 441–473.

Devlin, J. and Yap, N. (1994), 'Structural adjustment programmes and the UNCED agenda: explaining the contradictions'. In: Thomas, C. (ed.) *Rio: unravelling the consequences*. Frank Cass, London.

Dickens, P. (1992) *Society and nature – towards a green social theory*. Harvester Wheatsheaf, London.

—— (1996) *Reconstructing nature*. Routledge, London.

Dix, H.M. (1981) *Environmental pollution*. John Wiley & Sons, Chichester.

Dixon, M. (1990) *Textbook on international law*. Blackstone Press Ltd, London.

Dobson, A (1995) *Green political thought*, 2nd edn. Routledge, London.

Doran, P. (1995) 'Earth, power, knowledge: towards a critical global environmental politics'. In: MacMillan, J. and Linklater, A. (eds) *Boundaries in question*. Pinter Publishers, London, 193–211.

Dosi, G., Pavitt, K. and Soete, L. (1991), *The economics of technical change and international trade*. Harvester Wheatsheaf, Hertfordshire.

Downs, G.W., Rocke, D.M. and Barsoom, P.N. (1996) 'Is the good news about compliance good news about cooperation?' *International Organization* 50(3), 379–406.

Dudley, N., Barrett, M. and Baldock, D. (1985) *The acid rain controversy*. Earth Resources Research, London.

Dyer, H.C. (1993) 'EcoCultures: global culture in the age of ecology'. *Millennium* 22(3), 483–504.

Ehrlich, P. (1986) *The machinery of nature*. Paladin, London.

Elias, N. (1984) *Ueber die Zeit*. Suhrkamp, Frankfurt/Main.

Elsom, D. (1987) *Atmospheric pollution*. Basil Blackwell, Oxford.

Engels, B. (1988) 'Seerecht und Merespolitik – Vereinte Nationen und maritime Nord-Süd-Interessen'. *Nord-Süd aktuell* 2(2), 175–184.

Esty, D.C. (1994) *Greening the GATT*. Institute for International Economics (by Longman), Washington DC.

Evans, T. and Wilson, P. (1992) 'Regime theory and the English school of international relations: a comparison'. *Millennium* 21(3), 329–351.

Fagerberg, J. (1988) 'International competitiveness', *Economic Journal*, 98, 355–374.

Fawcett, J. (1970) 'The development of international law', *International Affairs*, November, 127–137, reprinted in Williams, M. (ed.) (1989), *International relations in the twentieth century: a reader*. Macmillan, London.

Feldman, D.L. (1992) 'Institutions for managing global climate change; compliance, fairness and universal participation'. *Global Environmental Change* 2(1), 43–58.

Feyerabend, P. (1993) *Against method*, 3rd edn. Verso, London.

Finkelstein, L.S. (ed.) (1988) *Politics in the United Nations system*. Duke University Press, London.

Fischer, F. and Forester, J. (eds) (1987) *Confronting values in policy analysis*. Sage Publications, Newbury Park/California.

Flinterman, C., Kwiatkowska, B. and Lammers, J. (eds) (1986) *Transboundary air pollution*. Martinus Nijhoff, Lancaster.

Forgacs, D. (ed.) (1988) *A Gramsci Reader, selected writings 1916–1935*. Laurence & Wishart, London.

Fraenkel, A. (1989) 'The Convention on Long-Range Transboundary Air Pollution: meeting the challenge of international cooperation'. *Harvard International Law Journal* 30(2), 447–476.

Francour, P. *et al.* (1994) 'Are the Mediterranean waters becoming warmer? Information from biological indicators'. *Marine Pollution Bulletin* 28(9), 523–526.

Freestone, D. (ed.) (1991) *The North Sea*. Graham & Trotman, London.

Freiberg, J., Hein, W., Hurtienne, T. and Mutter, T. (eds) (1984) *Drei Welten – eine Umwelt*. Verlag Breitenbach, Saarbrücken.

French, H.F. (1995) 'Wirksame Gestaltung von Umweltschutzabkommen'. *Spektrum der Wissenschaft* 16 (February), 62–66.

Gale, F. (1998) '*Cave "Cave hic dragones"*: a neo-Gramscian deconstruction and reconstruction of international regime theory'. *Review of International Political Economy* 5(2), 252–283.

Gehring, T. (1994) *Dynamic international regimes; institutions for international environmental governance*. Vol. 5. Peter Lang Europaeischer Verlag der Wissenschaften, Frankfurt/Main.

Giddens, A. (1990) *The consequences of modernity*. Stanford University Press, Stanford.

—— (1991) 'Structuration theory: past, present and future'. In: C. Bryant and D. Jary (eds) *Giddens' theory of structuration*. Routledge, London.

Gill, S. (ed.) (1993) *Gramsci, historical materialism and International Relations*. Cambridge University Press, Cambridge.

Gill, S. and Mittelman, J.H. (eds) (1997) *Innovation and transformation in International Studies*. Cambridge University Press, Cambridge.

Godard, O. (1992) 'Social decision making in the context of scientific controversies'. *Global Environmental Change* 2(3), 239–249.

Goldsmith, E. and Hildyard, N. (eds) (1986) *Green Britain or industrial wasteland*. Polity Press, Cambridge.

Goodland, R. and Daly, H. (1993) 'Why Northern income growth is not the solution to Southern poverty'. *Ecological Economics* 8, 85–101.

Gosovic, B. (1992) *The quest for world environmental cooperation: the case of the UN Global Environment Monitoring System*. Routledge, London.

Gough, C.A. *et al.* (1994) 'Environmentally targeted objectives for reducing acidification in Europe'. *Energy Policy* 22(12), 1055–1066.

Gourlay, K.A. (1988) *Poisoners of the sea*. Zed Books, London.

Gray, T. (ed.) (1995) *UK environmental policy in the 1990s*. Macmillan, Basingstoke.

Greene, O. (1995) *Coping with complexity: challenges for developing environmental regimes*. BISA conference paper, Southampton, 18–20 December 1995.

Grenon, M. and Batisse, M. (eds) (1989) *Futures for the Mediterranean Basin: the Blue Plan*. Oxford University Press, Oxford.

Gross, D. (1985) 'Temporality and the modern state'. *Theory and Society* 14, 53–82.

Grubb, M., Koch, M., Munson, A., Sullivan, F. and Thomson, K. (eds) (1993) *The Earth Summit Agreements – a guide and assessment*. RIIA, Earthscan, London.

Haas, P. (1989) 'Do regimes matter? Epistemic communities and Mediterranean pollution control'. *International Organization* 43(3), 377–403.

—— (1990) *Saving the Mediterranean*. Columbia University Press, New York.

Haas, P. and Haas, E.B. (1995) 'Learning to learn: improving international governance'. *Global Governance* 1/3, 255–284.

Haas, P. and McCabe, D. (1996) *International institutions and social learning in the management of global environmental risks*. ISA Conference, San Diego.

Haas, P., Hveem, H., Keohane, R. and Underdal, A. (eds) (1994) *Complex cooperation: institutions and processes in international resource management*. Scandinavian University Press, Oslo.

Haas, P.M., Keohane, R.O. and Levy, M.A. (eds) (1993) *Institutions for the earth: sources of effective international environmental protection*. MIT Press, Cambridge/Mass.

Haas, P.M. and Zuckman, J. (1990) 'The Med is cleaner'. *Oceanus* 33(1), 38–42.

Habermas, J. (1996) *Die Neue Unübersichtlichkeit*. Suhrkamp, Frankfurt/Main.

Haigh, N. (1989) 'New tools for European air pollution control'. *International Environmental Affairs* 1(1), 26–37.

—— (1990) *EEC Environmental Policy and Britain*, 2nd edn. Longman, London.

Hall, C. (1996) *Conservation and political effectiveness in international fisheries regimes*. ISA Conference, San Diego.

Ham, C. and Hill, M. (1993) *The policy process in the modern capitalist state*. Harvester Wheatsheaf, London.

Hannigan, J.A. (1995) *Environmental sociology*. Routledge, London.

Harrison, N. (1996) *The environmental challenge to International Relations theory*. ISA paper, San Diego.

Heij, G.J. and Erisman, J.W. (eds) (1995) *Acid rain research: do we have enough answers?* Elsevier, Amsterdam.

Hein, W. (1993) 'Die Neue Weltordnung und das Ende des Nationalstaats'. *Nord-Süd aktuell* 7(1), 50–59.

Helleiner, E. (1997) 'Braudelian reflections on economic globalisation: the historian as pioneer'. In: Gill, S. and Mittelman, J. (eds) *Innovation and transformation in International Studies*. Cambridge University Press, Cambridge, 90–104.

Helm, C. (1995) *Sind Freihandel und Umweltschutz vereinbar?* WBZ edition sigma, Berlin.

Herrick, C. and Jamieson, D. (1995) 'The social construction of acid rain'. *Global Environmental Change* 5(2), 105–112.

Hess, T. (1996) '1996 Jahr des Stillstands'. *Hamburger Abendblatt*, 28.12.96.

Hester, R.E. (ed.) (1986) *Understanding our environment*. The Royal Society of Chemistry, London.

Hetteling, J.-P., Downing, R.J. and de Smit, P.A.M. (eds) (1991) *Mapping critical loads in Europe*. UNECE Coordination Centre for Effect, Tech. Report No. 1.

Hinrichsen, D. (1990) *Our common seas: coasts in crisis*. Earthscan, London.

Hohmann, H. (1992) 'Umweltpolitik und Umweltrecht: national, regional und global'. *Politische Vierteljahreszeitschrift* 33(3), 489–509.

Hohn, H.-W. (1984) *Die Zerstörung der Zeit. Wie aus einem göttlichen Gut eine Handelsware wurde*. Fischer alternativ, Frankfurt/Main.

Hollis, M. and Smith, S. (1990) *Explaining and understanding International Relations*. Clarendon Press, Oxford.

Hovden, E. (1996) *Ecological thought and International Relations theory: the limits of regime theory*. Millennium Journal of International Studies 25th Anniversary Conference Paper.

Hunt, P. (1991) 'World Bank conservation record under fire'. *New Scientist* 13(1791), 14.

Hurrell, A. (1993), 'International society and the study of regimes: a reflective approach'. In: Rittberger, V. (ed.) *Regime theory and International Relations*. Clarendon Press, Oxford.

Hurrell, A. and Kingsbury, B. (eds) (1992) *The international politics of the environment*. Clarendon Press, Oxford.

Ikle, F.C. (1982) *How nations negotiate*. Harper & Row, New York.

Jackson, C.I. (1990) 'A tenth anniversary review of the ECE Convention on Long-Range Transboundary Air Pollution'. *International Environmental Affairs* 2(3), 217–226.

Jacobs, M. (1991) *The green economy*. Pluto, London.

Jacobson, H.K. and Brown Weiss, E. (1995) 'Strengthening compliance with international environmental accords: preliminary observations from a collaborative project'. *Global Governance* 1, 119–148.

Jäger, J. (1996) 'The use of integrated assessment models in the international negotiations for reducing sulphur emissions in Europe', IIASA John Mason Conference, Birmingham, 12 September 1996.

Jasanoff, S. (1990) *The fifth branch: science advisers as policymakers*. Harvard University Press, London.

—— (1995) 'Skinning scientific cats'. In: K. Conca, M. Alberty and G. Dabelko (eds) *Green planet blues*. Westview Press, Boulder/Colorado.

—— (1997) *Regulating environmental risk*. Environmental Futures Lecture Series, Cambridge, 25-2-1997.

Jeftic, L. (1990) 'The role of science in marine environmental protection of regional seas and their coastal areas – the experience of the Mediterranean Action Plan'. *Marine Pollution Bulletin* 25(1–4), 66–69.

Jeftic, L. and Saliba, L. (1987), 'The Mediterranean Action Plan: a regional approach to pollution control', *Water Science and Technology* 18 (9).

Jeftic, L., Keckes, S. and Perretta, J.C. (eds) (1996) *Climatic change and the Mediterranean*. Vol. 2. Edward Arnold, London.

Jeftic, L., Milliman, J. and Sestini, G. (eds) (1992) *Climatic change and the Mediterranean*. Vol. 1. Edward Arnold, London.

Joensson, C. (1993) 'International organisation and cooperation: an interorganisational perspective'. *International Social Science Journal* 138, 463–477.

Johnson, W. (1988) *The monk seal conspiracy*. Heretic Books, London.

—— (1994) *Captive breeding and the Mediterranean monk seal – a focus on Antibes Marineland*. International Marine Mammal Association Inc., Ontario.

—— (1995) *The Mediterranean monk seal – conservation guidelines*. International Marine Mammal Association Inc., Ontario.

Jones, P. (1991) 'Mediterranean oil spills'. *Marine Pollution Bulletin* 22(6), 260–261.

Jones, R.J.B. and Willetts, P. (eds) (1984) *Interdependence on trial*. Pinter, London.

Jordan, A. and O'Riordan, T. (1995) 'The precautionary principle in UK environmental law and policy'. In: *UK environmental policy in the 1990s* (ed: Gray, T.). Macmillan, Basingstoke, 57–84.

Joyce, F.E. and Schneider, G. (1988) *Environment and economic development in the regions of the European Community*. Avebury, Aldershot.

Judge, D. (ed.) (1993) *A green dimension for the European Community: political issues and processes*. Frank Cass, London.

Kaekoenen, J. (ed.) (1992) *Perspectives on environmental conflict and international politics.* Pinter, London.

Kahan, A.M. (1986) *Acid rain, reign of controversy.* Fulcrum Inc., Golden/Colorado.

Kakebeeke, W.J. (1991) 'Transboundary air pollution'. *International Environmental Law* 2, 103–106.

Kaplan, M.A. (1967) *System and process in international politics.* John Wiley Publishers, London.

Kay, D.A. and Jacobson, H.K. (eds) (1983) *Environmental protection, the international dimension.* Allansheld, Osmun & Co. Publishers, Totowa/New Jersey.

Keohane, R.O. (1984) *After hegemony: cooperation and discord in the world political economy.* Princeton University Press, Princeton.

—— (1986) *Neorealism and its critics.* Columbia University Press, New York.

Kiss, A. and Sheldon, D. (1991) *International environmental law.* Transnational Publishers, New York.

Kiss, C.A. (1985) 'Du nouveau dans l'air: des "pluies acides" à la couche d'ozone'. *Annuaire Français de Droit International* 31, 812–822.

Klaassen, G. (1994) 'Options and costs of controlling ammonia emissions in Europe'. *European Review of Agricultural Economics* 21(2), 219–240.

—— (1996) *Acid rain and environmental degradation; the economics of emission trading.* Edward Elgar, Cheltenham.

Knecht, R.W. (1995) *Institutional implications of sustainable development at the regional scale.* Conference paper, Genoa.

Knorr-Cetina, K.D. (1981) *The manufacture of knowledge.* Pergamon Press, Oxford.

Krasner, S.D. (ed.) (1983) *International regimes.* Cornell University Press, London.

Kratochwil, F. (1989) *Rules, norms and decisions.* Cambridge University Press, Cambridge.

Krumm, R. (1995) *Internationale Umweltpolitik, eine Analyse aus umwelt-ökonomischer Sicht.* Spring Verlag, Berlin.

Kuhn, T.S. (1982) 'Normal measurement and reasonable agreement'. In: Barnes, B. and Edge, D. (eds) *Science in context.* The Open University Press, Milton Keynes.

Kümmerer, K. (1996) 'The ecological impact of time'. *Time and Society* 5(2), 209–235.

Kütting, G.M.O. (1994), 'Mediterranean pollution: international cooperation and the control of pollution from land-based sources', *Marine Policy*, 18 (3), 233–248.

Kuwabara, S. (1984) *The legal regime of the protection of the Mediterranean against pollution from land-based sources.* Tycooly International Publishing, Dublin.

Labastille, A. (1981) 'Acid rain – how great a menace?' *National Geographic* 160 (11, November), 651–680.

Lash, S., Szerszynski, B. and Wynne, B. (eds) (1996) *Risk, environment and modernity.* Sage, London.

Lash, S. and Urry, J. (1987) *The end of organised capitalism.* Polity Press, Cambridge.

Lee, K. (1995) 'A neo-Gramscian approach to international organization: an expanded analysis of current reforms to UN development activities'. In: MacMillan, J. and Linklater, A. (eds) *Boundaries in question.* Pinter Publishers, London, 144–162.

Le Morvan, D. (1995) *Le littoral atlantique dans l'Union Européenne: vers quelle intégration?* Conference paper, Genoa.

Lempert, R.J. and Farnsworth, G. (1994) 'The Mediterranean environment: prospects for cooperation to solve the problems of the 1990s'. *Mediterranean Quarterly* 5(4), 110–124.

Levy, M.A. (1993a) 'Political science and the questions of effectiveness of international environmental institutions'. *International Challenges* 13, 17–35.

——— (1993b), 'European acid rain: the power of tote-board diplomacy'. In: Haas, P., Keohane, R. and Levy, M. (eds) *Institutions for the earth*. MIT Press, Cambridge/Mass.

Levy, M.A., Young, O.R. and Zuern, M. (1994) *The study of international regimes*. Working Paper 94–113. International Institute for Applied Systems Analysis, Laxenburg/Austria.

Lewis, L.A. and Barry, L. (1988) *African environment and resources*. Allen & Unwin, London.

Leys, C. (1996) *The rise and fall of development theory*. Indiana University Press, Bloomington/USA.

Liefferink, J.D., Lowe, P.D. and Mol, A.J.P. (eds) (1993) *European integration and environmental policy*. Belhaven Press, London.

Lipietz, A. (1997) 'The post-Fordist world: labour relations, international hierarchy and global ecology'. *Review of International Political Economy* 4(1), 1–41.

Lipschutz, R.D. (1996), *Global civil society and global environmental governance*. SUNY Press, New York.

Litfin, K. (1994) *Ozone discourses*. Columbia University Press, New York.

Lovelock, J. (1988) *The ages of Gaia – a biography of our living earth*. Oxford University Press, Oxford.

Luard, E. (1990) *Globalisation of politics: the changed focus of political action in the modern world*. New York University Press, New York.

Luciani, G. (ed.) (1984) *The Mediterranean region*. Croom Helm, London.

Luhmann, N. (1975), 'Weltzeit und Systemgeschichte'. In *Soziologische Aufklaerung*, Band II. Opladen.

Luke, A. (1991) 'Pollution chokes "lungs" of the Mediterranean'. *New Scientist* 132(1789), 11.

Lukes, S. (1974) *Power: a radical view*. Macmillan, London.

Macgarvin, M. (1997), 'Agriculture and the marine environment: what are the problems and how best to tackle them?'. Paper presented at the Wilton Park conference on securing the marine environment, 15 January 1997, Steyning, West Sussex.

Manos, A. (1990) *In defense of the coast. Coastal Ocean Space Utilisation – Proceedings International Symposium*. New York, Elsevier.

——— (1991) 'An international programme for the protection of a semi-enclosed sea – the Mediterranean Action Plan'. *Marine Pollution Bulletin* 23(-), 489–496.

Marchisio, S. (1995) *The emerging principle of common but differentiated responsibility and Mediterranean sea environmental protection*. Conference paper, Genoa, April 1995.

Martinez-Alier, J. (1987) *Ecological economics*. Blackwell, Oxford.

——— (1995) 'The environment as a luxury good or "too poor to be green"?' *Ecological Economics* 13, 1–10.

Mayer-Tasch, P. (1982) *Die Welt als Baustelle, Fragen an die politische Oekologie*. Edition Interfrom, Zürich.

——— (ed.) (1986) *Die Luft hat keine Grenzen*. Fischer Verlag, Frankfurt/Main.

——— (1990) 'Umweltinitiativen und internationale Umweltpolitik'. *Zeitschrift für Politik* 37(3), 172–180.

Mayer-Tasch, P., Mrass, W., von Weizsäcker, E.U. and Kohout, F. (1994) *Umweltpolitik und ihre Instrumente*. Economica Verlag, Bonn.

McCormick, J. (1989) *Acid earth*, 2nd edn. Earthscan, London.

——— (1991) *British Politics and the Environment*. Earthscan, London.

Merchant, C. (1992) *Radical ecology, the search for a livable world*. Routledge, London.

Metcalfe, S.E. and Whyatt, J.D. (1994) 'Modelling future acid deposition: a critical loads approach'. *Global Environmental Change* 4(2), 125–139.

Midgley, M. (1992) *Science as salvation: modern myth and its meaning*. Routledge, London.

Milner, H. (1992) 'International theories of co-operation among nations'. *World Politics* 44(3), 466–496.

Miloradov, M. (1986) 'Special issue on pollution of the Mediterranean Sea'. *Water Science and Technology* 18(9).

Mitchell, R.B. (1994) 'Regime design matters: intentional oil pollution and treaty compliance'. *International Organization* 48(3), 425–458.

Mlcoch, S. (1993) 'Silesia and the Black Triangle'. *Review of European Community and International Environmental Law* 2(1), 43–44.

Moore, W.E. (1963) *Man, time and society*. John Wiley & Sons, New York.

Morgenthau, H. (1993) *Politics among nations*. McGraw-Hill, New York.

Mouzelis, N. (1995) *Sociological theory – what went wrong?* Routledge, London.

Muntasser, M.A. (1995) 'Assessing the environmental impact of technology transfer and commercial oil and gas development in the Mediterranean area'. *OPEC Bulletin* 26(1), 11–14.

Nijkamp, P. and Perrels, A. (1994) *Sustainable cities in Europe*. Routledge, London.

Nowotny, H. (1989) *Eigenzeit, Entstehung und Strukturierung eines Zeitgefühls*. Suhrkamp Verlag, Frankfurt/Main.

Osborne, P. (1995) *The politics of time*. Verso, London.

Ostrom, E. (1990) *Governing the commons*. Cambridge University Press, Cambridge.

Paech, N. (1994) 'Von der Freiheit der Meere zum Common Heritage of Mankind'. *Nord-Süd aktuell* 8(3), 396–399.

Pallemaerts, M. (1988) 'The politics of acid rain control in Europe'. *Environment* 30(2), 42–44.

Park, C.C. (1987) *Acid rain, rhetoric and reality*. Methuen, London.

Parkin, S. (1994) *The life and death of Petra Kelly*. Pandora, London.

Pastor, X. (ed.) (1991) *Greenpeace – the Mediterranean*. Collins & Brown, London.

Paterson, M. (1995) 'Radicalizing regimes? Ecology and the critique of IR theory'. In: MacMillan, J. and Linklater, A. (eds) *Boundaries in question*. Pinter Publishers, London, 212–227.

—— (1996) *Global warming and global politics*. Routledge, London.

Pavasovic, A. (1995) *Integrated coastal and marine areas management in the Mediterranean: present state, problems and future*. Conference paper, Genoa, April 1995.

Pearce, D., Markandya, A. and Barbier, E.B. (1989) *Blueprint for a green economy*. Earthscan, London.

Pearce, D.W. and Turner, R.K. (1990) *Economics of natural resources and the environment*. Harvester Wheatsheaf, London.

Pearson, C.S. (1975) *International marine environmental policy; the economic dimension*. Johns Hopkins University Press, Baltimore.

Pesaro, E. (1995) *Marine specially protected areas: the Italian case*. Conference paper, Genoa.

Peters, H.-J. (1990) *Marine pollution in the Mediterranean: incidence, control issues and abatement options*. Gestion d'entreprises petrolieres, Montreal.

Pinkele, C.F. and Pollis, A. (1983) *The contemporary Mediterranean world*. Praeger, New York.

Pirages, D. (1988) *Global technopolitics, the international politics of technology and resources*. Brooks/Cole Publishing Company, Pacific Grove/California.

Ponting, C. (1991) *A green history of the world*. Penguin, London.

Porter, G. and Brown, J.W. (1996) *Global environmental politics*, 2nd edn. Westview, Boulder/Colorado.

Pridham, G. (ed.) (1984) *The new Mediterranean democracries: regime transition in Spain, Greece, Portugal.* Frank Cass, London.

Puchala, D. and Hopkins, R. (1983) 'International regimes: lessons from inductive analysis'. In: Krasner, S.D. (ed.) *International regimes.* Cornell University Press, London.

Putnam, R.D. (1988) 'Diplomacy and domestic politics: the logic of two-level games'. *International Organization* 42(3), 427–460.

Raftopoulos, E. (1992) 'The Barcelona Convention system for the protection of the Mediterranean Sea against pollution'. *International Journal of Estuarine and Coastal Law* 7(1), 27–41.

—— (1993) *The Barcelona Convention and Protocols, the Mediterranean Action Plan Regime.* Simmonds & Hill, London.

—— (1995) *Sustainable development and the Mediterranean Action Plan regime: legal and institutional aspects.* Conference paper, Genoa.

Rawlence, C. (ed.) (1985) *About time.* Jonathan Cape, London.

Redclift, M. (1984) *Development and the environmental crisis: red or green alternatives?* Routledge, London.

—— (1987) *Sustainable development, exploring the contradictions.* Routledge, London.

—— (1992) 'Sustainable development and global environmental change'. *Global Environmental Change* 2(1), 32–42.

—— (1995) 'The UK and the international environmental agenda: Rio and after'. In: Gray, T. (ed.) *UK environmental policy in the 1990s.* Macmillan, Basingstoke, 283–302.

—— (1996) *Wasted – counting the costs of global consumption.* Earthscan, London.

Redclift, M. and Benton, T. (eds) (1994) *Social theory and the global environment.* Routledge, London.

Redclift, M. and Woodgate, G. (1994), 'Sociology and the environment. Discordant discourse?' In: Redclift, M. and Benton, T. (eds) *Social theory and the global environment.* Routledge, London, 51–66.

Regens, J.L. and Rycroft, R.W. (1988) *The acid rain controversy.* University of Pittsburgh Press, Pittsburgh.

Reinhardt, U.J. (1989) *Meeresumweltpolitik.* Afes Press, Heidelberg.

Reynolds, P.A. (1980) *An introduction to International Relations.* Longman, New York.

Rhode, B. (ed.) (1988) *Air Pollution in Europe.* Vol. 1 (Western Europe). Vienna Centre, Vienna.

Rifkin, J. (1987) *Time wars.* Henry Holt, New York.

Rich, B. (1990) 'The emperor's new clothes: the World Bank and environmental reform', *World Policy Journal* 7 (2), 305–329.

Ritchie-Calder, Lord (1972) *The pollution of the Mediterranean Sea.* Herbert Lang & Co., Berne.

Rittberger, V. (ed.) (1990) *International regimes in East–West politics.* Pinter Publishers, London.

—— (ed.) (1993) *Regime theory and international relations.* Oxford University Press, Oxford.

Rittberger, V., Hasenclever, A. and Mayer, P. (1995) *Justice, equality and the robustness of international regimes: a research design.* Paper prepared for the 36th annual ISA convention, Chicago, 21–25 February 1995.

Riva, M. (1994) 'Local/global: literary postmodernism and the scientific rediscovery of time'. *Social Science Information* 33(4), 649–661.

Rodricks, J.V. (1992) *Calculated risks: understanding the toxicity and human health risks of chemicals in our environment*. Cambridge University Press, Cambridge.

Rollhansen, N. (1994) 'Science, politics and the mass media'. *Science, Technology and Human Values* 19(3), 324–341.

Rose, J. (1993) 'Environmental investment in the Mediterranean'. *Environmental Science and Technology* 27(8), 1494.

Rosenau, J.N. and Czempiel, E.O. (eds) (1992) *Governance without government: order and change in world politics*. Cambridge University Press, Cambridge.

Rosencranz, A. (1981) 'The ECE Convention of 1979 on Long-Range Transboundary Air Pollution'. *American Journal of International Law* 75, 975–982.

—— (1991) 'The European Conference on Acid Rain'. *Environment* 7(4), 158–160.

Rowlands, I.H. and Greene, M. (eds) (1992) *Global environmental change and international relations*. Macmillan, London.

Ruiz, J.J. (1995) *International law facing Mediterranean sustainable development: the revision of the Barcelona Convention and its related protocols*. Conference paper, Genoa.

Saliba, L. (1990) 'Coastal land use and environmental problems in the Mediterranean'. *Land Use Policy* 7(3), 217–230.

Samuelson, P. (1992) *Economics*, 14th edn. McGraw Hill, London.

Sancy, M. (1990) 'Law and the atmosphere: acid rain in Europe'. *Land Management and Environmental Law Report* 1(6), 189–192.

Sand, P.H. (1990) *Lessons learned in global environmental governance*. World Resources Institute, Washington DC.

—— (1990) 'Innovations in international environmental governance'. *Environment* 32(9), 16–44.

—— (1990), 'Regional Approaches to Transboundary Air Pollution'. In: *Energy: production, consumption and consequences*. Washington DC, National Academy Press

Sand, P.H. *et al.* (ed.) (1992) *The effectiveness of international environmental agreements*. Grotius Publications Ltd, Cambridge.

Sands, P. (1989) 'The environmental community and international law'. *Harvard International Law Review* 30, 393–420.

—— (ed.) (1993) *Greening international law*. Earthscan, London.

Saurin, J. (1995) *International theory and global environmental change*. BISA conference paper, Southampton, 18–20 December 1995.

Sayer, A. (1992) *Method in social science*, 2nd edn. Routledge, London.

Schachter, O. (1991) *International law in theory and practice*. Martinus Nijhoff, London.

Schipperges, H. (1995) *Hildegard von Bingen*. C.H. Beck, Munich.

Schlickman, J.A., McMahon, T.M. and van Riel, N. (eds) (1993) *International environmental law and regulation*. Butterworth Legal Publishers, London.

Schmidt, W. (1992) 'Empirical analysis of the trade effects of EC's global Mediterranean countries'. *Journal of Regional Policy* 12(2), 319–331.

Schumacher, E.F. (1973) *Small is beautiful*. Vintage, London.

Schwarzer, G. (1993) 'Das internationale Regime zur Bekämpfung der weiträumigen Luftverschmutzung'. *Aussenpolitik* 44(1), 13–22.

Schwieger, R.G. and Elliott, T.C. (eds) (1985) *Acid rain: engineering solutions, regulatory aspects*. McGraw-Hill, New York.

Scovazzi, T. (1996a) 'Recent developments in the Barcelona system for the protection of the Mediterranean against pollution'. *The International Journal of Marine and Coastal Law* 11(1), 95–100.

—— (1996b) 'Current legal developments: The amendments to the Protocol for the Protection of the Mediterranean Sea against Pollution from Land-Based Sources'. *The International Journal of Marine and Coastal Law* 11(4), 571–575.

Seager, J. (1995) *The state of the environment atlas.* Penguin, London.

Sebenius, J.K. (1992) 'Challenging conventional explanations of international cooperation: negotiation analysis and the case of epistemic communities'. *International Organization* 46(1), 323–365.

Sersic, M. (1989) 'Draft Protocol for the protection of the Mediterranean Sea against pollution resulting from offshore activities'. *Marine Policy Reports* 1(2), 161–165.

Singer, P. (1983) *Hegel.* Oxford University Press, Oxford.

Sjostedt, G. (ed.) (1993) *International environmental negotiation.* Sage Publications, London.

Skea, J. (1995) Acid rain: a business-as-usual scenario'. In: Gray, T. (ed.) *UK environmental policy in the 1990s.* Macmillan, Basingstoke, 189–209.

Skeffington, R. (1994) 'Critical; loads and energy policy'. In: Batterbee, R. (ed.) *Acid rain and its impact: the critical loads debate.* Ensis, London.

Skjaerseth, J.B. (1992a) 'The Mediterranean Action Plan: strenuous efforts – meagre results?' *International Challenges* 12(2), 54–59.

—— (1992b) *The Mediterranean Action Plan – More political rhetoric than effective problem-solving?* The Fridtjof Nansen Institute, Lysaker/Norway.

—— (1994) 'The effectiveness of the Mediterranean Action Plan'. *International Environmental Affairs* 6/4, 313–334.

—— (1995) *Methodological approaches in the study of implementation of international environmental commitments.* draft.

—— (1996a) *The impact of environmental institutions: implementing North Sea pollution control.* ISA paper, San Diego.

—— (1996b) 'The 20th anniversary of the Mediterranean Action Plan'. *Green Globe Yearbook,* 47–53.

Sklair, L. (1991) *Sociology of the global system.* Harvester Wheatsheaf, London.

Sliggers, J. and Klaassen, G. (1994) 'Cost sharing for the abatement of acidification in Europe: the missing link in the new sulphur protocol'. *European Environment* 4(1), 5–11.

Somsen, H. (1991) 'The regionalisation of EC marine pollution law: the example of the Mediterranean Sea'. *International Journal of Estuarine and Coastal Law* 6(3), 229–245.

Sorensen, J. (1995) *The Black Sea – an international environmental tragedy.* Conference paper, Genoa.

Sprinz, D.F. (1992) *Why countries support international environmental agreements: the regulation of acid rain in Europe.* PhD Dissertation, University of Michigan, Ann Arbor.

—— (1996) *Measuring the effectiveness of international environmental regimes.* ISA paper, San Diego.

—— (1998) *The effectiveness of global environmental regimes.* ISA paper, Minneapolis.

Sprinz, D. and Vaahtoranta, T. (1994) 'The interest-based explanation of international environmental policy'. *International Organization* 48(1), 77–105.

Stein, J.G. (1993), 'International cooperation and loss avoidance: framing the problem'. In: Stein, J.G. and Pauly, L.W. (eds) *Choosing to cooperate; how states avoid loss.* Johns Hopkins University Press, London.

Stein, J.G. and Pauly, L.W. (eds) (1993) *Choosing to cooperate; how states avoid loss.* Johns Hopkins University Press, London.

Stieger, R. (1995) *Internationaler Umweltschutz – eine politisch-oekonomische Analyse der Vertraege zum Schutz der Ozonschicht*. Peter Lang Europaeischer Verlag der Wissenschaften, Frankfurt/Main.

Stopford, J., Strange, S. and Henley, J.S. (1991) *Rival states, rival firms*. Cambridge University Press, Cambridge.

Strange, S. (1983), 'Cave hic dragones – a critique of regime analysis'. In: Krasner, S. (ed.) *International regimes*. Cornell University Press, New York.

Stubbs, R. and Underhill, G. (eds) (1994) *Political Economy and the changing global order*. Macmillan, London.

Suarez de Vivero, J.L. and Rodriguez, J.C. (1995) *The Alborean Sea: ocean management and international cooperation in the context of the Mediterranean political framework*. Conference paper, Genoa.

Sundgren, J. (1993) 'Lateral pressure theory as applied to global warming: an initial assessment'. *International Political Science Review* 14(1), 87–101.

Susskind, L. (1994) *Environmental diplomacy: negotiating more effective global agreements*. Oxford University Press, Oxford.

Sweet, J. (1994) 'Critical loads, the new sulphur protocol and European energy policy'. *European Environment* 4(1), 2–4.

Tanner, M. (1994) *Nietzsche*. Oxford University Press, Oxford.

Thomas, C. (1992), *The environment in International Relations*. Royal Institute of International Affairs, London.

—— (ed.) (1994), *Rio: unravelling the consequences*. Frank Cass, London.

Thomas, C. and Howlett, D. (eds) (1993) *Resource politics – freshwater and regional relations*. Open University Press, Buckingham.

Thunberg, B. and Hanneberg, P. (eds) (1993) *Acidification and air pollution*, 2nd edn. Swedish Environmental Protection Agency, Solna/Sweden.

Tollan, A. (1985) 'The Convention on Long-Range Transboundary Air Pollution'. *Journal of World Trade Law* 19(6), 615–621.

Underdal, A. (1992) 'The concept of regime effectiveness'. *Cooperation and Conflict* 27(3), 227–240.

Vallega, A. (1988) 'A human geographical approach to semienclosed seas: the Mediterranean case'. *Ocean Yearbook* 7, 372–393.

—— (1993) *The Agenda 21 for the Mediterranean*. ICCOPS Occasional Paper 1993/1, Genoa.

—— (1994a) 'Mediterranean Action Plan: Which futures?'*Ocean and Coastal Management* 23(3), 271–279.

—— (1994b) *The coastal use structure; a sustainable development consistent approach*. ICCOPS Occasional Paper 1994/2, Genoa.

—— (1995a) 'Towards the sustainable management of the Mediterranean Sea'. *Marine Policy* 19(1), 47–64.

—— (1995b) *Notes for a protocol on integrated coastal area management to the Barcelona Convention*. Conference paper, Genoa.

—— (1995c) *Pursuing the sustainable development of the Mediterranean*. ICCOPS Occasional Paper 1995/3, Genoa.

Vallejo, S.M. (1988) 'Development and management of coastal and marine areas: an international perspective'. *Ocean Yearbook* 7, 205–222.

VanDeveer, S.D. (1996) *Crossing the Mediterranean: the state in a transnational environment*. ISA paper, San Diego.

van Dyke, J.M., Zaelke, D. and Hewison, G. (eds) (1993) *Freedom for the seas in the 21st century*. Island Press, Washington.

Verstappen, H.T. (1995) *Natural and technical disasters in regional seas; an underestimated issue*. Conference paper, Genoa.

Vickery, J. (1997) 'Lime cuts insects to the quick'. *The Times Higher Education Supplement*, 14 February 1997.

Victor, D.G. and Skolnikoff, E.B. (1996) *Implementation and effectiveness of international environmental commitments*. ISA paper, San Diego.

von Prittwitz, V. (1984) *Umweltaussenpolitik, grenzüberschreitende Luftverschmutzung in Europa*. Campus Verlag, Frankfurt/Main.

—— (1990) *Das Katastrophen-Paradox, Elemente einer Theorie der Umweltpolitik*. Leske & Budrich, Opladen.

—— (ed.) (1993) *Umweltpolitik als Modernisierungsprozess*. Leske & Budrich, Opladen.

—— V. (1996) *Verhandeln und Argumentieren; Dialog, Interessen und Macht in der Umweltpolitik*. Leske & Budrich, Opladen.

von Weizsäcker, E.U. (1994) *Earth politics*. Zed Books, London.

Voss, G. (1987) *Argumente und Fakten zur Umweltpolitik*. Deutscher Instituts-Verlag, Cologne.

Wallerstein, I. (1984) *The politics of the world-economy*. Cambridge University Press, Cambridge.

—— (1991) *Unthinking social science*. Polity Press, Cambridge.

—— (1995) *After liberalism*. The New Press, New York.

Waltz, K. (1986), 'Political structures'. In: Keohane, R.O. (ed.) *Neorealism and its critics*. Columbia University Press, New York, 70–97 (reprint of Waltz, K. (1979), *Theory of international politics*. Addison-Wesley, Reading/Mass).

Weale, A. (1992) *The new politics of pollution*. Manchester University Press, Manchester.

Weidenfeld, W. (ed.) (1992) *Herausforderung Mittelmeer: Aufgaben, Ziele und Strategien europaeischer Politik*. Bertelsmann Stiftung, Guetersloh.

Weir, F. (1993) *From dirty man to drittsekk – UK acid rain policy*. Friends of the Earth, London.

Wetstone, G. and Rosencranz, A. (1983) *Acid rain in Europe and North America*. The Environmental Law Institute, Washington.

—— (1984) 'Transboundary air pollution: the search for an international response'. *Harvard Environmental Law Review* 8(89), 89–138.

Wettestad, J. (1995) *Nuts and bolts for environmental negotiators? Designing effective international regimes*. Fridtjof Nansen Institute, Lysaker/Norway.

Wettestad, J. and Andresen, S. (1991) *The effectiveness of international resource cooperation: some preliminary findings*. The Fridtjof Nansen Institute, Lysaker/Norway.

White, J.C. (ed.) (1988) *Acid rain: the relationship between sources and receptors*. Elsevier, New York.

Whitelegg, J. (1993) *Transport for a sustainable future – the case for Europe*. Belhaven Press, London.

Wilcher, M.E. (1989) *The politics of acid rain – policy in Canada, Great Britain and the United States*. Avebury, Aldershot.

Williams, M. (ed.) (1989), *International relations in the twentieth century: a reader*. Macmillan, London.

—— (1993) 'International trade and the environment: issues, perspectives and challenges'. *Environmental Politics* 2(4), 79–97.

—— (1994), *International economic organisations and the Third World*. Harvester Wheatsheaf, London.

Wright, L. (1991) 'Students in Mediterranean clean-up'. *Marine Pollution Bulletin* 22(9), 426–427.

Wynne, B. (1994), 'Scientific knowledge and the global environment', in Redclift, M. and. Benton, T. (eds) *Social theory and the global environment*. Routledge, London.

Yahia, L.A. (1995) *The law of the sea convention: a regulatory regime for the implementation of UNCED Agenda 21 in the Mediterranean area*. Conference paper, Genoa.

Yeroulanos, M. (1982) 'The Mediterranean Action Plan – a success story in international cooperation'. *Ekistics* 49(293), 171–175.

Young, M. (1988) *The metronomic society*. Thames & Hudson, London.

Young, O.R. (1982) *Resource regimes*. University of California Press, Los Angeles.

—— (1989) 'The politics of international regime formation: managing natural resources and the environment'. *International Organization* 43(3), 349–375.

—— (1992), 'The effectiveness of international institutions: hard cases and critical variables'. In: Rosenau, J. and Czempiel, E. (eds) *Governance without government: order and change in world politics*. Cambridge University Press, Cambridge.

—— (1994) *International governance, protecting the environment in a stateless society*. Cornell University Press, London.

—— (ed.) (1997) *Global governance – drawing insights from the environmental experience*. MIT Press, Cambridge/Mass.

Young, O. and von Moltke, K. (1994) 'The consequences of international environmental regimes: report from the Barcelona workshop'. *International Environmental Affairs* 6/4, 348–370.

Young, O.R. and Osherenko, G. (1993) 'Testing theories of regime formation: findings from a large collaborative research project'. In: Rittberger, V. (ed.) *Regime theory and international relations*. Oxford University Press, Oxford.

Zacher, M. and Sutton, BA (1996) *Governing global networks – international regimes for transportations and communications*. Cambridge University Press, Cambridge.

Zammit, A. (1995) 'Central Mediterranean Sea Permanent Watch'. *The Malta Sunday Times* 848 (8 January), 2.

Zehr, S.C. (1994) 'Flexible interpretations of "acid rain" and the construction of scientific uncertainty in political settings'. *Politics and the Life Sciences* 13(2), 205–216.

Zerubavel, E. (1981) *Hidden rhythms: schedules and calendars in social life*. University of Chicago Press, Chicago.

Ziegler, C.E. (1987) *Environmental policy in the USSR*. Pinter, London.

Index